THINKING FRENCH TRANSLATION

Second Edition

TITLES OF RELATED INTEREST

Thinking Arabic Translation: A Course in Translation Method: Arabic to English
James Dickins, Sándor Hervey and Ian Higgins

Thinking German Translation: A Course in Translation Method: German to English
Sándor Hervey, Ian Higgins and Michael Loughridge

Thinking Italian Translation: A Course in Translation Method: Italian to English
Sándor Hervey, Ian Higgins, Stella Cragie and Patrizia Gambarotta

Thinking Spanish Translation: A Course in Translation Method: Spanish to English
Sándor Hervey, Ian Higgins and Louise M. Haywood

Routledge Encyclopedia of Translation Studies
Mona Baker (ed.)

In Other Words: A Coursebook on Translation
Mona Baker

Becoming a Translator: An Accelerated Course
Douglas Robinson

The Scandals of Translation
Lawrence Venuti

Translation Studies
Susan Bassnett

THINKING FRENCH TRANSLATION

Second Edition

A Course in Translation Method:
French to English

Sándor Hervey
Ian Higgins

Routledge
Taylor & Francis Group

LONDON AND NEW YORK

First published in 1992,
second edition published 2002
by Routledge
2 Park Square, Milton Park, Abingdon, Oxon OX14 4RN

Simultaneously published in the USA and Canada
by Routledge
270 Madison Ave, New York, NY 10016

Reprinted with corrections in 2004, 2005
Reprinted 2006

Routledge is an imprint of the Taylor & Francis Group, an informa business

© 1992, 2002 Sándor Hervey, Ian Higgins

Typeset in Times New Roman by
Florence Production Ltd, Stoodleigh, Devon
Printed and bound in Great Britain by
TJ International, Padstow, Cornwall

British Library Cataloguing in Publication Data
A catalogue record for this book is available from the British Library

Library of Congress Cataloging in Publication Data
Hervey, Sándor G. J.
Thinking French translation: a course in translation method /
Sándor Hervey, Ian Higgins.–2nd ed.
p.cm.
Originally published: Thinking translation: a course in translation method,
French-English. New York: Routledge, 1992.
Includes bibliographical references and index.
1. French language–Translating into English.
I. Higgins, Ian. II. Hervey, Sándor G. J. Thinking translation. III. Title.
PC2498.H47 2002
428'.0241–dc21   2002021335

ISBN 10: 0–415–25521–X (hbk)
ISBN 10: 0–415–25522–8 (pbk)
ISBN 13: 978–0–415–25521–9 (hbk)
ISBN 10: 978–0–415–25522–6 (pbk)

To Catherine, Morris and Rosey

Contents

Contents

Acknowledgements

We owe a debt of gratitude to many people, above all to Chris Durban and Anne Withers. Although very busy professional translators, Chris and Anne gave extremely generously of their time and expertise in helping us find and deal with seemingly intractable material. It is no exaggeration to say that without their patience, skill and good humour this book would have been markedly poorer. We are deeply grateful to them. Many other people have helped us, in more ways than we can enumerate: Wendy Anderson, Lucille Cairns, Stéphane Calpena, Ian and Moira Christie, David Culpin, Anna Maria De Cesare, John Devereux, Rosalind Fergusson, Janet Fraser, Vince Fusaro, Chris Gledhill, Mathieu Guidère, Ian Henderson, Tammy Hervey, Lynn Johnstone, Richard Kimber, Lorna Milne, John Minchinton, Sylvain Pitiot, David Poppleton, Alison Rae, Peter Read, Mary Rigby, Alison Roy, Jim Supple, Julia 'Sweet Reason' Swales, Josine Thomas, Marie-José Tyler, Ceri Williams, Laurence Williams, Clare Wilson – from commas and contracts to perfume and wine, each of them knows just why we mention them here with a mixture of gratitude and brow-mopping relief.

The authors and publisher would like to thank the following people and institutions for permission to reproduce copyright material. Every effort has been made to trace copyright holders, but in a few cases this has not been possible. Any omissions brought to our attention will be remedied in future editions. Air France, for material from *Air France magazine*; A. Angevin, for material from 'La jeunesse d'Europe danse en Avignon'; Azzaro, for material from 'Eau belle'; Editions Bernard Grasset, for material from M. Cardinal, *Les Mots pour le dire*; Braun GmbH, for material from *The Cookbook for the Braun Multipractic Plus*; Calder Publications Ltd., for material from E. Ionesco, *Rhinoceros*, © this translation (by Derek Prouse) first published in 1960 by John Calder (Publishers) Ltd., London; Cambridge University Press: extracts from the Authorized Version of the Bible (The King James Bible), the rights in which are vested in the Crown, are reproduced by permission of the Crown's Patentee, Cambridge University Press; Jacques Coerten, for material from 'La Petite Provence du Paradou'; Editions Denoël, for material from R. Goscinny and J.-J. Sempé, *Le petit Nicolas*, © Editions Denoël, 1960; EADS, for material from *Rapport annuel Aerospatiale*, 1993; European Commission, for material from *Euroabstracts*; *L'Express*, for material, © *L'Express*, from articles by Alain Schifres and Roger Le Taillanter (propos recueillis par James Sarazin); Editions de Fallois, for material from M. Pagnol, *Jean de Florette*; Editions Gallimard, for material from S. de Beauvoir, *La Force de l'âge*, A. Camus, *L'Etranger*, J. Dutourd, *Au Bon Beurre*, E. Ionesco, *Rhinocéros* and J. Tardieu, *La Comédie de la comédie*; M. Guidère, for material from M. Guidère, *Publicité et traduction*, Editions L'Harmattan, 2000; Mercure de France, for material from A. Gide, *L'Immoraliste*; *Le Monde*, for M. Caste, 'Ma Mie'; Pelicula Films, for subtitles from *How to be Celtic*; Editions Plon, for material from C. de Gaulle, *Mémoires de guerre*; Random House, Inc., for material from A. Gide, *The Immoralist* (trans. D. Bussy); Les Salines de Guérande, for material from 'Fleur de Sel récolte 1997'; Editions du Seuil, for material from P. Emmanuel, *L'Arbre et le vent* and P. Grainville, *Les Flamboyants*.

Preface to the
second edition

This book is a completely revised and rewritten edition of *Thinking Translation*, a course in French–English translation method published in 1992. The change of title, to *Thinking French Translation*, takes account of subsequent adaptations of the course for German and Spanish and, more recently, Italian and Arabic. But this new edition is no less relevant to translation studies in general than the original edition was – if anything, it is more relevant and, I hope, more consistently convincing. The method is the same, but better explained.

Before presenting the changes, I want to record that the first instigation for a course along these lines came from Sándor Hervey. It is a matter of the greatest personal sorrow and professional regret that Sándor, who died suddenly in 1997 at the age of 55, has had virtually no hand in the changes I have made to our original concept. However, as far as one can be sure of anything in such matters, I am pretty confident that the changes are consistent with our thinking as it evolved over the thirteen years following our first pilot course in St Andrews. This is why, although the Preface is written in the first person, I have kept 'we' throughout the rest of the book. If anything in the book does redound to anyone's credit, let it be to the authors' credit jointly. Anything outrageous in this edition that is not present in the original is entirely my fault, not Sándor's.

The most notable conceptual refinements bear on the notions of compensation and genre, but all chapters benefit from sharper focus, clearer definitions and fuller and more relevant illustration. For example, in Chapter 2, our reservations about the term 'equivalence' are explained and illustrated more comprehensively, as is the important concept of translation loss. Such changes make for a longer chapter, but they have been made in response to consistent feedback from students and colleagues over the years.

Compensation has been given a chapter to itself. Our original section on compensation was an unhappy hybrid and already partly obsolescent, publication having been delayed for two years by a complicated series of takeovers in the publishing world. The result was an over-elaborate categorization of types of compensation which proved unnecessary in the classroom, and, in two of the categories, a conceptual fuzziness which was confusing for students and tutors. The new chapter is less ambitious taxonomically, more rigorously argued and more convincingly illustrated.

The other major change concerns genre. The first edition had two chapters on genre, positioned halfway through the book. Reflecting the current research interest of one of the authors, the two chapters paid disproportionate attention to differences between oral and written texts. These differences are vital, of course, but do not need so much space in a 250-page introduction to translation method. At the same time, there was not space enough for it to be made clear to students where to focus their textual analyses and their decision-making. A slimline, single-chapter format has worked much better in the Italian version of the course, and I have used this as the basis for the genre chapter in this book.

As for positioning the genre chapter, I have put it immediately between the one on compensation and those on the levels of textual variables. This makes for as coherent and progressive a course as before – but it was a difficult decision all the same. There are, after all, good reasons for keeping discussion of genre until Chapter 11. First, the genre-membership of a text cannot be finally decided until its other salient features have been isolated. These are features on the levels of textual variables (including literal and connotative meaning) and features of language variety. Second, students are often more confident in responding to genre requirements after working on these other features. The reason for siting the genre chapter earlier is that the defining element in genre is the relation between textual purpose and textual effect. This above all is what experienced translators respond to; and it is in turn the relation between this relation and the purpose of the TT that determines the translation strategy. Putting genre in Chapter 5 is in effect a forceful early statement of these fundamentals. That said, it would be no surprise, and need do no damage, if tutors felt happier keeping genre till later.

The six levels of textual variables are now presented in reverse order, from the phonic/graphic to the intertextual (Chapters 6–8). Given that the genre chapter now comes before these three, this order may seem perverse. In any case, linguistic orthodoxy requires a 'top-down' approach, from macro to micro. However, in teaching all versions of the course, we have found that students are more comfortable, and produce better work, with a 'bottom-up' approach. I must stress that this is purely a matter of pedagogic effectiveness, not of how translators set about their work. On the contrary, it is precisely to reflect professional practice that the genre chapter is placed so early, before discussion of textual variables.

In the first edition, there were also two chapters on language variety. After teaching different versions of the course, I feel that this was spinning things out too far, at the expense of other factors that needed more attention. As with compensation and genre, I have built a single chapter on the *Thinking Italian Translation* model, which has proved superior in class to the *Thinking Translation* one. And, as in the Italian course, these rearrangements have made space for an introductory chapter on legal and financial translation.

The revision and editing chapter has been completely rewritten, with more helpful analysis of examples to show the range of considerations and constraints that revisers and editors must always keep in mind.

As regards the illustrative and practical material, much has been retained from the first edition, but there is more that is new. A lot of what many colleagues regarded as marginal or over-specialized has been replaced with more 'real-world' material, notably from the fields of journalism, publicity, business, engineering and law. The real world has margins of its own, of course, and tutors who find that effective texts from the first edition have disappeared have every right to go on using those texts in classes.

Finally, a feature dropped from practicals in this edition is the speed translation. This is not meant to imply that translators do not work under fierce time pressure after all. It is more that the speed translations belong in a different sort of course. Perhaps they would be useful as a kind of bridge between an ESIT-type course and this one. As this course stands, though, the existing practicals are already more than enough for likely time available. In any case, it is open to tutors to impose any time limit they choose on any exercise they choose.

I think that – after vigorous discussion – Sándor Hervey would have agreed to these changes, which make the course clearer and more user-friendly, and so vindicate the original vision. If students and tutors enjoy using this new edition as much as we and our students enjoyed developing the original, his shade will be chuckling.

Ian Higgins
September 2001

Introduction

'Can translation be taught?' The question is asked surprisingly often – sometimes even by good translators, who you would think would know better. Certainly, as teachers of translation know, some people are naturally better at it than others. In this respect, aptitude for translation is no different from aptitude for any other activity: teaching and practice help anyone, including the most gifted, to perform at a higher level. Even Mozart had music lessons.

But most of us are not geniuses. Here again, anyone who has taught the subject knows that a structured course will help most students to become significantly better at translation – often good enough to earn their living at it. This book offers just such a course. Its progressive exposition of different sorts of translation problem is accompanied with plenty of practice in developing a rationale for solving them. It is a course not in translation theory, but in translation method, encouraging thoughtful consideration of possible solutions to practical problems. Theoretical issues do inevitably arise, but the aim of the course is to develop proficiency in the method, not to investigate its theoretical implications. When technical or theoretical terms are first explained, they are set in bold type; they are also listed in the Glossary of terms used (pp. 267–75).

If this is not a course in translation theory or linguistics, it is not a language-teaching course, either. The focus is on how to translate. It is assumed that the student already has a good command of French, and is familiar with the proper use of reference materials, including dictionaries and databases. The course is therefore aimed at final-year undergraduates, and at postgraduates or others seeking an academic or professional qualification in translation. That said, the analytical attention given to a wide variety of texts means that students do learn a lot of French – and probably a fair bit of English, too.

This last point is important. While our main aim is to improve quality in translation, it must be remembered that this quality requires the translator to have an adequate command of English as well as of

French. Assuming that this is the case, translator training normally focuses on translation into the mother tongue, because higher quality is achieved in that direction than in translating into a foreign language. Hence the predominance of unidirectional translation, from French into English, in this course. By its very nature, however, the course is also useful for French students seeking to improve their skills in translation into English: this is still an important part of English studies in France, and *Thinking French Translation* offers a distinctive and effective methodology and plenty of practical work in this area.

Since the course is an introduction to the interlingual operations involved in translating, we do not discuss machine translation, or how to use translation software on the Internet, etc. Only after learning to recognize what is at stake in a given translation task can one confidently accept or reject the sometimes disconcerting solutions proposed by translation software. Indeed, some of the service providers themselves implicitly acknowledge this, offering e.g. 'real live human translators' for 'more in-depth translation projects' (http://news.microsoft.co.uk/office1101018405). *Thinking French Translation* provides a basic training for those very people – human translators, capable of handling any in-depth project.

The course has a progressive structure. It begins with the fundamental issues, options and alternatives of which a translator must be aware: translation as process, translation as product, cultural issues in translation, and the nature and crucial importance of compensation in translation. Next, it looks at the question of genre, or text-type. It then moves, via a survey of translation issues raised on six layers of textual variables (from the phonic to the intertextual), to a series of semantic and stylistic topics – literal meaning, connotative meaning, register, sociolect and dialect. Further chapters are given to technical translation, legal and financial translation, consumer-oriented translation, and translation revision and editing.

Chapter by chapter, then, the student is progressively trained to ask, and to answer, a series of questions that apply to any text given for translation. Pre-eminent among these are: 'What is the purpose of my translation, and what are the salient features of this text?' No translation is produced in a vacuum, and we stress throughout the course that the needs of the target audience and the requirements of the person commissioning the translation are primary factors in translation decisions. For this same reason, when students are asked in a practical to do a translation, we always include a translation brief in the assignment. As for the salient features of the text, these are what add up to its specificity as typical or atypical of a particular genre or genres. Once its genre-membership and purpose have been pinned down, the translator can decide on a strategy for meeting the translation brief. The student's attention is kept focused on this issue by the wide variety of genres found in the practicals – in addition to technical, legal and business texts, students are asked to work on various sorts of journalistic and literary text, song, film subtitling, publicity brochures, customer leaflets, etc.

The sorts of question that need to be asked in determining the salient features of any text are listed in the schema of textual matrices on p. 5. The schema amounts to a checklist of potentially relevant kinds of textual feature. These are presented in the order in which they arise in the course, in Chapters 3 and 5–11. (Compensation, the subject of Chapter 4, is not a textual feature, and therefore does not figure in the schema.) The student would be well advised to refer to the schema before tackling a practical: it is a progressive reminder of what questions to ask of the text set for analysis or translation.

While the course systematically builds up a methodical approach, we are not trying to 'mechanize' translation by offering some inflexible rule or recipe. Very much the opposite: translation is a creative activity, and the translator's personal responsibility is paramount. We therefore emphasize the need to recognize options and alternatives, the need for rational discussion, and the need for decision-making. Each chapter is intended for class discussion at the start of the corresponding seminar, and a lot of the practicals are best done by students working in small groups. This is to help students keep in mind that, whatever approach the translator adopts, it should be self-aware and methodical.

The course is divided into a series of units intended to fit into an academic timetable. Each of the first eleven units comprises a chapter outlining a coherent set of notions and problems, and a practical or practicals in which students are set concrete translation tasks relevant to the chapter. These units are designed to be studied in numerical order, and are the essential foundation for the rest of the course. Chapters 12–14 give practice in various genres which commonly provide the bread and butter of professional translators. Ideally, all of these should be worked through, but local conditions may oblige the tutor to leave one out. Chapter 15 focuses on revision and editing. Chapters 16–19 are different from the others. They can be studied at whatever points in the course seem most opportune. These chapters are devoted to four areas of 'contrastive linguistics' in which French–English translation problems commonly occur.

Each unit needs about two hours of seminar time. It is vital that every student should have the necessary reference books in class: a *c.*2000-page monolingual French dictionary, such as the *Petit Robert*, a similar-sized French–English/English–French dictionary, an English dictionary and an English thesaurus. Some of the practical work will be done at home – sometimes individually, sometimes in groups – and handed in for assessment by the tutor. How often this is done will be decided by tutors and students between them. Full suggestions for teaching and assessment can be found in Sándor Hervey and Ian Higgins, *Thinking French Translation: Tutor's Handbook* (Routledge, 2002).

Note that Practical 5 involves work on oral texts. These are supplied to tutors with the *Tutor's Handbook*. Many of the practicals involve work on texts that are not contained in the present volume, but are intended for distribution in class. These texts are found in the *Tutor's Handbook*.

Students doing the course often inquire about the possibility of translation as a career. The Postscript (pp. 264–6) outlines the nature, attractions and drawbacks of translation work, and contains information about professional bodies which can give detailed help and advice.

The abbreviations used in the book are explained in Chapter 1. As for symbols, there are only two that need any comment, the slash and the brace in examples where alternative translations are given. Basically, we use slashes, with no space before or after, to indicate the different possibilities, as in:

'Promenade' can be translated as 'walk/ride/drive/sail' etc.

Where necessary, we use braces to make the division between units in the alternatives absolutely clear, e.g.:

In this context, 'approfondir' means 'to go {deeper/further} into'.

Here, the braces show that the alternatives are 'to go deeper into' and 'to go further into', not 'to go deeper' and 'to go further into'.

Note that a slash with a space before and after it does not indicate alternatives, but simply a division between e.g. lines of verse, as in 'There was a young fellow from Warwick / Who had reason for feeling euphoric'.

SCHEMA OF TEXTUAL MATRICES		
QUESTION TO ASK ABOUT THE TEXT	MATRIX OF FEATURES	EXAMPLES OF TYPICAL FEATURES
	GENRE MATRIX (Chapter 5)	
What genre(s) does this text belong to:	Genre types: empirical philosophical religious persuasive literary hybrid Oral vs written	scientific paper, balance sheet, etc. essay on good and evil, etc. biblical text, etc. constitution, advertisement, etc. short story, etc. sermon, parody, job contract, etc. dialogue, song, subtitles, etc.
	CULTURAL MATRIX (Chapter 3)	
Are there significant features presenting a choice between:	Exoticism Calque Cultural borrowing Communicative translation Cultural transplantation	wholesale foreignness idiom translated literally, etc. name of historical movement, etc. public notices, proverbs, etc. Paris recast as Glasgow, etc.
	FORMAL MATRIX (Chapters 6–8)	
Are there significant features on the:	Phonic/graphic level Prosodic level Grammatical level: lexis syntax Sentential level Discourse level Intertextual level	alliteration, layout, etc. vocal pitch, rhythm, etc. archaism, overtones, etc. simple vs complex syntax, etc. sequential focus, intonation, etc. cohesion markers, etc. pastiche, allusion to Racine, etc.
	SEMANTIC MATRIX (Chapters 9–10)	
Are there significant instances of:	Literal meaning Allusive meaning Attitudinal meaning Associative meaning Collocative meaning Reflected meaning Affective meaning	synonymy, etc. echo of proverb, etc. hostile attitude to referent, etc. gender stereotyping of referent, etc. collocative clash, etc. homonymic echo, etc. offensive attitude to addressee, etc.
	VARIETAL MATRIX (Chapter 11)	
Are there significant instances of:	Tonal register Social register Sociolect Dialect	ingratiating tone, etc. intolerant right-wing bourgeois, etc. Paris *banlieue* working class, etc. Chtimi accent, etc.

1

Preliminaries to translation as a process

This chapter examines translation as a process – what it is the translator actually does. But first, we must note a few basic terms that will be used throughout the course:

Text   Any given stretch of speech or writing assumed to make a coherent whole. A minimal text may consist of a single word preceded and followed by a silence or a blank, e.g. 'Zut!', or the road sign 'Stop'. A maximal text, such as Proust's *A la recherche du temps perdu*, may run into volumes.

Source text (ST)   The text to be translated.

Target text (TT)   The text which is a translation of the ST.

Source language (SL)   The language in which the ST is spoken or written.

Target language (TL)   The language into which the ST is to be translated.

Strategy   The translator's overall 'game-plan', consisting of a set of strategic decisions taken after an initial reading of the ST, but before starting detailed translation of it.

Strategic decisions   The first set of reasoned decisions taken by the translator. These are taken before starting the translation in detail, in response to the following questions: 'What is the translation brief, i.e. what are the purpose and intended audience of my translation? What is the purpose of this ST? What genre does it belong to, and what audience is it aimed at? What is its message content? What are its salient linguistic features? What are its principal effects? What are the implications of all these factors? If a choice has to be made among them, which ones should be given priority in ensuring that the TT is fit for its purpose?'

Decisions of detail   Reasoned decisions concerning the specific problems of syntax, vocabulary, etc. encountered in translating particular expressions or stretches of text in their particular context. Decisions of detail are made in the light of the strategy. However, problems of detail may well arise during translating which raise unforeseen strategic issues and oblige the translator to refine the original strategy somewhat.

With these terms in mind, the translation process can be broken down into two types of activity: understanding an ST and formulating a TT. These do not occur successively, but simultaneously; indeed, it is often only when coming up against a problem in formulating the TT that translators realize they have not fully understood something in the ST. When this happens, the ST may need to be reinterpreted in the light of the translator's new understanding of it. This reinterpretation sometimes entails revising the original strategy, the revision in turn necessitating changes to some of the decisions of detail already taken. Nevertheless, it is useful to discuss ST interpretation and TT formulation as different, separate processes.

The processes of translation are no different from familiar things that everyone does every day. Comprehension and interpretation are processes that we all perform whenever we listen to or read a piece of linguistically imparted information. Understanding even the simplest message potentially involves all our accumulated experience – the knowledge, beliefs, suppositions, inferences and expectations that are the stuff of personal, social and cultural life. Understanding everyday messages is therefore not all that different from what a translator does when first confronting an ST – and it is certainly no less complicated.

In everyday communication, evidence that a message has been understood may come from appropriate response, for example, if your mother asks you for a spoon, and you give her a spoon and not a fork. Or it may come from appropriate *linguistic* response – such things as returning a greeting correctly, answering a question satisfactorily, or filling in a form. None of these are translation-like processes, but they do show that the comprehension and interpretation stage of translation involves an ordinary, everyday activity that simply requires an average command of the language used.

However, one everyday activity that does resemble translation proper is what Roman Jakobson actually calls 'inter-semiotic translation' (1971: 260–6), that is, translation between two semiotic systems (systems for communication). 'The green light means go' is an act of inter-semiotic translation, as is 'The big hand's pointing to twelve and the little hand's pointing to four, so it's four o'clock'. In each case, there is translation from a non-linguistic communication system to a linguistic one. To this extent, everyone is a translator of a sort.

Still more common are various sorts of linguistic response to linguistic stimuli which are also very like translation proper, even though they actually take place within a single language. These sorts of process are what Jakobson (ibid.) calls 'intralingual translation'. A brief look at the two extremes of intralingual translation will show what its major implications are. Take the following scenario. Jill is driving Jack through the narrow streets of a small town. A policeman steps out and stops them. As he leans in to speak to Jill, she can see over his shoulder that, further on, a trailer has tipped over and blocked the street. At one extreme of intralingual translation lies the kind of response typified in this exchange:

POLICEMAN   There's been an accident ahead, Madam – I'm afraid you'll have to turn left down St Mary's Lane here, the road's blocked.
JILL   Oh, OK. Thanks.
JACK   What did he say?
JILL   We've got to turn left.

The policeman's essential message is 'Turn left'. But he does not want to sound brusque. So he mollifies the driver with a partial explanation, 'There's been an accident', and then cushions his instruction with 'I'm afraid you'll have to'. 'Down St Mary's Lane' gives a hint of local colour and fellow-citizenship; but he does add 'here', just in case the driver is a stranger. Finally, he completes his explanation.

When Jack asks what he said, however, Jill *separates the gist* of the policeman's message from the circumstantial details and tonal subtleties, and *reports it in her own words*. This type of intralingual translation we shall call **gist translation**. The example also shows two other features which intralingual translation shares with translation proper. First, Jill's is not the only gist translation possible. For instance, she might have said 'We've got to go down here.' Among other things, this implies that at least one of them does not know the town: the street name has no significance. A third possibility is 'We've got to go down St Mary's Lane': if Jack and Jill do know the town, the policeman's gist is accurately conveyed.

The other feature shared by intralingual translation and translation proper is that the situation in which a message is expressed and received affects *how* it is expressed and received. By 'situation' here we mean a combination of three elements: the circumstances in which speaker and addressee find themselves (such as being stopped in a car and having to take a diversion), the accumulated experience they carry with them all the time (knowing or not knowing the town; familiarity or unfamiliarity with conventions for giving and receiving instructions; liking or disliking the police, etc.), and the linguistic **context**. 'Context' is often used metaphorically in the sense of 'situation' (and sometimes even in the sense of 'meaning'). In this book we shall use it specifically to denote the rest of a text in which a given expression or stretch of text occurs. For example, the context of Jack's question is the exchange between Jill and the policeman and her reply to Jack; the context of the policeman's words is everything that follows them; the context of Jill's reply to Jack is everything that precedes 'We've got to turn left'. As will become clear, the whole context is an important consideration in translation; but the more immediate the context, the more crucial a factor it becomes in making decisions of detail.

There are always so many variables in the message situation that it is impossible to predict what the gist translation will be or how the addressee will take it. For example, Jill might simply have said 'Turn left', a highly economical way of reporting the gist – no bad thing when she has to concentrate on driving. However, depending on how she says it and how Jack receives it, it could give the impression that the policeman was brusque.

Another reason why 'Turn left' could sound brusque is that, grammatically, it looks like direct speech (an imperative), whereas all the other gist translations we have given are clearly indirect speech (or 'reported speech'). Now *all* translation may be said to be indirect speech, inasmuch as it does not repeat the ST, but reformulates it in the translator's words. Yet most TTs, like 'Turn left', mask this fact by omitting the typical markers of indirect speech, e.g. 'The author says that . . .', or change in point of view (as in changing '*I'm* afraid *you'll* have to turn left' into '*he's* afraid *we'll* have to turn left'). As a result, it is easy for reformulation consciously or unconsciously to become distortion, either because the translator misrepresents the ST or because the reader misreads the TT, or both.

In other words, gist translation, like any translation, is a process of *interpretation*. This is seen still more clearly if we take an example at the other extreme of intralingual translation. Jill might just as easily have interpreted the policeman's words by expanding them. For example, she could build on an initial gist translation as follows:

We've got to go down St Mary's Lane – some fool's tipped a trailer over and blocked the High Street.

This puts two sorts of gloss on the policeman's message: she adds details that he did not give (the tipping over, the name of the street ahead) and her own judgement of the driver. We shall use the term **exegetic translation** to denote a translation that explains and elaborates on the ST in this way. The inevitable part played by the translator's accumulated experience becomes obvious in exegetic translation, for any exegesis by definition involves explicitly bringing considerations from outside the text into one's reading of it – here, the overturned trailer, Jill's knowledge of the town, and her attitude towards other road-users.

An exegetic translation can be shorter than the ST, as in this example, but exegesis is usually longer, and can easily shade into general observations triggered by the ST but not really explaining it. Knowing the town as she does, Jill might easily have gone on like this:

The street's just too *narrow* for a thing that size.

This explanation is admissible as exegesis, but it probably goes beyond the limit of exegetic translation.

Finally, gist translation and exegetic translation often occur in close association with one another. Sometimes, they seem to be inseparable, especially in the rewording of metaphor (see the *Macbeth* examples on p. 11). But this is not confined to intralingual translation or to literary texts. Here is an example from the statement of accounts of a big firm. In France, the accounts must be accompanied by a *rapport général des commissaires aux comptes* (statutory auditors' report), and by a *rapport spécial des commissaires aux comptes sur les conventions réglementées*. This ST and TT refer to the latter (the ST report is addressed to the shareholders):

ST	TT
En application de l'article 103 de la loi du 24 juillet 1966, nous vous informons que le Président de votre conseil d'administration ne nous a donné avis d'aucune convention visée à l'article 101 de cette loi.	In accordance with corporate legislation, we are required to submit a report to the Annual General Meeting of Shareholders with respect to certain agreements entered into by the Company with managers or directors of the Company, or with companies in which such persons exercise similar functions. Agreements of this nature require prior approval of the Board of Directors.
(Aerospatiale 1994a: 86)	No such agreements or transactions arising therefrom have been brought to our attention.
	(Aerospatiale 1994b: 86)

Clearly, the ST reader is expected to know what this law requires. The TT may have been produced, as such texts often are, in accordance with standard translations issued by the International Accounting Standards Committee (IASC). However it was arrived at, the strategy has clearly been to assume that the TL reader will not understand an unglossed reference to the law of 24 July 1966. The TT is basically exegetic, but it is also a gist translation, in that it does not even mention the law by name.

As these examples show, it is not only sometimes hard to keep gist translation and exegetic translation apart, it can be hard to see where translation shades into comment pure and simple. It certainly seems very difficult to achieve an ideal rephrasing, a halfway point between gist and exegesis that would use terms radically different from those of the ST, but add nothing to, and omit nothing from, its message content. And yet, with its constant movement between gist and exegesis, intralingual translation happens all the time in speech. It is also common in written texts.

Students regularly encounter it in annotated editions. A good example is G.K. Hunter's edition of *Macbeth*, in which the text of the play is followed by about 50 pages of notes. Here are the opening lines of the Captain's report on how the battle stood when he left it, followed by Hunter's notes and rephrasings and, in square brackets, our comments on them:

> Doubtful it stood,
> As two spent swimmers that do cling together
> And choke their art. The merciless Macdonwald –
> Worthy to be a rebel, for to that
> The multiplying villainies of nature
> Do swarm upon him – from the Western Isles
> Of kerns and galloglasses is supplied [. . .].

choke their art   make impossible the art of swimming. [An exegetic rephrasing, in so far as it makes explicit what is only implicit in the metaphor: neither army holds the advantage. At the same time, it only conveys the gist, losing the crucial implications of the image of 'choking'.]

to that   as if to that end. [Exegetic rephrasing, explaining Shakespeare's elliptical formulation.]

multiplying villainies of nature / Do swarm upon him   hosts of rebels join him like noxious insects swarming. [Exegetic rephrasing which gives the gist of Shakespeare's image, but also distorts it, turning the metaphor into an explanatory simile: in the ST, the rebels are not *like insects*, they *are* villainous manifestations of nature.]

Western Isles Hebrides   [Synonymous rephrasing, for readers unfamiliar with Scottish geography: a good example of how any rewording involves presuppositions regarding the target audience's accumulated experience.]

kerns and galloglasses   light and heavy-armed Celtic levies. [Virtually synonymous rephrasing, this time for readers unfamiliar with medieval Irish and Scottish armies. However, 'levies' may not be accurate in respect of galloglasses, who were mercenaries – even the simplest rephrasing may be misleading, intentionally or not.]

(Shakespeare 1967: 54, 140)

In all the examples we have been discussing, the dividing lines between gist, exegesis, translation and comment are blurred. Things could not be otherwise. If one thing has become clear in this chapter, it is the difficulty of controlling (and even of seeing) how far an intralingual TT omits from, adds to or faithfully reproduces the ST message content. And, as we shall see in the next chapter and throughout the course, what applies to intralingual translation applies a fortiori to translation proper: the ST message *content* can never be precisely reproduced in the TT, because of the very fact that the two *forms of expression* are different.

There are other important respects in which the three types of intralingual translation are on an equal footing with translation proper. They all require knowledge of the subject matter of the source text, familiarity with the source language and source culture in general, and interpretive effort. But they also require knowledge of the nature and needs of the target public, familiarity with the target culture in general — and, above all, mastery of the target language. Synopsis-writing, reported speech, intralingual rephrasing and exegesis are therefore excellent exercises for our purposes, because they develop the ability to find and choose between alternative means of expressing a given message content. This is why the first exercise in this course is a piece of intralingual translation in English.

PRACTICAL 1

1.1 Intralingual translation

Assignment
  (i)   Identify the salient features of content and expression in the following ST, and say what its purpose is.
  (ii) Recast the ST in different words, adapting it for a specific purpose and a specific public (i.e. a specific readership or audience). Say precisely what the purpose and the public are. Treat the ST as if you were recasting the whole book of Genesis, of which it is a part. (As a rule, *whenever* you do a translation as part of this course, you should proceed as if you were translating the whole text from which the ST is taken.)
  (iii) Explain the main decisions of detail you took in making the textual changes. (Insert into your TT a superscript note-number after each expression you intend to discuss, and then, starting on a fresh sheet of paper, discuss the points in numerical order. This is the system you should use whenever you annotate your own TTs.)

Contextual information
The text is from the Authorized Version of the Bible, published in 1611. The best way of making sense of it is to read the rest of Genesis 3, of which it is the start. In Chapter 2, God has told Adam that he may eat of every tree in the Garden of Eden except the tree of the knowledge of good and evil, on pain of death. Subsequently God has made a woman as a helper for Adam (she is not called Eve until later in Chapter 3). At the end of Chapter 2, they are both naked, and not ashamed.

ST

Now the serpent was more subtil than any beast of the field which the
LORD God had made. And he said unto the woman, Yea, hath God said,
Ye shall not eat of every tree in the garden?

And the woman said unto the serpent, We may eat of the fruit of the
5 trees of the garden:

But of the fruit of the tree which is in the midst of the garden, God
hath said, Ye shall not eat of it, neither shall ye touch it, lest ye die.

And the serpent said unto the woman, Ye shall not surely die:

For God doth know that in the day ye eat thereof, then your eyes shall
10 be opened, and ye shall be as gods, knowing good and evil.

And when the woman saw that the tree was good for food, and that it
was pleasant to the eyes, and a tree to be desired to make one wise, she
took of the fruit thereof, and did eat, and gave also unto her husband with
her; and he did eat.

15 And the eyes of them both were opened, and they knew that they
were naked; and they sewed fig leaves together, and made themselves
aprons.

And they heard the voice of the LORD God walking in the garden in
the cool of the day: and Adam and his wife hid themselves from the pres-
20 ence of the LORD God amongst the trees of the garden.

And the LORD God called unto Adam, and said unto him, Where art
thou?

And he said, I heard thy voice in the garden, and I was afraid, because
I was naked; and I hid myself.

(Genesis 3, v. 1–10)

1.2 Gist translation

Assignment

(i)   You have been commissioned to translate the following text for *Air
France magazine*, in abridged form. The publisher has specified that
the TT will be printed below the ST, in smaller type. The ST contains
349 words. The TT should contain between 250 and 270 words.
Discuss the strategic decisions that you have to take before starting
detailed work on this ST, and outline and justify the strategy you
adopt.

(ii) Produce a gist translation of the specified length.

(iii) Discuss the main decisions of detail you took, concentrating on
explaining your omissions and any exegetic elements that you introduced.

(iv) Compare your TT with the published one, which will be given you
by your tutor. Concentrate on the omissions, and on whether they
have entailed introducing any exegetic elements.

Contextual information
Printed on the first page as a kind of editorial, the text is an introduction
to the main contents of the magazine.

ST

Bonjour, et bienvenue à bord.
« J'ai simplement le sentiment qu'il me faut entendre d'autres voix. Toutes
celles qu'on ne laisse pas venir jusqu'à nous, celles de ces gens qu'on a
trop longtemps dédaignés, dont on trouvait le nombre trop infime mais
5   qui, pourtant, ont tellement à nous apporter. » Ce propos de **J.M.G. Le
Clézio** illustre à souhait les œuvres de deux grandes voix de notre époque
dont les échos résonnent dans ce numéro.
    La première est, bien sûr, celle de l'écrivain lui-même, éblouie par le
Mexique, par les grands textes sacrés amérindiens, la langue, les rites et
10   l'éclat d'une pensée interrompue avec l'arrivée des conquérants espag-
nols. « Ce que je découvrais ainsi, écrira-t-il dans *La fête chantée*, c'est
l'intelligence de l'univers, son évidence, sa sensibilité. » Les Amérindiens
ne nous sont pas étrangers. Ils sont une partie de nous-mêmes, de notre
destinée.
15   **Louis Armstrong**, oui, le trompettiste dont on fête cette année le
centième anniversaire de la naissance, a-t-il dit autre chose tout au long
de sa carrière à propos du peuple noir ? Il était petit-fils d'esclaves.
Hollywood a essayé d'en faire le « bon noir », naïf jovial aux roulements
d'yeux de bouffon. Dans les années 1960, quand le gouverneur de
20   l'Arkansas, Faubus, utilise la garde nationale pour empêcher les enfants
noirs d'aller à l'école, Louis Armstrong est le premier à protester. Fiché
pour ses interventions contre la ségrégation raciale, celui qui est alors une
star mondiale refusera de retourner à la Nouvelle-Orléans, sa ville natale,
soumise à des lois racistes.
25   Ecouter la voix de ceux qu'on n'entend pas ou si peu, c'est aussi ce
que proposent, dans ce numéro, les habitants de **l'île grecque de
Kárpathos** qui, à l'occasion de Pâques, revivent les traditions millénaires
qu'ils ont su préserver. C'est encore, dans un registre tout à fait différent,
le projet du photographe **Thierry des Ouches** qui nous donne à voir une
30   France rurale, sentimentale, que l'on regarde avec un brin de nostalgie.
    N'hésitez pas à emporter ce magazine, il vous appartient.
    Merci de voyager en notre compagnie. Bonne lecture et bon vol.

                                              (Air France 2001: 5)

2

Preliminaries to translation as a product

Chapter 1 viewed translation as a process. However, the evidence we had for the process was *products* – gist translations and exegetic translations. It is as a product that translation is viewed in the present chapter. Here, too, it is useful to examine two diametric opposites: in this case, two opposed degrees of freedom of translation, showing extreme SL bias on the one hand, and extreme TL bias on the other.

DEGREES OF FREEDOM OF TRANSLATION

At the extreme of SL bias is **interlinear translation**, where the TT does not necessarily respect TL grammar, but has grammatical units corresponding as closely as possible to every grammatical unit of the ST. Here is an example:

Je persiste à croire qu'elle n'avait pas tort de le dire.
I persist to think that she not had no wrong to it say.

Interlinear translation is of no practical use for this course. It is normally only used in descriptive linguistics or language teaching. Even then it has its limitations – witness the difficulty of finding a counterpart for 'pas' here. Interlinear translation is actually an extreme form of the much more common **literal translation**, where the literal meaning of words is taken as if straight from the dictionary (that is, out of context), but TL grammar is respected. (The **literal** – or 'cognitive' or 'denotative' – **meaning** of an expression is the appropriate conventional referential meaning given for it in the dictionary, regardless of any connotations or nuances it has in a particular context.) A possible literal translation of our example is:

'I persist in thinking that she was not wrong to say it.' For practical purposes, we shall take literal translation as the extreme of SL bias.

At the opposite extreme, TL bias, is **free translation**, where there is only an overall correspondence between the textual units of the ST and those of the TT. Between the two extremes, the degrees of freedom are infinitely variable. However, in assessing translation freedom, it can be useful to situate the TT on a scale between extreme SL bias and extreme TL bias, with notional intermediate points schematized as in the following diagram, heavily adapted from Newmark (1981: 39):

The five points on the scale can be illustrated from the example we have just used, 'Je persiste à croire qu'elle n'avait pas tort de le dire':

LITERAL	I persist in thinking that she wasn't wrong to say it.
FAITHFUL	I still think she wasn't wrong to say it.
BALANCED	I still don't think she was wrong to say it.
IDIOMIZING	I still think she hit the nail on the head.
FREE	No way should she retract.

Before going any further, we should define what we mean by an **idiomizing translation**. This is one that respects the ST message content, but typically uses TL idioms or familiar phonic and rhythmic patterns to give an easy read, even if (as in our example) this means sacrificing nuances of meaning or tone. By **idiom** we mean a fixed figurative expression whose meaning cannot be deduced from the literal meaning of the words that make it up, as in 'football's not *my cup of tea*', 'that's *a different kettle of fish*', 'you've *hit the nail on the head*', etc. Note that 'idiomizing' is not synonymous with 'idiomatic': throughout this course, we use the term **idiomatic** to denote what sounds 'natural' and 'normal' to native speakers – a linguistic expression that is unexceptional and acceptable in a given context. Thus, in our five examples of degrees of freedom, the last three are certainly idiomatic, but only one of them is an idiomizing translation.

The five examples call for comment. First, it should be noted that, since literal translation respects TL grammar, it very often involves **grammatical transposition** – the replacement or reinforcement of given parts of speech or grammatical categories in the ST by others in the TT. In the literal translation given here, there are two grammatical transpositions: (1) the infinitive 'croire' is rendered by the gerund 'thinking'; (2) the noun 'tort' is rendered by the adjective 'wrong'. But this adoption of TL grammar still has not made for a very plausible TT. Not surprisingly, there are more grammatical transpositions in the faithful and balanced translations.

In the faithful translation, there are three grammatical transpositions: (1) the verb 'persister' becomes the adverb 'still'; (2) the infinitive 'croire' becomes the finite 'I think'; (3) there is no conjunction corresponding to 'que'. This translation is less implausible than the literal translation, but it would still sound odd in most contexts.

In the balanced translation, two more grammatical transpositions are added to those in the faithful translation: (1) the negation is transferred from 'avoir tort' to 'croire', and (2) it is rendered with an auxiliary verb ('do'), where the ST has none. Five grammatical transpositions, then, but they are unexceptional and acceptable: this balanced translation is more idiomatic and more convincing than the literal and faithful translations.

Another important point about the degrees of freedom is that the dividing lines between them are fluid. Each of the TTs is open to query, and others could be suggested. For instance, is 'I persist in thinking' really an accurate literal rendering of 'Je persiste à croire'? Do 'I think she wasn't wrong' and 'I don't think she was wrong' mean the same thing? Similarly, the suggested idiomizing translation corresponds to 'I think she was right', which perhaps means something else again. Depending on the answers to these questions, it might even be argued that, in this case, the suggested balanced translation is the only accurate literal translation. As for the free translation, it only gives a partial overlap with the ST: the overall message is the same – 'She was right to say what she said', but it loses the explicit expression of an opinion, and adds the implication that she is under pressure to withdraw her statement. If all these issues are discussed in class, it will become clear that the five categories are fluid, and that, depending on context, any of these TTs – or others – could be the preferred choice.

However, some contexts offer less choice than others. This brings us to our final point: in certain circumstances, the freest TT may in fact hardly be a free choice at all! This is often the case if the ST contains an SL idiom, proverb, or other expression standard for a given situation, and the TL offers an idiom, proverb, or other expression standard for an equivalent target-culture situation. In such cases, using the TL equivalent is often inescapable. So, in most contexts, the following TTs will generally seem mandatory:

ST	TT
C'est une autre paire de manches.	That's another kettle of fish.
J'ai d'autres chats à fouetter.	I've got other fish to fry.
Faute de grives, on mange des merles.	Half a loaf is better than no bread.
Objets trouvés.	Lost property.
Je vous en prie.	You're welcome/don't mention it.

importance de la culture [handwritten]

We shall call this sort of rendering a **communicative translation**. A communicative translation is produced when, in a given situation, the ST uses an SL expression standard for that situation, and the TT uses a TL expression standard for an equivalent target-culture situation. We will discuss communicative translation in more detail in Chapter 3. For the moment, we will just point out a seeming paradox: inasmuch as they diverge greatly from ST literal meanings, these ready-made communicative translations are examples of free translation; yet the translator seems to have little free choice as to whether or not to adopt them.

Note that although 'No way should she retract' is very free and colloquially plausible, it is not a communicative translation, because it is not the standard expression in the given situation. (There *is* no standard expression for this situation.) So its freedom is gratuitous, and might well be considered excessive: it might be out of character for the speaker to use 'no way' in this sense, and the TT is in any case avoidably different in message content and tone from the ST.

élaborer [handwritten] It should also be noted that a free translation does not have to be a colloquial one. It could just as easily be highly formal, as in: 'I remain of the unshakeable conviction that she should on no account withdraw her observation.'

EQUIVALENCE AND TRANSLATION LOSS

In introducing the notion of communicative translation, we referred to 'equivalent' idioms and proverbs, and 'equivalent' target-culture situations. As a matter of fact, most writers on translation use the terms 'equivalence' and 'equivalent', but in so many different ways that equivalence has become a confusing concept even for teachers of translation, let alone their students. So we need to say what we mean, and what we do not mean, by 'equivalence' and 'equivalent'. We shall not go in detail into the philosophical implications of the term 'equivalence': this is not a course on translation theory. Hermans (1999), Holmes (1988), Koller (1995), Nida (1964), Toury (1980 and 1995) and Snell-Hornby (1988) between them provide a useful introduction to the question.

The many different definitions of equivalence in translation fall broadly into two categories: they are either descriptive or prescriptive. Descriptively, 'equivalence' denotes an observed relationship between ST utterances and TT utterances that are seen as directly corresponding to one another. According to this view, each of the TTs illustrating degrees of freedom (p. 16) is equivalent to 'Je persiste à croire qu'elle n'avait pas tort de le dire', and the TT of the accountants' report on p. 10 is equivalent to the ST. Prescriptively, 'equivalence' denotes the relationship between an SL expression and the standard TL rendering of it, for example as given in a dictionary, or as required by a teacher, or as consonant with a given theory or methodology of translation. So, prescriptively, the following pairs of utterances are equivalents:

ST	TT
I'm hungry.	J'ai faim.
Merci de ne pas fumer.	Thank you for not smoking.
Ce n'est qu'une broutille.	It's nothing.
Où est l'entrée des artistes ?	Where's the stage door?
Chat échaudé craint l'eau froide.	Once bitten, twice shy.
Don't teach your grandmother to suck eggs.	On n'apprend pas à un vieux singe à faire des grimaces.

An influential variant of prescriptive equivalence is the 'dynamic equivalence' of the eminent Bible translator Eugene Nida. This is based on the 'principle of equivalent effect', the principle that 'the relationship between receptor and message should be substantially the same as that which existed between the original receptors and the message' (Nida 1964: 159). Nida's view does have real attractions. As we have just seen, and shall suggest throughout the course, there are all sorts of good reasons why a translator might not want to translate a given expression literally. A case in point is communicative translation, which may be said to be an example of 'dynamic equivalence' (cf. Nida 1964: 166: 'That is just the way we would say it'). However, there is a danger of 'dynamic equivalence' being seen as giving *carte blanche* for freedom to write more or less anything as long as it sounds good in the TL and does reflect, however tenuously, something of the ST message content. This danger is very real, as most teachers of translation will confirm. It is in fact a symptom of theoretical problems contained in the very notion of 'equivalent effect', most notably the normative implications.

To begin with, who is to *know* what the relationship between ST message and source-culture receptors is? For that matter, is it plausible to speak of *the* relationship, as if there were only one: are there not as many relationships as there are receptors? And who is to know what such relationships can have been in the past? *Phèdre*, the *Déclaration des droits de l'homme*, *L'Etranger*: each is, and has been, different things to different people in different places at different times – and indeed, different to the same person at different times. In any case, most texts have *plural* effects even in one reading by one person; the less technical the text, the more likely this is. And these problems apply as much to the TT as to the ST: who is to foresee the multiple relationships between the TT and its receptors? Finally, whatever the relationships between the ST and source-culture receptors, and between the TT and target-culture receptors, can we be satisfied that bites and scalded cats, or grandmothers and monkeys, produce 'equivalent effects' on their respective receptors? And the connotations of 'entrée des artistes' surely produce a significantly different effect from those of 'stage door'.

The discussion so far suggests that, the more normative the use of 'equivalence', the more the term risks being taken to imply 'sameness'. Indeed, it is used in this way in logic, mathematics and sign-theory, where an equivalent relationship is one that is objective, incontrovertible and – crucially – reversible. In translation, however, such unanimity and such reversibility are unthinkable for any but the very simplest of texts – and even then, only in respect of literal meaning. For example, 'Merci de ne pas fumer' translates as 'Thank you for not smoking', but will **back-translation** (i.e. translating a TT back into the SL) automatically give 'Merci de ne pas fumer'? This French expression is a polite *request* not to smoke. But the English expression can just as easily be used to thank a smoker for having refrained. If that is the intention, the appropriate French form is 'Merci de n'avoir pas fumé' (or 'Merci de ne pas avoir fumé'). Similarly, back-translation of 'It's nothing' could just as easily give 'Ce n'est rien', 'C'est pas grave', or even 'Ça ne coûte rien', as 'Ce n'est qu'une broutille'. Even the three possible back-translations of 'J'ai faim' – 'I'm hungry', 'I am hungry', 'I feel hungry' – are not exact equivalents of one another.

In so far as the principle of equivalent effect implies 'sameness' or is used normatively, it seems to be more of a hindrance than a help, both theoretically and pedagogically. Consequently, when we spoke of 'an equivalent target-culture situation', we were not intending 'an equivalent' to have a sense specific to any translation theory, but were using it in its everyday sense of 'a counterpart' – something different, but with points of resemblance in the aspects judged to be most relevant. This is how the term will be used in this book.

Given the problems associated with 'equivalence', we have found it more useful, both in translating and in teaching translation, to avoid an absolutist ambition to *maximize sameness* between ST and TT, in favour of a relativist ambition to *minimize difference*: to look, not for what is to be put into the TT, but for what might be saved from the ST. There is a vital difference between the two ambitions. The aim of maximizing sameness encourages the belief that, somewhere out there, there is the 'right' translation, the TT that is 'equi-valent' (has 'equal value') to the ST, at some ideal halfway point between SL bias and TL bias. But it is more realistic, and more productive, to start by admitting that, because SL and TL are fundamentally different, the transfer from ST to TT *inevitably* imposes difference – or, as we shall argue, loss.

It may be helpful here to draw an analogy with 'energy loss' in engineering. The transfer of energy in any machine necessarily involves energy loss. Engineers do not bewail this as a theoretical anomaly, but simply see it as a practical problem which they confront by striving to design more efficient machines, in which energy loss is reduced. We shall give the term **translation loss** to non-replication of the ST in the TT – that is, the inevitable loss of culturally relevant features. By 'culturally relevant' features, we mean features which are specific to the SL and the source culture and which make the ST what it is. The term 'translation loss' is intended to suggest that translators should not agonize over the loss, but should concentrate on 'reducing' it, i.e. controlling and channelling it.

The analogy with energy loss is not perfect, of course: whereas energy loss is a loss (or rather, a diversion) *of* energy, translation loss is not a loss *of* translation, but a loss *in* the translation process. It is a loss *of* textual effects. Further, since these effects cannot be quantified, neither can the loss. So, when trying to 'reduce' it, the translator never knows how far still to go. This is why one can sometimes go on infinitely translating the same text and never be completely satisfied.

Nevertheless, despite the limitations of the analogy, we have found it practical both in translating and in the classroom. Once the concept of inevitable translation loss is accepted, a TT that is not, in all culturally relevant respects, a replica of the ST is not a theoretical anomaly, and translators can forget the unrealistic aim of seeking the 'right' TT, and concentrate instead on the realistic one of channelling translation loss. Indeed, one of the attractions of the notion is that it frees translators actually to *exploit* translation loss – to introduce any loss, however major, that enables them to implement the strategy fully. Quite apart from any need for compensation in actually doing the translation, the brief itself may require a gist translation, or an exegetic translation, or an adaptation for children or immigrants, or for the stage or radio, etc. We saw a good example of deliberately introduced translation loss in the accountants' report (p. 10): the TT incurs great lexical and grammatical loss, but this is less serious than the incomprehensibility of a literal TT would have been. In sum, as we shall see throughout the course, translation loss is only to be regretted when it prevents successful implementation of the translator's strategy, i.e. if it means that the TT is not fit for its purpose.

Using the term 'loss' rather than e.g. 'difference' may seem unduly negative. It is indeed meant to be negative, but constructively so. The danger in talking of 'translation difference' is that 'difference' might be understood in a trivial sense: 'Of course the ST and TT are different – just look at them, one's in French and the other's in English.' 'Loss' is more likely to direct attention to the *relation between* ST and TT as terms in a system of relationships, rather than to the texts in themselves (cf. 'just look at them') as static, substantial, autonomous entities. Crucially, 'loss' is a reminder that, if you read a translation of *L'Etranger*, you are not reading *L'Etranger*, you are reading a reading of it.

To show some of the implications of translation loss for the translator, it is enough to take a few very simple examples, at the primitive level of the sounds, rhythm and literal meaning of individual words.

There is translation loss even at the seemingly most trivial level. For instance, true SL–TL homonymy rarely occurs, and rhythm and intonation are usually different as well. So, in most contexts, 'cheval' and 'horse' will be synonyms, and there will be no loss in literal meaning in translating one by the other. But 'cheval' and 'horse' sound completely different: there is total phonic and rhythmic loss. The immediate and obvious question is whether such losses actually *matter*. The equally obvious answer is that, in a veterinary manual and in most other contexts, they matter not at all. But if the ST word is part of an alliterative chain in a literary text, or if it rhymes (e.g. 'I know two things about the horse, and one of them is rather coarse'), then the loss may be crucial.

Translation loss in respect of sound is virtually certainly entailed even in cases where the ST word has already entered the TL. For instance, French 'cloisonné' and English 'cloisonné' sound different from one another. Similarly, if French 'leader' is translated as English 'leader', there is palpable loss in terms of sound and rhythm. Nor would it help if the French loan-words were pronounced in authentic French fashion in an English oral TT. On the contrary, pronouncing 'cloisonné' or 'pas de bas' in an authentically French way would actually increase the translation loss: it would increase the phonic and rhythmic foreignness (which are absent from the ST), and it would introduce a comic or off-putting pretentiousness (again absent from the ST).

In respect of meaning, too, there is clear translation loss in using loan-words. Quite apart from the sound of the words, using 'cloisonné', 'joie de vivre', etc. in an English TT introduces a semantic foreignness that is not present in the ST: that is, the TT *loses* the cultural neutrality of the ST expression. Conversely, translating French 'leader' as English 'leader' *loses* the cultural foreignness of the ST expression. In the case of a loan-word from a third language, it may well have different connotations in the two borrowing cultures. For example, English 'Gauleiter' and French 'Gauleiter' do not only sound different: in English, 'Gauleiter' will tend to have slightly facetious connotations, whereas in French, it will have altogether more painful connotations, arising from personal and collective memories of the Nazi Occupation.

An important implication of the concept of translation loss is that it embraces any non-replication of an ST, whether this involves *losing* features in the TT or *adding* them. Take the word 'borgne'. Suppose this is translated as 'blind in one eye'. There is obvious lexical loss, in that 'borgne' can also mean 'one-eyed' – the TT loses the semantic breadth of 'borgne'. But there is translation loss in other respects as well. Although the TT is acceptable in terms of literal meaning, it has added three words and it makes explicit reference to blindness and eyes. Conversely, rendering 'blind in one eye' as 'borgne' not only loses the semantic narrowness and explicitness of the ST expression, but is also more economical (or less weighty) in terms of number of words and syllables.

Such losses are extremely common. Two more examples will suffice to illustrate this. First, rendering 'chapardeur' as 'light-fingered' incurs translation loss because the TT does not have the concision of the ST (even though there is a gain in vividness). Translating in the other direction, rendering 'light-fingered' as 'chapardeur' entails an equally obvious translation loss, in that the TT does not have the vividness of the ST (even though there is a gain in concision). The second example exhibits still more sorts of translation loss – translating 'capital transfer tax' by 'impôt sur le transfert des capitaux', and vice versa. The English is more concise, but its grammar is a potential source of ambiguities for a lay person: is this a transfer tax that is capital, or a tax that is a capital transfer, or a tax on transfers that are capital, or a tax on the transfer of capital? The grammar of the French expression eliminates all such ambiguity, but it is more cumbersome than the English. As all these examples show, translation loss, as we have defined it, is inevitable, even if the TT gains in economy, vividness, avoidance of ambiguity, semantic breadth or narrowness, etc.

Before drawing conclusions for the practice of translation from this discussion of equivalence and translation loss, we should briefly explain the advantages for apprentice translators of insisting that there is, always and everywhere, translation loss. After all, we have just given examples of *gain*.

There are two main reasons for calling these so-called 'gains' losses. One is theoretical, the other practical. The theoretical one has to do with the concept of equivalence. In so far as equivalence implies sameness, or degree zero, 'gain' implies a plus value, 'loss' a minus value. And this three-valued view is what engenders our practical reason for insisting on translation loss: the belief in gain makes it very difficult for student translators to resist the temptation of gratuitously adding or altering detail, either to 'improve on' the ST, or in the vague hope that the losses will be outweighed by a greater volume of gains. Here are two examples from student translations, for discussion in class. The first is from a text on mergers and takeovers:

ST	TT
La même tendance se note dans la construction aéronautique, où Boeing vient d'acquérir de Havilland Canada et recherche des partenaires, japonais et suédois, pour le 737.	The same trend can be seen in aircraft construction, where Boeing has just acquired de Havilland Canada and is hunting down Japanese and Swedish partners for the 737.

The translator preferred 'hunting down' to 'seeking' or 'looking for' because it is 'more vivid' and 'more appropriate in a context of predatory takeovers'. The second example is from a text on the transport of nuclear materials. Here, the correct order of the adjectives and the correct terminology were altered to 'make the text sound better and more idiomatic':

ST	TT
Les équivalents de dose effectifs collectifs différentiels annuels reçus par les riverains et par les passagers d'autres véhicules sont 5 du même ordre de grandeur.	The different annual collective efficacious equivalent doses received by people living along the route and passengers in other vehicles are of the same order of magnitude.

(For analysis of this ST, see pp. 176–8.)

In both examples, the translator was looking for what can be put into the TT to make it a more dramatic or elegant TL text, rather than how to preserve what is important from the ST. In our experience, this approach is likely to be encouraged if translation is seen as the pursuit of equivalence as equi-valence or 'substantial sameness'. Student translators will strive to maximize sameness, haunted by the idea that somewhere out there the *right* TL equivalent to the ST is waiting to be found. Failing attainment of that right TT, they will be encouraged by the three-valued system (loss ~ gain ~ equivalence) to try to outweigh losses by accumulating 'gains'. The practical advantages of the two-valued system (loss ~ no loss) – i.e. the notion that translation loss is inevitable, and that even a so-called gain is a loss – are therefore the following. First, translators are unburdened of the demoralizing supposition that, if only they were clever enough or lucky enough to find it, the right TT is just round the corner, and that if they do not find it, they are failures. And, second, seeking to minimize difference, to save ST elements from disappearance, requires a closer attention to the properties of the text: to know what can and should be saved, one has to know what features are there, and what their functions are.

As some of the examples in this chapter suggest, if translation loss is inevitable even in translating single words, it is obviously going to feature at more complex levels as well – in respect of sentence-structure, for example, or discourse, language variety, and so on. There is no need to give further examples of these just now: plenty will arise, chapter by chapter, as we deal with these and other topics. For the moment, all we need do is point out that, if translation loss is inevitable, the challenge to the translator is not to eliminate it, but to control and channel it by deciding which features, in a given ST, it is most important to respect, and which can most legitimately be sacrificed in respecting them. This is where the classroom advantages of the translation loss approach lead directly to its advantages for the practising translator. For the translator has always to be asking, and answering, such questions as: does it *matter* if 'leader' is foreign in French and not in English, and sounds different in each? Does *it matter* if 'blind in one eye' is semantically more limited than 'borgne'? If 'On n'apprend pas à un vieux singe à faire des grimaces' is phonically, rhythmically, grammatically, lexically and metaphorically totally different from 'Don't teach your grandmother to suck eggs'? There is no once-and-for-all answer to questions like these. Everything depends on the translation brief, the nature of the target audience, and what role the textual feature has in its context. Whether the final decision is simple or complicated, it does have to be made, afresh, every time, and the translator is the only one who can make it.

As we have seen, this decision is not whether to replicate all the culturally relevant ST features in the TT, which is impossible, but how to control translation loss by channelling it in such a way as to respect the ones that are most relevant. This very often involves deliberately introducing blatant translation losses in order to avoid even bigger ones; we saw a simple example in the accountants' report. This kind of compromise and compensation will be the subject of Chapter 4.

PRACTICAL 2

2.1 Degrees of freedom; translation loss

Taking the first half of the ST below:

(i) Identify the salient features of its content and expression.
(ii) Taking the TT (printed next to it) as a whole, place it on the scale of degrees of freedom given on p. 16, and explain your decision.
(iii) Taking the detail of the TT, discuss the main differences between it and the ST, paying special attention to cases where it incurs, or manages to avoid, unacceptable translation loss.
(iv) Where you think the TT can be improved, give your own revised version and explain the revision.
(v) In the light of this work on the first part of the ST, outline and justify a strategy for translating the rest of it.
(vi) Translate the rest of the text (the section entitled 'Le marché') into English.
(vii) Paying special attention to cases where you managed to avoid unacceptable translation loss, discuss the main decisions of detail you took, explaining what the threatened loss was and how you avoided it.
(viii) Compare your TT with the published one, which will be given to you by your tutor.

Contextual information

The ST is from the annual report for 1995 of Schneider, one of the biggest suppliers of electrical equipment in the world. The TT was published in the English version of the report. This part of the report is elaborately illustrated and precedes the detailed financial statements and balance sheets. It thus combines publicity with information on the company's main activities. Among other things, Schneider supply high-tension equipment (for national grids, etc.), transformers and low-tension wiring systems in buildings; 'basse tension terminale' refers to the final level of equipment – switches, circuit breakers, etc.

ST

BASSE TENSION TERMINALE
Les produits et systèmes de basse tension terminale permettent de garantir la sécurité, d'améliorer le
5 confort, de réaliser des économies, bref de bénéficier de toutes les possibilités offertes par l'énergie électrique dans les bâtiments industriels, tertiaires et résiden-
10 tiels.
    L'offre de Schneider se décline en deux activités : d'une part, la distribution terminale constituée de l'ensemble des produits et
15 systèmes assurant les fonctions de protection des personnes et des biens et de contrôle-commande ; d'autre part, la sécurité et le contrôle du bâtiment constitués de
20 l'ensemble des produits et services liés à l'intrusion, l'incendie, le contrôle d'accès et la gestion technique du bâtiment.
                (Schneider 1996a: 22)

TT

FINAL LOW VOLTAGE
Final low voltage products and systems deliver the full benefits of electricity to industrial, commercial and residential buildings. They ensure user safety, enhance comfort and reduce costs. Schneider serves this market through two activities.
    We make final distribution products and systems to protect people and property, and to perform control and monitoring functions.
    We also supply products and services for building security and control, which comprises anti-intrusion, fire prevention, access control, and building management services.
                (Schneider 1996b: 22)

ST (continued)

Le marché

Le marché de la basse tension terminale représente 30 milliards de francs en 1995. Quoique stagnant en Europe et aux Etats-Unis, le marché mondial offre des perspectives de forte croissance, pour répondre aux besoins
5 d'électrification, de sécurité et de confort des pays à fort potentiel de développement.

Schneider occupe la 1re place mondiale sur ce marché. Cette position s'appuie sur plusieurs leaderships en Asie (Chine, Indonésie, Thaïlande, Singapour...), qui s'ajoutent aux positions dominantes détenues en
10 Amérique du Nord et en Europe. Ce résultat est le fruit de l'avance technologique de Schneider et de prix de revient très compétitifs. Les usines à vocation mondiale, très automatisées, sont complétées par des unités locales chargées d'adapter les produits aux différents marchés.

(Schneider 1996a: 23)

2.2 Degrees of freedom; translation loss

Assignment

Here is an ST for comparison with two published TTs. Your tutor will tell you which of the TTs to discuss.

(i)   Identify the salient features of content and expression in the ST.
(ii)   Taking each TT as a whole, place it on the scale of degrees of freedom given on p. 16, and explain your decision.
(iii) Taking the detail of each TT, discuss the main differences between it and the ST, paying special attention to cases where it incurs, or manages to avoid, unacceptable translation loss.
(iv) Where you think the TT can be improved, give your own revised version and explain the revision.

Contextual information

The ST is from Camus's *L'Etranger* (1942). Salamano is an old man with a skin condition who lives in the next-door flat to the narrator, Meursault. Meursault's mother has recently died. Salamano has a dog, with which he has a love–hate relationship. The two men meet on the landing, and Salamano says that his dog has disappeared. When Meursault tells him he can easily get it back from the pound for a small fee, he shouts and blusters and refuses to countenance the possibility. He and Meursault go into their respective flats. This is when the ST starts. TT (i) was published in 1946, TT (ii) in 1982. Note that TT (i) was produced from the original edition of the ST, which finished with 'souper'; this was amended to 'dîner' in later editions.

ST

Un moment après, j'ai entendu le pas du vieux et il a frappé à ma porte. Quand j'ai ouvert, il est resté un moment sur le seuil et il m'a dit : « Excusez-moi, excusez-moi. » Je l'ai invité à entrer, mais il n'a pas voulu. Il regardait la pointe de ses souliers et ses mains croûteuses tremblaient.
5 Sans me faire face, il m'a demandé : « Ils ne vont pas me le prendre, dites, monsieur Meursault. Ils vont me le rendre. Ou qu'est-ce que je vais devenir ? » Je lui ai dit que la fourrière gardait les chiens trois jours à la

disposition de leurs propriétaires et qu'ensuite elle en faisait ce que bon lui
semblait. Il m'a regardé en silence. Puis il m'a dit : « Bonsoir. » Il a fermé
10   sa porte et je l'ai entendu aller et venir. Son lit a craqué. Et au bizarre petit
bruit qui a traversé la cloison, j'ai compris qu'il pleurait. Je ne sais pas
pourquoi j'ai pensé à maman. Mais il fallait que je me lève tôt le lende-
main. Je n'avais pas faim et je me suis couché sans dîner.

     (A. Camus *L'Etranger*, © Editions GALLIMARD, 1947: 59–60)

TT (i)
A minute or two later I heard Salamano's footsteps and a knock on my
door.
    When I opened it, he halted for a moment in the doorway.
    'Excuse me . . . I hope I'm not disturbing you.'
5   I asked him in, but he shook his head. He was staring at his toe-caps,
and the gnarled old hands were trembling. Without meeting my eyes, he
started talking.
    'They won't really take him from me, will they, Monsieur Meursault?
Surely they wouldn't do a thing like that. If they do – I don't know what
10   will become of me.'
    I told him that, so far as I knew, they kept stray dogs in the Pound for
three days, waiting for their owners to call for them. After that they
disposed of the dogs as they thought fit.
    He stared at me in silence for a moment, then said, 'Good evening.'
15   After that I heard him pacing up and down his room for quite a while.
Then his bed creaked. Through the wall there came to me a little wheezing
sound, and I guessed that he was weeping. For some reason, I don't know
what, I began thinking of Mother. But I had to get up early next day; so,
as I wasn't feeling hungry, I did without supper, and went straight to bed.

    (Camus 1946: 39)

TT (ii)
A minute later I heard the old man's footsteps and he knocked at my door.
When I opened it, he stood for a moment in the doorway and said, 'Excuse
me, excuse me.' I asked him in, but he didn't want to. He was looking down
at his boots and his scabby hands were trembling. Without looking up at
5   me, he asked, 'They won't take him away from me, will they, Mr Meursault.
They will give him back to me. Otherwise what will I do?' I told him that
they kept dogs at the pound for three days for their owners to collect them
and that after that they dealt with them as they saw fit. He looked at me in
silence. Then he said, 'Goodnight.' He closed his door and I heard him
10   pacing up and down. Then his bed creaked. And from the peculiar little
noise coming through the partition wall, I realized that he was crying. For
some reason I thought of mother. But I had to get up early in the morning.
I wasn't hungry and I went to bed without any dinner.

    (Camus 1983: 41–2)

2.3 Translation loss

Assignment

(i) You are translating the novel from which the following ST is taken. Discuss the strategic decisions that you have to take before starting detailed translation of this ST, and outline and justify the strategy you adopt.

(ii) Translate the text into English.

(iii) Paying special attention to cases where you managed to avoid unacceptable translation loss, discuss the main decisions of detail you took, explaining what the threatened loss was and how you avoided it.

Contextual information

The passage is from Jean Dutourd's *Au Bon Beurre* (1952), a satirical novel about the Nazi occupation of France in 1940–44. The passage begins when the naive Léon, a prisoner of war in Germany, having unintentionally escaped from captivity and survived for a week by stealing food and clothes, eventually finds himself in a crowded street in Hamburg. Lélé is Léon's nickname.

ST

Une belle fille lui sourit. Le cœur de Lélé battit comme il n'avait pas battu dans les plus grands périls.

Elle était un peu grande, cette fille ; son manteau de loutre élargissait singulièrement sa carrure. Avec ses chaussures à hauts talons, elle dépas-
5 sait Lélé d'une demi-tête. Lélé pensa : « C'est une walkyrie », et il manœuvra pour s'approcher d'elle. La walkyrie sourit encore ; le cœur de Lélé résonnait jusque dans ses oreilles.

– *Liebling !* murmura la walkyrie en le prenant sans façon par le bras. Léon défaillit presque quand il pénétra dans un petit studio situé au sommet
10 d'une maison neuve de la Michaëlisstraße. Qu'allait-il devenir ? Léon était vierge, sans le sou, et ne parlait pas allemand. Le studio empestait le patchouli. La walkyrie enleva son manteau de fourrure et apparut dans une robe de jersey bleu. Lélé s'écria :

– Je suis français !
15 Elle le regarda avec surprise et partit d'un rire un peu grave.

– *Man spricht französisch !* Prisonnier évadé tu es, je crois ? dit-elle d'une voix de contralto extrêmement émouvante.

– *Ja wohl !* dit Lélé.

– Je devrais avoir douté, avec ton habit et barbe.
20 – Vous êtes très *schön*, dit Lélé en tremblant. Je n'ai jamais vu une aussi belle *Fräulein*.

– Embrasse-moi, Français !

Jusqu'à ce moment, Lélé n'imaginait pas ce que c'était qu'un baiser. Celui qu'il reçut dura cent vingt secondes et lui causa les sensations les

25 plus exaltantes. La femme qu'il serrait dans ses bras était ferme, dure,
bien musclée, quasi anguleuse ; il ne concevait pas qu'on pût être plus
séduisante. Cette bouche peinte, ces joues poudrées, ce cou de lutteur l'en-
flammaient. Il demanda :

– Comment vous appelez-vous ?

30 – J'appelle Helmuth Krakenholz.

– Helmuth ? dit Lélé, badin, ce n'est pas un nom de femme.

– Aussi femme ne suis-je pas, mais *Oberleutnant* dans la Luftwaffe.

– Quoi, dit Léon, subitement glacé, vous êtes un homme ?

– Oui, mais une âme tendre et mélancolique j'ai, comme une dame.

35 J'aime militaires, même militaires français.

(J. Dutourd, *Au Bon Beurre*, © Editions GALLIMARD 1972: 29–30)

3

Cultural issues in translation

In this chapter, we complete the introduction to translation loss by looking at implications of the crucial fact that translating involves not just two languages, but a transfer *from one whole culture to another*. Of course, one of the defining characteristics of a culture is its language or languages: among the 'culturally relevant features' (p. 21) that make a text what it is are linguistic features. To that extent, the degrees of freedom considered on p. 16 all reflect a greater or lesser degree of constraint in transferring messages from culture to culture. We shall take it as read that if a literal translation is acceptable (as it so often is), the translation operation is culturally neutral. In this chapter, we look at translation procedures that are less neutral, chosen by the translator in the light of general cultural differences that go beyond purely linguistic differences. The two overlap, of course, and are often inseparable (especially in communicative translation, which we look at both in Chapter 2 and here).

Nevertheless, it is useful to discuss general cultural differences as such, because they are sometimes bigger obstacles to successful translation than linguistic ones. Indeed, a useful recent book is devoted entirely to the notion that translators and interpreters must 'change from being seen as inefficient human dictionaries to facilitators for mutual understanding between people. The proposal is for a new role [...], that of "cultural mediator"' (Katan 1999: 1). The idea is not altogether new, of course. It is precisely out of such considerations that the translator of the accountants' report (p. 10) opted for an exegetic TT. The Dutourd ST (Practical 2.3) is less challenging, but you will have had to consider whether Valkyries and the German language itself have the same impact in the source and target cultures, and the cultural resonances of 'man spricht französisch' needed a bit of careful thought. The 1946 translation of *L'Etranger* (p. 28) is an example of the very strong influence that target-culture conventions can exert. Even Harry Potter has caused a cultural stir in France, some people taking offence at the perceived choice of French-sounding names for the villains – Voldemort, Malfoy (and Pettigrew!).

Proper names actually offer some of the most straightforward examples of the basic issues in cultural transposition. Dealing with names in translation is not usually a major issue, but it does provide a useful introduction to the cultural dimension of translation. There are two main alternatives in dealing with names. The name can be taken over unchanged into the TT, or it can be adapted to conform to the phonic/graphic conventions of the TL. Assuming that the name is an SL name, the first alternative introduces a foreign element into the TT. This loss will not usually matter; most often it will actually be welcomed as a reminder of the origin of the text. More serious is the sort of case where using the ST name introduces into the TT different associations from those in the ST. Brand names are a typical danger area. French motorists were not attracted by the Toyota MR2. Translating an (admittedly unlikely) French ST in which someone snacked on a Crap's bar washed down with Pschitt, it would be prudent to drop the brand names altogether, or perhaps invent English ones with more product-enhancing associations. With fictional names, there is more latitude, as we shall see in a moment.

Simply using the ST name unchanged in the TT may in any case sometimes be impracticable, if it actually creates problems of pronounceability, spelling or memorization. This is unlikely with 'Chirac' or 'Jospin', but it can easily happen with, say, Polish or Russian names. The second alternative in dealing with names, **transliteration**, to some extent solves these problems by using TL conventions for the representation of an ST name. This is the standard way of coping with Russian and Chinese names in English texts. How a name is transliterated may be entirely up to the translator, if it has never been put into the TL before. Or it may be necessary to follow a precedent established by earlier translators. Standard transliteration varies from language to language, as is easily seen with place names: compare Venezia/Venice/Venise/Venedig, Salzburg/Salzbourg/Salisburgo, etc.

Some names do not need transliteration at all, but have standard TL equivalents. Compare French 'Saint Jean', German 'St Johannes', Italian 'S. Giovanni'; or Flemish 'Luik', French 'Liège', German 'Lüttich' and Italian 'Liegi'; or French 'la Manche' and German 'der [Ärmel]kanal': in these cases there is little choice but to use 'St John', 'Liège' and 'the Channel', unless the translator wants deliberately to draw attention to the foreign origin of the text. The same applies to initials and acronyms: compare French 'ONU' and English 'UNO' (or 'the UN'), French 'OMS' and English 'WHO', French 'TVA' and English 'VAT', etc. Keeping the French form here would normally introduce needless obscurity and undermine confidence in the translator. So would failure to spot differences between SL and TL geographical conventions: compare 'le golfe de Naples' and 'the Bay of Naples', 'le détroit du Pas de Calais' and 'the

Strait of Dover'. French journalists, by analogy with 'Versailles', often refer to Buckingham Palace simply as 'Buckingham'; but translating the headline 'Charles et Camilla: bouche cousue à Buckingham' as 'Charles and Camilla: Sealed Lips in Buckingham' would be confusing, to say the least.

Another alternative in dealing with names is cultural transplantation. SL names are replaced by indigenous TL names that are not their conventional or literal equivalents, but have similar cultural connotations. In the English translations of Hergé's Tintin books, 'Dupont et Dupond' have become 'Thompson and Thomson'. This ingeniously anglicizes the two characters, retains the connotations of commonness of the names, and imitates the ST play on different spellings. There is some clever cultural transplantation of names in the French Harry Potter translations: Ravenclaw > Serdaigle, Hufflepuff > Poufsouffle, Scabbers > Croûtard, Malfoy > Malefoy, Neville Longbottom > Neville Londubat, etc. Many of the names remain unchanged, however (not least Harry Potter). This seemingly arbitrary mixture of French and English names does seem odd, but in Rowling's double world it probably leaves readers unfazed. Cultural transplantation of names must be done with care, however; if Hergé's illustration showed two detectives called Thompson and Thomson having a drink at an obviously Continental *brasserie*, the effect would be incongruous.

CULTURAL TRANSPOSITION ≠ *literal*

The question of names in translation is enough to show that there may be ST expressions that, for cultural reasons, must be taken over unchanged into the TT, or need to be 'naturalized' in some way. Sometimes, they are best dropped altogether. We shall use the general term **cultural transposition** for the main types and degrees of departure from literal translation that may be resorted to in transferring the contents of an ST from one culture into another. Any degree of cultural transposition involves the choice of features indigenous to the TL and the target culture in preference to features with their roots in the source culture. The result is to reduce foreign features in the TT, thereby to some extent naturalizing it into the TL and its cultural setting. Whether this is desirable or not depends on the purpose of the TT.

The various degrees of cultural transposition can be visualized as points along a scale between the extremes of exoticism and cultural transplantation:

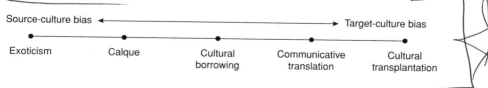

Source-culture bias ← → Target-culture bias

Exoticism — Calque — Cultural borrowing — Communicative translation — Cultural transplantation

Exoticism — cultural, ? strange

The extreme options in signalling cultural foreignness in a TT fall into the category of **exoticism**. A TT marked by exoticism is one which consistently uses grammatical and cultural features imported from the ST with minimal adaptation, thereby constantly signalling the exotic source culture and its cultural strangeness. This may be one of the TT's chief attractions, as in this translation of an Arabic *maqamat*:

> I went from Irak to Damascus with its green water-courses,   in the day when I had troops of fine-bred horses   and was the owner of coveted wealth and resources,   free to divert myself, as I chose,   and flown with the pride of him whose fullness overflows.   When I reached the city after toil and teen   on a camel travel-lean,   I found it to be all that tongues recite   and to contain soul's desire and eye's delight.
>
> (Nicholson 1987: 119)

A TT like this, however, has an impact on the TL public quite unlike any that the ST could have had on an SL public, for whom the text has fewer features of a different culture.

[margin note: so the audience can understand]

Cultural transplantation

At the other end of the scale from exoticism is **cultural transplantation**, whose extreme forms are hardly translations at all, but more like adaptations – the wholesale transplanting of the ST setting, resulting in the entire text being rewritten in a target culture setting. Examples include Craig Raine's *'1953'* (a transplantation of Racine's *Andromaque* into a Rome where the claimant to the British throne is held captive after Britain's defeat by the Axis), and Jim McBride's adaptation of Godard's *A bout de souffle* into *Breathless*. Cultural transplantation on this scale is not normal translation practice, but it can be a serious option, as long as no points of detail have knock-on effects that make the TT as a whole incongruous. A successful example is Siân Reynolds's translation of Louis Pergaud's 'L'argument décisif' (set in the Franche-Comté) into a *Huckleberry Finn* idiom (Cross 1988: 286–7); another is Liz Lochhead's *The Patter Merchants*, which transplants *Les Précieuses ridicules* into Glasgow.

By and large, normal translation practice avoids the two extremes of exoticism and cultural transplantation. In avoiding the extremes, the translator will consider the alternatives lying between them on the scale given on p. 33.

Calque

One alternative, even where the TT as a whole is not to be marked by exoticism, is to introduce a momentary foreignness in the form of calque.

not the same meaning when translated! (handwritten annotation)

A **calque** is an expression that consists of TL words and is acceptable as TL syntax, but is unidiomatic in the TL because it is modelled on the structure of an SL expression. This lack of idiomaticity may be purely lexical and relatively innocuous, or it may be more generally grammatical. The following calques illustrate decreasing degrees of idiomaticity:

ST	TT
Il n'est pire eau que l'eau qui dort.	There is no water worse than the water that sleeps.
Vous sentez-vous une âme de sculpteur?	Do you feel a spirit of sculptor?
Elle s'est vu remettre le bijou par le voleur lui-même.	She has seen herself to hand back the jewel by the thief himself.

For most translation purposes, it can be said that a bad calque imitates ST features to the point of being ungrammatical in the TL, while a good one compromises between imitating ST features and offending against TL grammar. It is easy, through haste or ignorance, to mar the TT with bad calques. However, it is conceivable that in some TTs the momentary foreignness of calque may be desirable or necessary, even if its effects need to be palliated by some form of compensation. We shall return to this point in a moment, when looking at communicative translation.

Sometimes, what was originally a calqued expression actually becomes a standard TL cultural equivalent of its SL original. An English example is 'world-view', calqued on 'Weltanschauung'. French examples are 'poids mouche', calqued on English 'flyweight', 'jardin d'enfants', calqued on German 'Kindergarten', 'objet volant non identifié' ('ovni'), calqued on 'unidentified flying object' ('UFO'), 'sortir du placard', calqued on 'to come out of the closet', and French-Canadian 'bienvenue' (in response to 'merci bien'), calqued on 'you're welcome'.

Cultural borrowing

Another alternative introducing an element of foreignness is to transfer an ST expression verbatim into the TT. This is termed **cultural borrowing**. Certainly, something foreign is by definition exotic; this is why, when the occasion demands, it can be useful to talk about *exotic elements* introduced by various translation practices. But cultural borrowing is different from exoticism and calque, because it does not involve adaptation of the SL expression into TL forms. Translators often turn to cultural borrowing when it is impossible to find a suitable indigenous TL expression. As with calque, such borrowings sometimes become standard TL terms – think of all the English ballet terms that are loan-words from French. Cultural borrowing is most frequent in texts on history or legal, social or political matters, where the simplest solution is to insert into the TT a definition of terms like 'Polytechnique', 'département' or pre-Revolution 'parlement', and thereafter to use the SL word as a loan-word in the TT.

Cultural borrowing only presents the translator with a true choice in cases where previous translation practice has not already firmly established the ST expression in the TL. So unless the context militates against it, it is virtually mandatory to render loan-expressions like 'joie de vivre', 'savoir-faire', 'dérailleur', 'pétanque' or 'cloisonné' verbatim into an English TT, because they have become the standard conventional equivalents of the SL expressions.

However, caution needs to be exercised in translating SL words that have become TL loan-words, and vice versa. To begin with, they may be spelt differently, e.g. 'derailleur' has no accent in English. Then they may be used differently in the two languages: French 'cloisonné' more often means 'divided up', 'partitioned off' or 'compartmentalized' than it does 'cloisonné'; 'de rigueur' ('obligatory', 'essential') is used in a much wider range of situations in French than in English, where it usually applies to the (socially) done thing; 'piste' ('track', 'trail', 'runway', 'parking strip', etc.) only denotes a ski-run in English; 'entrepreneur' has more meanings in French ('contractor', businessman', 'entrepreneur') than it has in English, etc. Conversely, in French, 'une girl' is a chorus girl; 'look' means 'style/look/image', and you can even be 'looké punk/sixties' etc.; a 'baby-star' is a 'child star', 'un palace' a plush hotel, etc.

Communicative translation

As we saw on p. 18, communicative translation is usually adopted for all those clichés, idioms, proverbs, etc. which have readily identifiable communicative equivalents in the TL. Only special contextual reasons could justify not choosing communicative translation in such cases as the following:

Chien méchant.	Beware of the dog.
Sens interdit.	No entry.
Légitime défense.	Self-defence.
Une hirondelle ne fait pas le printemps.	One swallow doesn't make a summer.
Maigre comme un clou.	As thin as a rake.

Literal translation of expressions like these would introduce a potentially comic or distracting foreignness not present in the ST. Sometimes, however, the obvious communicative equivalent will not be appropriate in the context. It will not be possible to translate 'les giboulées de mars' as 'April showers' if the action is taking place in March. In a TT clearly set in France and involving only French characters, it would be unhelpful to translate 'Charbonnier est maître chez soi' as 'An Englishman's home is his castle'. If this comic effect were not wanted, the translator would have either to substitute something like 'My home is my castle', or to invent a generalization with a proverbial ring to it ('Every man's home is his castle', 'Every man is master in his own house', etc.), or to substitute a related proverb ('Every dog is a lion at home', etc.). Each of these has its own connotations; which (if any) is appropriate will depend on what nuance is required in the context.

This example lies halfway between cases where communicative translation is virtually inescapable (as for 'Maigre comme un clou'), and cases where a set phrase in the ST does not have a standard communicative equivalent in the TL. In cases like these, the translator has a genuine choice between literal translation and some degree of communicative translation. Take the following scenario. Pierre is discussing his daughter, a quiet, self-contained child, with a meddling neighbour. To emphasize his misgivings, the neighbour wags a finger and sententiously says 'N'oubliez pas: il n'est pire eau que l'eau qui dort'. The temptation is to render proverb with proverb and to translate: 'Just remember: still waters run deep.' This translation is indeed the one given in the dictionaries. But in this case it does not work. Literally, the French proverb explicitly says that calm water is a bad thing, presumably because it gives a false sense of security. Figuratively, it refers to quiet people who cunningly and treacherously hide their true nature behind a mask of reserve. It is clearly pejorative. Originally, the English proverb may have had similar force. But nowadays it is clearly meliorative: it means that quiet people have deeper thoughts and feelings than noisy ones, even if it takes time to discover these admirable qualities. It is conceivable that in certain situations the TL proverb would overlap with the French one and be usable in the context: but it would have to be clear from the context that the person in question is dangerous or untrustworthy, and the proverb would have to spoken in a suitably critical tone of voice. But this would be a lucky chance, and in most cases 'Still waters run deep' is not a communicative translation of 'Il n'est pire eau que l'eau qui dort'.

Given that there is no standard communicative equivalent here, what are the translator's options? Literal translation is one possibility: 'There is no water worse than the water that sleeps'. However, this calque introduces an exotic element, and it also makes the neighbour into some kind of whimsical wordsmith or parodist instead of someone simply quoting a well-worn saying. Whether these effects were acceptable would depend on the context.

A less stylistically marked option is an exegetic paraphrase – something like 'It's the quiet ones you've got to watch'. In most cases, this would be the safest solution, and it does have the advantage of being an established saying. But it is not a true proverb, which could be a significant loss if a notable part of the neighbour's character is that he regularly uses proverbs. If that were the case, the solution might be a paraphrase stylized like a proverb and preceded by an exegetic clause making it clear that the neighbour is quoting an existing proverb, e.g.: 'Remember the saying: "Water asleep is water too deep".' As there is no such English proverb, this TT combines communicative paraphrase (in the hint of 'Still waters run deep'), exegesis (in 'Remember the saying', and especially in 'too', which conveys the danger expressed by ST 'pire'), and a touch of exoticism (in the pseudo-calque of an SL proverb).

Translators themselves clearly need to navigate ST waters with care. It is easy to spoil the ST message with ill-judged attempts at communicative translation. As usual, it is ultimately the context and the strategy that will determine the final decision. Here are two TTs for comparison and discussion. The ST is from the opening scene of Molière's *Tartuffe*. The shrewish and dogmatic Mme Pernelle has just told her grandson that he is a fool and a ne'er-do-well. His gentle sister tries to intercede, but Mme Pernelle interrupts her:

> Mon Dieu, sa sœur, vous faites la discrète,
> Et vous n'y touchez pas, tant vous semblez doucette;
> Mais il n'est, comme on dit, pire eau que l'eau qui dort,
> Et vous menez sous chape un train que je hais fort.
>
> (Molière 1990: 34)

TT (i)

> His sister now! A startled fawn,
> Too sweet to understand what's going on.
> Still waters may run deep; they're rarely pure.
> You can't fool me by acting so demure.
>
> (Molière 1967: 242)

TT (ii)

As for you, my girl, you're his sister, but you seem sensible enough. You behave very sweetly and you don't make tongues wag. But you know what they say: still waters run deep. You carry on behind our backs and I don't like it.

> (Molière 2000: 34)

PRACTICAL 3

3.1 Cultural issues

Assignment
Here is an ST for comparison with the published TT.

(i) Concentrating on the sorts of cultural issue introduced in Chapter 3, compare the texts, commenting on necessary changes that have been made in the TT. Sometimes, these changes will have been imposed by cultural differences, sometimes by linguistic differences. You should discuss both types, because they may on occasion be connected.

(ii) Discuss any cases where you think that the TT may not have taken differences between source culture and target culture sufficiently into account.

(iii) Where you think the TT can be improved, give your own revised version and explain the revision.

Contextual information

The texts are taken from an illustrated publicity leaflet for La Petite Provence du Paradou, a miniature village with 400 *santons* illustrating everyday life as it used to be. A *santon* is a clay figure, about 30 cm high. They are a Provençal speciality. Originally they were made for crib sets at Christmas, but nowadays they represent people from all walks of life. Among the illustrations in the leaflet, for example, are 1920s' card players outside a café, and a farrier, bearded and bucolic, from around the same time. The miniature village is situated in the village of Le Paradou, not far from Les Baux.

ST   *TT*

La Petite Provence du Paradou

Le village des santons — ornamental figure

	ST	TT
	Daudet, Mistral, Giono, Pagnol lui-même, s'y seraient trompés en retrouvant leurs personnages aussi	Daudet, Mistral, Giono, and even Pagnol himself might be deceived into thinking they were seeing
5	vrais que nature dans un adorable vieux village de la Provence profonde.	their characters true to life in a delightful old village deep in the heart of the Province region of
	8.000 heures de travail ont été nécessaires pour réaliser avec une	France. "of Texas" – Chausau. It took 8,000 hours of work to
10	authenticité incroyable les 32 vieilles bâtisses (50.000 tuiles en argile, toutes faites, une à une, à la main) de ce mini-village provençal où plus de 400 santons	create the 32 incredibly authentic old buildings (50,000 clay tiles, hand-made, one by one) for this miniature Provencal village where more than 400 figurines are seen
15	évoluent dans des scènes de la vie quotidienne, saisissantes de pittoresque, de rire ou d'émotion, à une époque où l'on prenait encore le temps de vivre.	going about their daily business in astonishingly picturesque scenes, filled with laughter and emotion, at a time when life went on at a more leisurely pace.

20   **La Boutique**

La Boutique propose à ses visi-
teurs... santons, poteries, tissus
provençaux, huiles d'olive, herbes
de Provence... Toute une gamme
25   de souvenirs, de cadeaux et de
produits du terroir.

'The Boutique' offers 'Santon'
ornamental figures, pottery,
Provençal fabrics, olive oil, herbes
de Provence... A wide range of
souvenirs, gifts and products from
rural France.

mass v. count nouns   his/her

L'atelier

L'atelier du Paradou est à la
30   disposition de ceux qui veulent
mettre la main à la pâte et
réaliser eux-mêmes un Santon.
Sur réservation seulement.

The Paradou studio is available to
anyone wishing to get their hands
on some clay and make their own
Santon figurine. By reservation
only.

Sur le site, le restaurant « La
35   Treille » vous accueillera avec
plaisir et vous fera découvrir ses
spécialités aux senteurs de
garrigue.

'La Treille' welcomes you and
lets you enjoy her highly seasoned
dishes.
its

*"clunky   our
translation"*   (Coertens 2001)

3.2   Cultural issues

Assignment

(i)   You are translating a publicity booklet entitled *Tables et saveurs de Bretagne*, which gives details of about forty top restaurants in the area. The two STs below are representative of the booklet. Discuss the strategic decisions that you have to take before starting detailed translation of these STs, and outline and justify the strategy you adopt.

(ii)   Translate the texts into English.

(iii)   Discuss the main decisions of detail you took.

(iv)   Compare your translations with the published TTs, which will be given you by your tutor.

Contextual information

Each entry in the booklet comprises details of location, prices, specialities, etc., and a brief text profiling the chef(s) and encapsulating the style
and ambience of the establishment. All the texts are written by the same
person. It may be helpful to know the locations of the restaurants:
L'Amphitryon is in Lorient, and the Auberge « Grand'Maison » is in
Mur-de-Bretagne (not far from Pontivy).

ST (i)

L'Amphitryon

M. et Mme Abadie   Chef : M. Abadie

Ici se rejoignent les Pyrénées et la Bretagne, le foie gras et le beurre salé, la terre et la mer, mais, proximité des arrivages oblige, le poisson a largement pris la vedette : on est chez un amphitryon marin. La maison sort d'un salutaire lifting complet qui la fait trancher encore plus avec son
5 environnement. L'Amphitryon est une bulle douillette où Jean-Paul Abadie, le Bigourdan, pointu et régulier, démontre son obsession perfectionniste. Sur un fond classique, une cuisine précise où tout semble rigoureusement maîtrisé. Forcément personnalisée car, ainsi qu'il aime à le rappeler, le seul restaurant étoilé où il ait travaillé c'est le sien.

(Cabon 1999: n.p. [29])

ST (ii)

Auberge « Grand'Maison »

M. et Mme Guillo   Chef : M. Guillo

Un apôtre en Argoat, voilà Jacques Guillo qui, venu tard à la gastronomie, maîtrise totalement son art après avoir jugulé ses audaces, réfléchi et personnalisé sa cuisine de mille trouvailles. Beaucoup d'associations terre-mer avec des poissons atlantiques et des crustacés de Manche. De son
5 auberge au cœur géographique de la Bretagne, l'hyper-sensible maître Jacques a fait une « Grand'Maison » de cœur et de rencontre, où une clientèle dispersée se retrouve pour se laisser conduire sur les chemins sensoriels d'une cuisine épicurienne à travers des menus conçus comme des étapes du tour de France cycliste. Des plats, des montées et des
10 descentes. Mais que des bons plats !

(Cabon 1999: n.p. [44])

 3.3 Cultural issues

Assignment

(i) You are translating the article from which the following ST is taken for publication in a broadsheet newspaper, as part of a series entitled 'How the Continentals see us' (or 'How Continental Europeans see the British', etc.). Discuss the strategic decisions that you have to take before starting detailed translation of this ST, and outline and justify the strategy you adopt.

(ii) Translate the text into English.

(iii) Discuss the main decisions of detail you took.

Contextual information

The article, entitled 'Dix poids, dix mesures', appeared in August 2000, when legislation on metrication in the United Kingdom made it illegal to sell most goods by imperial measure (pounds, feet, pints, etc.). The article is dedicated to the 'Anglais courageux qui fondent chaque week-end sur les magasins de Calais, afin de s'initier à l'incroyable complexité du système métrique'. After all, the author suggests, in an era of globalization 'il est sain de maintenir un certain niveau d'incompréhension entre les peuples'. It may be helpful to note that the rubric under which this weekly column appears is 'L'humeur d'Alain Schifres'.

DIX POIDS, DIX MESURES

[...] Vous êtes quand même un peu là pour nous faire rire. La Grande-Bretagne est le pays exotique le plus proche de Paris. [...]

Quand vos journaux en appellent au « bon sens » et dénoncent l'« incroyable complexité du système métrique », ça me touche, forcément. Le bon
5 sens, c'était nous, bon sang, et voilà que c'est vous ? Cela mérite enquête. Pour commencer, le mètre et le yard. Défini par un morceau de méridien, ou encore par la vitesse de la lumière dans le vide, le mètre, autant l'avouer, est bien abstrait. Alors que la première expression du yard est à la portée d'un bambin : soit la distance qui sépare le nez d'Henri Ier du bout de son majeur
10 quand il a le bras tendu. Henri Ier (1069–1135) eut 24 enfants, comme il convient à un maître étalon, et mourut d'une indigestion de lamproies, ce qui n'a rien à voir avec mon sujet. Certes, on n'a pas toujours un roi sous la main et le premier monarque lancé dans le vide à la vitesse de la lumière n'est pas pour aujourd'hui. Aussi, votre fameux bon sens vous donna-t-il l'idée
15 de reporter le yard sur une grande règle en bois. Ce qui fait d'Henri Ier, à ma connaissance, l'unique souverain qui serve à mesurer les moquettes.

La suite obéit à la même logique implacable. Le pouce n'est pas un pouce, mais sa largeur mesurée à la base de l'ongle. Le pied n'est pas un pied (c'est grand, 30 cm 48, même pour un Anglais), mais 12 largeurs
20 de pouce. Ensuite, vous avez la brasse, mesure nautique de 1 m 829, d'abord calculée de majeur à majeur sur le bras étendu d'un homme (« corpulent », précisent les auteurs). Pendant ce temps, à la campagne, vous inventez l'acre (soit 43 560 pieds carrés, un chiffre facile à retenir), en multipliant 66 sillons larges de 1 pied chacun par la longueur d'un
25 sillon creusé par un attelage de bœufs avant qu'il n'observe, précisent encore les auteurs, une « petite pause » (*brief rest*). [...]

Vous reste le mile, qui donne au Français l'illusion de se traîner sur de courtes distances, alors qu'il va très loin et roule beaucoup trop vite. L'essence, en revanche, est passée au litre, mais pas sa consommation,
30 calculée en gallons aux 100 miles, ce genre de choses très claires qui rendent à peu près fou.

(Schifres 2000: 70)

4

Making up for the translation loss somehow.

Compensation

In Chapter 3, we said it may be necessary to palliate certain TT effects *make up for* by using compensation. To see what is meant by this, we can return to the meddling neighbour (p. 37). One way of translating the proverb was: 'Remember the saying: "Water asleep is water too deep".' 'Remember the saying' is added to show that the aphorism is an established proverb and not a flight of poetic creativeness on the part of the neighbour. Without the addition, the unfamiliarity of the pseudo-calque would have an exotic quality that is completely absent from the ST, and it would also imply something about the neighbour's personality that the ST does not imply at all. Depending on the purpose of the TT, these two effects could be instances of serious translation loss, a significant betrayal of the ST effects. Adding 'Remember the saying' does not make 'water asleep is water too deep' any less unfamiliar in itself, but it does make it less likely to have these misleading effects. And giving it a quasi-proverbial style preserves the sententious tone, which would be lost in a literal translation.

These procedures together are a good example of **compensation**: that is, where any conventional translation (whether literal or otherwise) would entail an unacceptable translation loss, this loss is reduced by the freely chosen introduction of a less unacceptable one, such that important ST effects are rendered approximately in the TT by means other than those used in the ST. In other words, one type of translation loss is mitigated by the deliberate introduction of another. In this example, adding 'Remember the saying' incurs great translation loss in terms of economy and cultural presupposition, but this is accepted because it significantly reduces the greater loss in terms of message content that would be incurred by a literal translation or a misleading communicative translation. And the pseudo-proverb is grammatically, rhythmically and phonically very far from the ST proverb; but this loss, too, is welcomed because it preserves the sententious tone, which a literal translation would lose.

Note that these departures from literal translation have not been *forced on* the translator by the dictates of TL grammar. The changes have been deliberately and freely chosen to compensate for the lack of a TL proverb that does what the ST one does. This question of choice versus constraint is vital to the understanding of compensation, as we shall see.

There is another example in TT (i) on p. 38. The translator has preserved Mme Pernelle's dogmatic moralizing by using the equally aphoristic 'Still waters run deep'. But he has seen that, on its own, this means the opposite to what Mme Pernelle says in the ST. So he adds the concessive 'may', and then the exegetic 'they're rarely pure'. The rhyme in 'demure' then clinches the strident, critical sarcasm. Grammatically, prosodically and phonically, these two sentences in TT (i) incur greater translation loss than the corresponding ones in TT (ii). Yet the deliberate changes bring it closer than TT (ii) to the tone and meaning, the overall impact, of the ST. Keeping what is lost would have incurred even greater translation loss.

Translators make this sort of compromise all the time, balancing loss against loss in order to do most justice to what they think is most important in the ST. Our aim in this book is to encourage student translators to make these compromises as the result of deliberate decisions taken in the light of strategic factors such as the nature and purpose of the ST, the purpose of the TT, the nature and needs of the target public, and so on. In taking these decisions, it is vital to remember that compensation is not a matter of putting any old fine-sounding phrase into a TT in case any weaknesses have crept in, but of countering a specific, clearly defined, serious loss with a specific, clearly defined, less serious one. Compensation illustrates better than anything else the imaginative rigour that translation demands.

Compensation is more of a concern in non-technical texts than in technical ones. Normally, in translating e.g. a legal document, a financial statement or a paper on electrolysis, the need for compensation is minimal: the translator identifies the relevant TL expressions and uses them. (There is more to technical translation than that, of course, but compensation rarely comes into it.) In most genres, however, successful translation is impossible without compensation. Like so many translation issues, compensation is most clearly and economically illustrated from literary texts, so most of our examples here will be from such texts. But, as the course progresses, it will be found that hardly any of all the wide variety of texts will be properly translatable without the use of compensation.

The question of how to compensate can never be considered in and for itself, in isolation from other crucial factors: context, style, genre, the purpose of the ST, the purpose of the TT. Compensation is needed whenever consideration of these factors confronts the translator with inevitable, but unwelcome, compromise. Simply put, it is a less unwelcome compromise. It virtually always entails a difference in kind between the ST textual effect and the TT textual effect. For instance, it may involve making explicit what is implicit in the ST, as in 'Still waters *may* run deep; *they're rarely pure*'. An area where the implicit quite often needs to be made explicit is in the differences between French and English verb systems, especially the narrative tenses. The contrast between imperfect and past historic frequently causes problems. There were examples in Practical 2.3. In the following extract from a text about a schoolteacher in the French Resistance, it is the contrast between past historic and perfect that has the crucial effect, an effect which literal translation cannot get across:

passé simple

Arrêtée avec un convoi d'enfants qu'elle accompagnait en Suisse, elle fut emprisonnée à Annemasse. Refusant l'offre d'être libérée sans les enfants, elle continua de leur prodiguer ses soins en prison.

Quelques jours après la Libération, on retrouva son corps dans un charnier. Elle a été fusillée le 8 juillet 1944 à l'âge de 23 ans.

Elle fut une militante exemplaire [...]

les effets de l'extrait   (Audisio 1945: 57)

e.g. had been shot

The use of the perfect tense in this passage is striking, for two reasons. First, it would have been more usual in French to use the pluperfect: she was shot *before* her body was found. Second, the perfect contrasts vividly with the predominant past historic. The contrast intensifies the emotional charge, as if the writer is still reeling from the impact of this event. The final past historic then brusquely distances us again, definitively separating the girl's life from the present – she is dead and gone and nothing can bring her back, however moved we still are by her fate.

The English verb system does not in itself permit the expressive power which this ST derives from switching between tenses. One way of overcoming this lack might be to compensate in kind, by translating the last two sentences as follows: 'This girl was shot on 8 July 1944, at the age of 23. She was an exemplary *résistante*.' In this TT, the emotional impact of the ST's play on tenses is conveyed by three things. 'This girl' and the rhetorical comma stress her youth; and using '*résistante*' instead of 'resister' is a cultural borrowing which has a distancing effect, locating the event in a specific period of the past history of another country.

Here is an example in which an ST connotative meaning is conveyed through literal meaning in the TT:

ST	TT
[La mer] ne sort jamais de ses bornes qu'un peu, met *elle-même* un frein à la fureur de ses flots. (Ponge 1965: 66; Ponge's italics)	[The sea] never oversteps its bounds by much, and needs no God to help it bridle its wild waves.

The ST contains an allusion to Racine's *Athalie*: 'Celui qui met un frein à la fureur des flots / Sait aussi des méchants arrêter les complots.' To an English-speaking reader, the implicit reference to the Almighty would be lost if '*elle-même*' were translated by 'itself'. The TT thus drops 'itself' and the connotation, and compensates for this by inserting the explicit reference to God.

So far, we have seen examples in which compensation makes the implicit explicit. Sometimes it does the opposite, as in these lines from the subtitles of the film *Tirez sur le pianiste*:

ST	TT
Monsieur Charlie, permets-moi de te tutoyer ; Monsieur Charlie, tu vas mourir.	Charlie, old man, no formalities; Charlie, old man, I'm going to kill you.

Here, ST 'permets' explicitly uses the familiar form, 'tutoyer' explicitly denotes such use, and 'tu' explicitly denotes 'familiar addressee'. As the English verb system has nothing corresponding to the *tu/vous* distinction, these things have to become implicit in the TT, in 'old man' and 'no formalities'.

Something that is notoriously difficult to translate without using compensation is humour. Successful examples abound in the *Astérix* books. In this example from *Astérix en Corse*, the humour hinges on people speaking different dialects. Without cultural transplantation, this is impossible to convey in the TL, so the TT derives its humour from puns instead.

ST	TT
ABRARACOURCIX Eh bien, vous pourrez en constater les effets ! Pour fêter l'anniversaire de Gergovie, nous allons attaquer le	VITALSTATISTIX You'll soon notice its effects. We're going to attack the Roman camp of Totorum before dinner. A little
5 camp romain de Babaorum avant le dîner ! Ça nous ouvrira l'appétit.	punch-up by way of an aperitif.
PLAINCONTRIX Ouais !	INSTANTMIX Punch-up!
BEAUFIX Bravo !	JELLIBABIX I'm pleased as punch!
ALAMBIX L'ARVERNE Cha	
10 ch'est caujé !	WINESANSPIRIX THE AVERNIAN That's the ticket!
LABELDECADIX (DE MASSILIA) Vé ! C'est un peu bieng organisé, cette fÂlte !	DRINLIKAFIX (FROM MASSILIA) Tickety-boo, eh?
ALAMBIX Chette quoi ?	WINESANSPIRIX Tickety what?
15 LABELDECADIX Cette fÂlte ! Effeu – ê – té –	DRINLIKAFIX This is what makes us tick.
ALAMBIX Ah ! Chette fête !	WINESANSPIRIX Ah, punching Romans! They're the ticket!
LABELDECADIX Vouaye. Cette sÔterie si vous préférez.	DRINKLIKAFIX Not a bad punchline.
(Goscinny and Uderzo 1973: 11)	(Goscinny and Uderzo 1980: 11)

As in the ST, there is a touch of incomprehension in the TT ('Tickety what?'), but otherwise the humour is different. In the ST, we chuckle as the characters unintentionally reveal their provincial differences; in the TT, we appreciate their deliberate puns. But the overall effect is not *significantly* different: they are cheerily looking forward to having a party punching up the Romans.

Another common feature of compensation is that the loss of a particular effect found at a given place in the ST is compensated for by creating a corresponding effect at an earlier or later place in the TT. This is partly because compensation very often entails grammatical transposition, but there are often other factors involved. A simple example is that of compensating for the loss of an unreproducible pun by using a related pun on another word at a different place in the TT, as in *Asterix the Gaul*:

ST	TT
Ton idée de les envoyer aux *fraises* n'est pas mal non plus… Ça nous fait des vacances aux *frais* de César !	That was a *fruitful* suggestion of yours, sending them off after *strawberries*! We're having a nice holiday at Caesar's expense!
(Goscinny and Uderzo 1961: 32; our italics)	(Goscinny and Uderzo 1969: 32; our italics)

In literary, political or journalistic STs, a significant part of the effect is often produced through the sounds of words. If the strategy is to produce similar effects in similar ways in the TT, this will almost certainly only be possible using different sounds in different places, as in the following example from a speech by General de Gaulle in 1944:

> **V**oilà ce que **v**eulent dire les **vir**iles acclamations de nos **vill**es et de nos **vill**ages, purgés enfin de l'ennemi.

Here, the rhetoric is obviously reinforced by the alliteration and assonance, and by the phonic resemblance of 'villes' and 'villages', which mirrors their semantic resemblance. This phonic reinforcement cannot be replicated in an English TT: the key words do not alliterate, and 'towns' and 'villages' have no sound in common except the final [z]. The following TT compensates for this loss by using phonic reinforcement in different places from the ST:

> This is what the cheering mea**ns**, re**soun**ding through **our towns** and villages clean**s**ed at last of the **enemy**.

All these sorts of substitution may be confined to single words, but they more usually extend to whole phrases, sentences, or even paragraphs. Sometimes, an entire text is affected. For instance, quite apart from lexical and grammatical considerations, if a poem is heavily marked by rhyme, and the translator decides that rhyme would lead to unacceptable translation loss, compensation might consist of heavily marking the TT with something different, such as rhythm, assonance or expressive breaks between lines. Ted Hughes's 1998 translation of *Phèdre*, which deliberately introduces translation loss on every level, is a resoundingly successful example of wholesale compensation on this scale.

Compensation also very often involves a change in 'economy', ST features having to be spread over a relatively longer (or sometimes shorter) length of TT. The following sentence, adapted from the writer Jacques Dupin, provides an excellent example:

> L'écriture ne comble pas mais au contraire approfondit toujours davantage le manque et le tourment qui la suscitent.

For both 'comble' and 'approfondit', the context mobilizes more than one of their potential meanings. This is because the two verbs are used together. If 'comble' were used on its own with these abstract direct objects ('manque' and 'tourment'), it would be taken in its regular figurative senses, 'to fill (a gap/lack)', 'to meet/satisfy (a need)':

ST	TT
L'écriture ne comble pas le manque ni le tourment qui la suscitent.	Writing satisfies neither the need nor the torment that prompt it.

The figurative expression 'combler le manque' is an established collocation, a dead metaphor, and is not a translation problem. Interestingly, however, 'combler le tourment' stretches and revitalizes the metaphor somewhat. It would be more usual to use 'calmer'. 'Comble' gives 'tourment' a nuance of lack, emptiness or hunger, as if writers actually need torment as part of their inspiration. Fortunately, 'satisfies the torment' is as unusual as the ST collocation, and has a similar effect. In this case, there is no need for compensation: the ST exploits established SL lexical usage for a particular effect, and established TL lexical usage can be exploited for a closely similar effect.

'Approfondit' too, if used on its own with these abstract direct objects, would be taken in its regular figurative sense, 'to go {deeper/further} into', 'to investigate (a problem/question)':

ST	TT
L'écriture approfondit toujours davantage le manque et le tourment qui la suscitent.	Writing investigates ever more deeply the lack and the torment that prompt it.

aider avec les effets d'autres mots 49

There is no renewal of the dead metaphor here, no translation problem, and no need for compensation. The effect of the established TT expression is acceptably close to that of the established ST expression.

However, the verbs are not used singly, but together. The fact that both verbs are used, and in opposition to one another, triggers their latent opposed *concrete* meanings, 'to fill up (a hole)' and 'to deepen (a hole)'. This in turn triggers the latent concrete sense of 'tourment', '(physical) agony'. The result is a very concentrated sentence with a complex meaning. It says first that writing springs from an anguished spiritual/intellectual need experienced as some kind of painful, physical void or wound. But it also says that, far from meeting the need and soothing the pain, writing makes them ever worse by probing further into them in its effort to understand and explain them.

Unfortunately, for neither 'comble' nor 'approfondit' does there seem to be an English verb that will on its own convey the multiple meanings found in this particular case. One way of translating the sentence would therefore be to compensate by splitting the ST verbs into more units:

Writing does not soothe or heal the lack and the torment that prompt it, but opens and probes them ever more deeply. – *plus de mots*

'Comble' is divided between 'soothe' and 'heal': 'soothe' corresponds to the figurative sense, 'to satisfy (a need)'; 'heal' implies the closing up of a wound, and corresponds to the concrete sense, 'to fill up'. 'Approfondit' is divided between 'opens' and 'probes': 'opens' corresponds to the concrete sense, 'to deepen'; 'probes' corresponds to the figurative sense, 'to investigate further'. The physical dimension of 'tourment' is rendered by the medical connotations of 'soothe', 'heal' and 'probes'. This context also gives 'opens' the connotation of an open wound. So as well as splitting two SL verbs into four TL ones, the TT also substitutes connotative meaning for literal meaning. Compound compensation like this is the rule rather than the exception.

This complex example raises the issue of the parameters of compensation. What we have done is deliberately introduce loss in economy and grammar in order to avoid more serious loss in message content. Now, since it is after all the translator's job to convey the message content, it could be reasonably argued that making these changes is not strictly speaking compensation at all, but simply a constraint. That is, to do full justice to the ST's semantic complexity, the translator does not have a choice, because the splitting and grammatical rearrangement is the only adequate solution – anything else would simply have been a mistranslation.

It is true that if, in this context, 'comble' and 'approfondit' are seen as having a particular nexus of literal meanings and connotations, a TT that does not in some way convey them all should be considered defective. In deciding whether the changes introduced amount to compensation, the crucial factor is the role of context. If an ST expression has a standard TL counterpart that, regardless of context, spreads it over a relatively longer or shorter stretch of TT, then this is a constraint, an instance of canonic expansion or contraction, not of compensation. So, for instance, 'capital gains tax' will always be translated as 'impôt sur le transfert des capitaux', and vice versa, whatever the context. In every case, the translation is predictable. That is, the differences between the ST expression and the TT expression only reflect standard lexical and syntactic differences between English and French. The same is true where the translator does have a choice between possibilities for an ST expression but the context dictates the choice unambiguously. Thus, in most contexts, the following translations will be more or less automatic:

ST	TT
il a comblé son retard	he (has) made up the lost time
c'est un homme comblé	he has everything he could wish for
elle est morte comblée d'honneurs	she died laden with honours
je suis un professeur comblé	{I'm/I've been} a very lucky teacher/I've had a most fulfilling career, etc.

In the last example, the choice will again usually be clear from the context. If the context does *not* anywhere make it absolutely clear which is meant, the translator can be pretty sure that it does not matter, and simply choose the rendering that fits in best.

The example with 'combler' and 'approfondir' is not like this, however. Certainly, it reflects lexical differences between French and English; certainly, it forces the translator's hand. But our expansions, rearrangements and exploitation of connotations are not canonic or predictable; in fact they are virtually unrepeatable. To the extent that these are specific reactions to specific occurrences of the ST expressions in specific contexts, they are instances of compensation.

The difference between constraint and compensation can be finally confirmed by looking briefly at communicative translation. Communicative translation could be said to involve compensation, in that it reduces translation loss by deploying resources like those in the examples we have been discussing. But the element of compensation is, in a sense, 'automatic': the original compensation was created long ago, by the first person who decided that, say, 'Chat échaudé craint l'eau froide' was best rendered with a TL equivalent like 'Once bitten, twice shy'. Certainly, ever since then, translators confronted with this proverb have had to be alert enough to recognize the need for communicative translation. To that extent, producing the TL equivalent does involve choice, as all translation does. But in cases like this one, the translator is not required to devise the TT expression from scratch. The element of decision is minimal. Therefore, in discussing TTs, such cases are generally more usefully noted as communicative translations, instances of constraint, than analysed as instances of compensation.

The same is true of the myriad cases where the canonic literal translation involves grammatical transposition. Take a simple exchange like 'Je n'ai pas faim. – Moi non plus': there is little option but to translate as '"I'm not hungry." "Neither am I/Me neither"'. In most contexts, the unidiomatic exoticism of '"I do not have hunger." "Me no more"' would create grievous translation loss. So preserving TL idiomaticity does in a way compensate for the loss of the ST grammatical structures. But this compensation is even more automatic than that involved in communicative translation. In so far as the canonic literal translation is unavoidable, it is a constraint, and there is no point in discussing such cases as examples of compensation.

In both these sorts of mandatory translation, then, the only element of choice is in the decision *not* to depart from the standard rendering. Occasionally, however, it will be necessary to depart from the norm. This more often happens with communicative translation than with canonic literal translation. Here is an example, from an article on translation:

D'ailleurs ce n'est pas le traducteur, chat échaudé du langage, qui se moquera des traductions des autres.   *once bitten, twice shy*

The meaning is clear: one bloody encounter with language is enough to make you wary of tangling with it again, and certainly of criticizing other translators' work. How can this be put into English? The first response is obviously is to try something with 'once bitten'. But there is a problem with this expression. 'Once bitten by language' is going to sound as if it means 'once you've got the language bug', i.e. 'once you've developed an enthusiasm for language'. Not even adding 'twice shy' later in the sentence will prevent this misleading implication. Something like 'once bitten by language, twice shy of laughing at other people's translations' sounds like a heavy-handed pun, and is unclear. And incorporating this into the sentence as a whole makes things worse, e.g.:

In any case, the translator has been bitten once by language and is twice shy of laughing at the efforts of others.

In any case, the translator has so often been bitten by language that he is many times shy of laughing at the efforts of others.

expliquer l'expression

In a case like this, drawing on the established communicative translation creates unacceptable translation loss, so the translator does have a real choice. Here is a possible TT:

> In any case, translators bear too many scars from past battles with language to laugh at the efforts of others.

Where the ST has an allusion to a proverb ('chat échaudé'), the TT uses a stock metaphor ('to bear scars'). The TT makes explicit what is implicit in the ST. This makes the TT more cumbersome than the ST, and it is tempting to omit 'with language'. But then it might look as if the battles were quarrels with other translators, not struggles with language. A slicker possibility, using a different stock metaphor, is:

> In any case, translators have fought too many losing battles with language to laugh at the efforts of others.

The drawback to this is that the ST does not imply losing battles, only getting hurt in them. (And, as our concept of translation loss shows, we do not accept that the translator *ever* need lose the battle.) Luckily, the problem can be solved by adjusting the stock metaphor into a different one:

> In any case, translators have fought too many bruising battles with language to laugh at the efforts of others.

Each of these TTs is an example of compensation, because a one-off, *ad hoc* decision has been taken to reject the mandatory communicative translation and to render the important ST effects by different means.

Compensation, then, is a matter of choice and decision. It is the reduction of an unacceptable translation loss through the calculated introduction of a less unacceptable one. Or, to put it differently, a deliberately introduced loss is a small price to pay if it is used to avoid the more serious loss that would be entailed by conventional translation of the expression concerned. Compensation is unlikely to be successful if inspiration is not allied with analytical rigour. So, before deciding on how to compensate for a translation loss, it is best to assess as precisely as possible what the loss is and why it matters both in its immediate context and in the TT as a whole. This reduces the likelihood of inadvertently introducing more serious translation losses than the one that is being compensated for. The answer to these questions depends, of course, on what the purpose of the translation is. When all the possibilities have been reviewed, the decisive question is: 'Will the proposed compensation make the TT *more* fit for its purpose, or *less*?'

PRACTICAL 4

4.1 Degrees of freedom; cultural issues; compensation

Assignment

(i) This assignment is unorthodox, because it comprises translation from English into French, and the text is of a type sometimes said to be 'untranslatable'. It is a limbering-up exercise, combining elements of revision with the central concern of compensation. Of course, every practical in *Thinking French Translation* involves revision: the assumption is that you have read the previous chapters and done the corresponding practicals. However, compensation is the issue that raises most clearly of all the question of the limits of translatability. In explicitly mentioning degrees of freedom and cultural issues in the assignment, we want to confront you squarely with the question of these limits; and in asking you to translate into French, we want to force the question of cultural and linguistic foreignness to the fore-front of your strategic attention. In this way, the ST raises especially clearly problems that are fundamental to translation of all but the most purely empirical texts. The basic question is that of the purpose of the text. If the key to the whole thing is the punning punchline, a productive approach might be to find a French dictionary definition of 'panda' and work backwards from there. This probably implies wholesale changes to the story, so that the TT details lead up to the punchline, just as the ST details do. The TT may well be shorter or longer than the ST. Bearing this preamble in mind, discuss the strategic decisions that you have to make before starting detailed translation of this ST, and outline and justify the strategy you adopt.

(ii) Translate the text into French.

(iii) Explain the main decisions of detail you took.

Contextual information

The ST is quite simply a story that was told, over a glass of wine, as an example of an untranslatable joke.

ST

A panda goes into a pub and orders a ploughman's and a pint of stout. The barman's a bit surprised, but he shouts through the order and starts pulling the pint. The other drinkers are as taken aback as the barman, and for a few moments there's an awkward silence in the pub. But it triggers
5 no reaction in the panda, who just twitches his muzzle and fixes his atten-tion on the filling glass. The barman passes him the pint, and, as the panda waits patiently for the head to settle, the silence is followed by an excited buzz. No one's ever seen anything like it, and an animated argument starts. Some are adamant that pandas only drink lager, others that they're strictly

10   vegan. Bets are laid on whether he'll really drink the stout, and odds of
      seven to four are agreed that he'll take the cheese out of the ploughman's
      before he eats it. Silence falls again when the food arrives. Everyone stares
      as the panda devours the whole thing in a couple of mouthfuls. Then
      suddenly, before anyone can say a thing, he looks up, glares at the gaping
15   punters, whips out a revolver, fires six shots into the ceiling and storms
      out of the pub.
          His keeper, who's waiting for him outside in the car, says 'What the
      hell's the matter? I've never known you do a thing like that, it's not like
      you at all.'
20   'What do you mean, it's not like me?' says the panda, 'Of course it is
      – haven't you ever looked me up in the dictionary?'
          The keeper's not much one for books, so the panda hands him his own
      dictionary. Screwing up his eyes in concentration, the keeper looks up
      'panda', and laboriously reads:
25   '**Panda**. Asian mammal; eats shoots and leaves.'

4.2   Compensation

Assignment
   (i)   It is 1981. You have been commissioned to translate this ST for a
          quality newspaper, as part of a regular series showing different reac-
          tions to the latest nine-days wonder on the Continent. In thinking
          about your strategy, you may find it useful to compare the text with
          the ST in Practical 4.3. Discuss the strategic decisions that you have
          to make before starting detailed translation of this ST, and outline
          and justify the strategy you adopt.
   (ii)   Translate the text into English.
   (iii) Discuss the main decisions of detail you took, paying special atten-
          tion to cases where you used compensation to avoid unacceptable
          translation loss.

Contextual information
The whole text is given here. It appeared in *Le Monde* on 24 December
1980. It refers to a price war between bakers in France, which began when
a baker in the south cut the price of his baguettes from the going rate of
around FF 1,40 to one franc. Others rapidly offered baguettes for 85
centimes, then 80.

ST

MA MIE

Les boulangers qui vendent le pain à un franc ont certes du pain sur la
planche, disent leurs concurrents, mais à force de proposer leur baguette
pour une bouchée de pain et de n'avoir pour tout bénéfice que des miettes,
ils risquent fort de se retrouver bientôt au pain sec.

5 Pour une fois que ce n'est pas nous que l'on roule dans la farine et que
l'on fait marcher à la baguette, nous voudrions pourtant bien que ces
boulangers, pour avoir voulu nous faire manger notre pain blanc, ne se
retrouvent pas ensuite dans le pétrin.

10 Quoi qu'il en soit, nous leur devrons d'avoir, au moins pendant un
moment, pensé que la tartine pouvait ne pas toujours tomber du côté du
beurre, et, ne serait-ce que pour cela, nous avons envie d'embrasser ces
boulangers... comme du bon pain.

(Caste 1980: 1)

4.3 Compensation

(i) You are translating for the same newspaper as in Practical 4.2 the
article from which the following ST is taken. The TT will appear
with the TT of 'Ma mie'. It may be useful to compare the ST with
'Ma mie' in considering your strategy. Discuss the strategic decisions that you have to take before starting detailed translation of
this ST, and outline and justify the strategy you adopt.

(ii) Translate the text into English.

(iii) Discuss the main decisions of detail you took, paying special attention to cases where you used compensation to avoid unacceptable
translation loss.

Contextual information

The article, by the poet and *académicien* Pierre Emmanuel (1916–84),
appeared in *France catholique* on 9 January 1981. It is entitled 'Le pain
et le livre'. A leitmotif is that we live in 'un monde qui a perdu le goût
du pain' (cf. l. 27). In the first half of the article, Emmanuel expresses
his jaundiced view that, behind the bread war, there is an alliance of big
business and government ministers, the aim being to squeeze the life out
of small bakers; as a result, 'presque tous les Français mangeront de
l'éponge, comme les Anglais ou les Américains'. The second half begins:
'Un autre pain dont nous risquons de perdre le goût est celui de l'esprit,
l'œuvre littéraire.' Emmanuel foresees a similar hijacking of the book
trade by the supermarkets, and the consequent disappearance of serious
writing: 'les lettres mourront d'une mort assez vilaine : mais qui, au fond,
se soucie dans un monde qui a perdu le goût du pain ?' The extract is
from the first third of the article. It begins with the opening paragraph;
the omitted material is on the politics and economics of the situation. It
may be helpful to know that René Monory was chubby-featured.

ST

La guerre du pain vient d'être déclarée entre petits boulangers, et je
soupçonne M. Monory, ministre de l'Economie, et les « grandes surfaces »

d'être les puissances qui tirent les marrons du feu. Même la semaine des bûches de Noël n'a pas incité les combattants à la trêve, et les médias,
5 comme il fallait s'y attendre, prêtent leur grosse artillerie aux partisans de la baguette à un franc. Le ministre de l'Economie s'était fait une tête de brioche pour déclarer, en toute neutralité, que ce conflit entrait dans le jeu normal de la compétition dans notre système « libéral ». [. . .]

Qu'il me pardonne, mais ces choses-là font rire. Une campagne si bien
10 menée à la baguette, cela ne fait pas que s'entendre, cela se voit. Si les Français ne mangent pas autant de pain que jadis, ils vivent encore de symboles : et le pain en est un. Pour un mot malheureux sur lui, Marie-Antoinette a sans doute perdu la tête. La phrase du *Notre Père* : « Donne-nous aujourd'hui notre pain de chaque jour », est celle que la
15 plupart des chrétiens prononcent avec la conviction la plus immédiate. Qui parle du pain, mot concret s'il en est, évoque par lui toute nourriture. Il va de soi comme ce pain à midi sur la table que la baguette à un franc symbolise une baisse générale de la nourriture, même si cette baisse – justement parce que cette baisse – ne se produit pas.
20 Mais l'art de symboliser a des limites que les poètes connaissent mieux que les stratèges de l'économie. Une aussi *visible* émulation à la baisse, qui nous vaudra peut-être un pain – mais lequel ? – à soixante-dix centimes avant la fin du mois, se fait voir pour ce qu'elle est, une opération de propagande, auprès de gens qu'elle prend pour des imbéciles, en l'espèce
25 chacun de nous. Cette propagande n'a qu'un but : hâter la disparition de la boulangerie artisanale, l'une des rares qui subsiste, et la meilleure, dans un monde qui a perdu le *goût du pain*.

(*L'Arbre et le vent*, P. Emmanuel, 1ère publication
Editions du Seuil, 1982: 199, 200)

5

Textual genre and translation issues

type de communication

comment doit-on interpréter tout ça?

It will have become clear by now that different STs require different strategic priorities. In deciding which textual variables to prioritize, the translator has always to ask: what is the purpose of the ST, and what is the purpose of the TT? These questions imply two others: what kind of text is the ST, and what kind of text should the TT be? The texts we have used as examples and in practicals all illustrate the importance of these four inseparable questions in deciding a strategy. At issue here is a fundamental consideration in translation: all texts are defined in terms of **genre**. By genre we mean what Hymes calls a 'type of communicative event' (quoted in Hervey 1992: 199) – that is, a category to which, in a given culture, a given text is seen to belong and within which the text is seen to share a type of communicative purpose and effect with other texts. In this definition, the term also covers the traditionally identified genres of literature, and genres bearing what Mona Baker calls 'institutionalized labels' such as 'journal article', 'science textbook', 'newspaper editorial' or 'travel brochure' (1992: 114).

L'effet

The term **text-type** is often used in a similar sense to 'genre'. The best-known classification of text-types has been that of Katharina Reiss, who distinguishes three, each characterized by a different function of language – artistic and creative self-expression, conveying information, and persuading somebody to do something (1989: 105–15). Snell-Hornby (1988) sees this classification as too limited, and suggests a much more complex 'prototypology' – certainly too complex for our purposes. Neubert and Shreve (1992: 125–35) also try to get round the problem with a concept of 'prototype'. Yet another classification is proposed by Hatim and Mason (1990: 153–8), who distinguish between argumentative, expository and instructional text-types, found functioning alongside one another as what amount to multiple texts within texts.

3 fonctions de la langue

In all these taxonomies, a decisive factor in distinguishing text-type is the author's intention. This is something they have in common with genre as we have defined it. However, in foregrounding intention rather than event, these writers may be laying less stress than we do on the text as outcome, perhaps implying that the author's purpose and the actual effect of the text coincide, or that, where they do not, this does not matter. From the translation point of view, this in turn may imply a normative assumption that there are certain archetypal invariants that can and should be transferred without loss from ST to TL. However legitimate or illegitimate these possible inferences may be, the term 'text-type' is used so variously that we shall stick to 'genre', because the element of 'event' in its definition ensures that the definable qualities of a text are seen as dynamic, as together constituting an attempt to realize a particular communicative purpose.

Most texts belong to a genre or genres. Some innovative texts arguably do not, when they first appear: but even these are defined by contrast with genres they do *not* belong to. Innovative texts aside, it can be said that any ST shares some of its properties with other texts of the same genre, and is perceived by an SL audience as being what it is on account of such genre-defining properties. Therefore, in order to assess the nature and purpose of the ST, the translator must have some sort of overview of genre-types in the source culture, and be familiar with the characteristics of relevant genres within those types.

What is true of SL texts is true of TL texts. Since the nature and the purpose of a given text imply one another, the translator has to be as familiar with target-culture genre-types and genres as with those of the source culture. Paying due attention to the nature and purpose of the TT guarantees a degree of TL bias which helps to prevent the excessive SL bias that so often defeats the purpose of the TT.

Since translators need to consider these genre-related questions before translating a text, it is useful for them to have a framework of broad genre-types. This will help students to identify salient genre characteristics of the ST, and to check those of the TT they are producing. At this training stage, it will take some time to learn how to pick out the features that signal a particular genre and – just as important – what the TL expectations are for that genre. However, once this ability has been developed, applying it takes very little time. This is especially true in many professional situations: in areas like technical, legal or financial translation, the translator knows in advance what genre most STs are likely to belong to, and it only takes a quick look at the text to confirm this.

We shall suggest five broad genre-types. Within each type, there are innumerable genres. And many texts have important characteristics from more than one genre and more than one genre-type. So we are not going to attempt an exhaustive typology of genres; that would be far too elaborate for our purposes. In determining the genre of a text, two essential factors need to considered. The first is the author's attitude to the treatment of the subject matter of the text. (We use 'author' to denote the originator of the text, whether it is oral or written.) The second is the question of whether the text is an oral one or a written one.

ATTITUDE TO TREATMENT OF SUBJECT MATTER

Subject matter in itself is not a useful criterion for describing genres, because the same subject matter can figure in very different genres. What is at issue is the author's attitude, implicit or explicit, to treatment of the subject matter. This attitude comprises three things. First, there is the author's attitude to the subject matter itself. Second, there is the author's intention or desire that the text should have a particular sort of effect on the reader or listener. And third, there is an acceptance by the author of the likelihood – i.e. the probability or improbability – of this intention being achieved. On this basis, we shall distinguish five broad categories of genre.

The first category is that of empirical genres. Genres in this category deal with the real world as it is experienced by observers. An empirical text is more or less informative, and it is understood to take an objective view of observable phenomena. Scientific, technological and many scholarly texts fall into this category. It therefore goes on diversifying into new genres and sub-genres as new scientific and academic disciplines are created. While there is always scope for specialists to disagree with one another about the broader implications of, say, a text on the transport of nuclear waste, the author of an empirical text will nevertheless be pretty confident that, as long as it is written in a particular way, it will fulfil its purpose of unambiguously relaying a body of facts and a conclusion drawn from them.

The second category comprises philosophical genres. These have as their subject matter a 'world' of ideas. Pure mathematics is the best example of the kind of subject matter that defines philosophical genres. Even in the field of metaphysics, however original the text, the author is understood not to be free to develop theoretical structures at will, but to be constrained by some standard of rationality. This does not, of course, prevent it being easy for the reader to misunderstand the point; hence the elaborate t-crossing and i-dotting with which philosophical authors try to reduce the uncertainty of effect. Philosophical genres have not proliferated as much as empirical ones, but they are strikingly diverse nonetheless.

The third category comprises religious genres. In terms of the author's attitude, the subject matter of religious texts implies the existence of a spiritual world that is not fictive, but has its own external realities and truths. The author is understood not to be free to create the world that animates the subject matter, but to be merely instrumental in exploring it. Even so, the author can never be certain that the desired effect will be produced. The fiercely proselytizing or threatening tone of many religious texts is testimony to precisely that uncertainty. The category of religious genres has perhaps diversified less than any of the others, but, certainly in the field of Christianity, it still has a wide range of styles, including Authorized Version and happy-clappy.

The fourth category is that of persuasive genres. The essence of these is that they aim at making listeners or readers behave in prescribed or suggested ways. This aim can be pursued through various means: we are classifying in a single category the entire gamut of texts from instruction manuals, through laws, rules and regulations to propaganda leaflets and advertisements. The very many genres and sub-genres in this category have a common purpose, that of getting an audience to take a certain course of action, and perhaps explaining how to take it. The very notion of trying to persuade implies an inbuilt element of uncertainty as to whether the text will succeed. From video manuals to election propaganda, the history of persuasive genres is lit by failure as well as success. This is a crucial factor in the selection of a style for such texts.

Finally, there is the category of literary genres. Literary genres have subdivided and diversified very greatly over the centuries. There are innumerable sub-genres of poetry, prose narrative and drama, each with its characteristic style. However, all texts in this category have two essential features. First, they concern a world created autonomously in and through the texts themselves, and not controlled by the physical world outside. However close a literary text is to history or autobiography, it still approaches its subject matter by recreating experience in terms of a subjective, internal world, which is fundamentally perceived as fictive, for all its similarities to the world outside the text. Second, whatever other characteristics they have, and whatever their subject matter, literary texts contain features of *expression* that emphasize, modify or actually create features of *content*. There are examples in Practical 2. In the Camus text in Practical 2.2, the stripped-down, somewhat disjointed style gives an impression of detachment or alienation, which accords perfectly with the idea of Meursault as 'étranger'. And in Practical 2.3, Helmut's unorthodox grammar emphasizes Lélé's anxiety and excitement at being in a hostile country, mirrors Helmut's unorthodox sexuality, and perhaps introduces the theme of Lélé's inability to cope with the unexpected.

With their reliance on suggestion – through e.g. connotation, imagery or analogy – literary genres are especially vulnerable to chance and subjectivity. However carefully the author tries to control the reactions of the reader or listener, it is less possible than with most other genre-types to be certain that the effect will be the one the author desired or intended. An acceptance of this uncertainty is part of the literary author's attitude to treatment of subject matter.

Consideration of the author's attitude to treatment of the subject matter concentrates the translator's mind on four groups of vital strategic questions. First, what are the salient features of the ST? What do these features imply about its purpose? What genre do the features and purpose suggest it belongs to? Second, does the ST have recognizable genre-specific characteristics that require special attention? If so, which of them should be retained in translation? Third, what TL genre(s) provide a match for the ST genre? What do existing specimens of these TL genres suggest regarding formulation of the TT? Fourth, what genre should the TT ultimately belong to, and what genre-specific features should it have?

Two words of caution are needed here. First, it is easy for student translators to begin their strategic considerations something like this: 'This text belongs to genre A, therefore it has characteristics x, y and z.' This is putting the cart before the horse. It is much more useful to identify the text's characteristics first, and then, on that basis, to assign it to a genre. Of course, in many professional situations translators know in advance what genre the text will belong to. But they still have to serve an apprenticeship in mastering the particularities of that genre. In any case, many other professional translators do not get such predictable work, and have to decide what genre-features the latest text has before getting down to detailed work. This is why, at this stage, we urge students to look at the text first, decide what its defining features are, and only then allot it to a genre.

This approach does not only result in a more sensitive appraisal of the true purpose of the text. It also makes it easier to be flexible and to recognize cases where, as very often happens, the ST actually has a blend of features – it may be predominantly typical of one genre, but also have features from other genres or even other genre categories. So, for example, instruction manuals may vary in character between the empirical and the persuasive categories. Advertising very commonly shares features with literary texts, as do religious and philosophical texts. Religious texts often share features with persuasive texts. Many legal or administrative texts – contracts or memoranda of agreement, for instance – combine empirical and persuasive genre-features. Texts often contain quotations from texts that belong to other genres, or parodies of other genres.

This 'hybridization' in genre is common in journalism, parody and satire. Such blends may theoretically constitute sub-genres and subdivisions of sub-genres, but that is not our concern: our aim here is to encourage and enable students to isolate the salient features and the purpose of an ST, so that they can relate these to the purpose of the TT and thus be in a position to develop an appropriate translation strategy.

The second word of caution is that it is essential for translators to be familiar with the characteristic features of the TL genre or genres that they decide correspond most closely to the ST genre(s). If in doubt, examine sample texts from the chosen TL genre before the translation is started. Professional translators tend to specialize in particular fields, and one of the first things they do is acquire an awareness of relevant TL genre characteristics. Before embarking on any of the exercises in Practical 5, the student should where necessary do some of this preliminary TL genre-sampling.

ORAL TEXTS AND WRITTEN TEXTS

The relevance of these words of caution becomes even clearer when the second factor in defining a genre is taken into account: is the text an oral one or a written one? Each of the five genre categories includes both oral and written texts. In truth, it is almost impossible not to distinguish an oral text as belonging to a discrete oral genre, and a written text as belonging to a discrete written genre, even where the texts share the same subject matter: the difference in medium generally entails a difference in attitude to treatment of the subject matter. Thus, a story told in a pub is in a different genre from a story printed in a magazine. A sermon on the Beatitudes, a talk on the Fifth Republic, a tutorial explanation of quarks – each is in a different genre from any kind of written reflection on the topic. A complicating factor is that many oral genres also involve written texts: songs, plays, sermons, lectures, a salesperson's patter – all may be performed on the basis of a written text that is either read out, or spoken from memory, or used as the basis for improvisation. To get an idea of the significance of these factors for translation, it is helpful first to look at some of the specific characteristics of oral texts as distinct from written ones.

An oral text is a fleeting event. This has important consequences. First, vocal utterance is usually accompanied by visual cues, such as gestures or facial expressions, that may be secondary to it but certainly form part of the overall text and often play a crucial role in creating its meaning. Significant features of intonation, voice stress and tempo are often reinforced by such visual cues. Second, effective oral texts obey the 'rules' of a spoken language first and foremost. In particular, an effective oral text avoids long sentences, information overload, elaborate cross-referencing, excessive speed, etc., because these make the text hard to follow. In all these respects, what is true for oral STs is true for oral TTs as well.

A third implication of orality is the appearance of spontaneity that generally characterizes oral texts. This goes not only for impromptu conversation or narrative, but also for prepared texts, such as memorized lines in a play. Even in a speech or a lecture where the speaker sticks closely to a script, the delivery may imitate that of an unscripted text. Similarly, dramatized reading, recited verse and song lyrics, if well performed, can all give the audience a chance to enter into the illusion of spontaneous vocal utterance. An oral text is in fact always quite different in nature and impact from even the most closely corresponding written version.

An awareness of these properties of oral texts is a necessary starting-point for translating an oral ST into an oral TT. Spoken communication has characteristics that are very much language-specific. Oral translation is not simply a matter of verbal transposition: the genre-related body-language of the target culture must be respected as well, including gestures, facial expressions, and so on. Translating a joke, for instance, will generally involve quite different genres from conference interpreting. Both, however, make it clear that an oral text in any genre is not only an utter-ance, but also a dramatic performance.

Another genre helps to highlight a second set of difficulties peculiar to oral translation. This is the genre of the song lyric. Assuming that the TT is to be sung to the same tune as the ST, there will be major translation problems on the phonic/graphic and prosodic levels as well as the gram-matical level. As we shall see in Chapter 6, the phonic and prosodic properties of different languages are very different. This poses real prob-lems, as Michael Irwin points out:

> A language prolific in short vowel-sounds, awkward consonantal clus-ters and sudden shifts of tempo does not lend itself easily to musical drama. No singer is likely to relish tackling a word such as 'strengths' or 'relapsed'. 'To be or not to be' could be splendidly singable; 'that is the question' would be taxing. Presumably Rodolfo was given the absurd phrase, 'your tiny hand is frozen', because the natural adjective, 'little', is a terrible throat-closer.
>
> (Irwin 1996: 96–7)

Clearly, anyone translating a lyric or libretto needs to understand the prosodic features not only of the SL, but also of the TL. On the phonic level, the song-translator must pay attention to how vowels correspond with notes in the score: on certain musical notes, certain vowels are hard to sing without distortion. Consonant clusters must also be attended to, not only so that the performer is not given a tongue-twister to sing, but also to avoid nonsense. This is hard enough in speech, let alone singing. Auberon Waugh, who was hard of hearing, tells of being telephoned one day and asked to go to an African country to give a lecture on breast feeding. He was a bit surprised, because he knew nothing about the subject. But he swotted it up, flew out and was some way into the lecture before realizing that what they wanted was a lecture on press freedom. And Malachy McCourt claims to have been mystified as a lad by the weekly assertion in the Hail Mary: 'Blessed art thou, a monk swimming'. Given these factors, it is not surprising that translators of songs and libretti take such liberties with ST literal meaning.

It is interesting to compare different musical settings of a pre-existing text such as a poem. Take the settings of Baudelaire's 'L'invitation au voyage' by Duparc and Chabrier. As a written and as a spoken text, the poem has the tone of a man entranced, aware of the awe-inspiring mystery of love and its kinship with death, a man who wants to believe – and wants the girl he is addressing to believe – in the reality of an impossible dream. The tone of Duparc's setting is very close to this. Listen to the Chabrier, though, and the same words have a completely different effect: here is no mystery, just a young gentleman from an operetta trying to sweet-talk a village girl into a romp in the hay. If the brief is to translate the songs, as distinct from the poem, then two different TTs are required. Reading either, you would in effect be reading the translator's reading of the composer's reading of Baudelaire's text . . .

Translators actually do a great deal of their work in a written medium, even when it involves an oral text. Inevitably, the cross-over from written to oral and vice versa results in changes. These changes are essentially due to the fact that writing is such a pale copy of speech in terms of expressive nuance. Cross-over may take a number of forms. We shall mention four, and there will be a chance to try some of these out in the practical.

In the first type of cross-over, the translator starts with an oral ST, and then uses a written transcript to compose a TT which is on paper, but suitable for oral performance: song lyrics are typically translated in this way. In the second type, the translator starts with a written ST, considers how it might be performed orally, and then composes a TT which is on paper, but suitable for oral performance: this is generally how plays are translated. Third, the translator may start with a written script, try out the ST orally, and then produce a TT suitable either for silent reading or for oral performance, or for both: poetry is usually translated like this. In the fourth type, the translator starts with an oral ST and its transcript, and produces a TT for silent reading: this is how film subtitles are generally produced.

Like translating song, subtitling is a very useful exercise in a course like this, having special requirements that force the student to focus especially sharply on many of the issues raised in this chapter and throughout the course. And, while working in a written medium, under very tight constraints of time and space, the translator will often want to hint at some of the oral characteristics of the ST. This is especially true of feature films, where it might be misleading to suggest that all the characters talk the same, or like a book.

Even without the equipment for subtitling film or videotape, it is possible to do a useful introductory exercise using an ordinary audiocassette. There will be a chance to do such an exercise in Practical 5. To help in preparation for this, here are some general notes on subtitling as practised by professionals, followed by a sample of the amateur version using audio material.

NOTES ON SUBTITLING

The subtitler/translator usually has a transcript of all the verbal content of the film, known as a 'dialogue list'. The dialogue list does not include details of cuts. The subtitler runs the film on a viewing/editing table, measuring the time of each phrase, sentence and shot to determine when titles should start and stop. This process is called 'spotting'. The technicalities vary, depending on whether the subtitler is working with film or videotape, but the essential rules are the same (throughout, subtitles are referred to as 'titles'):

- A single-line title requires at least two seconds' viewing time.
- A double-line title requires at least four seconds.
- Never show a title for less than two seconds or more than six seconds.
- Avoid carrying a title over a cut (except in newsreel with many cuts).
- Voices off, such as telephone voices or narrations, are in italics (unless the speaker is present but simply not in camera view).
- Observe the basic rules of punctuation but, where the end of a title coincides with the end of a sentence, omit the full stop.
- In two-line titles, try to make the second line shorter than the first, but do not be inflexible: the first line should read well and not end clumsily.
- Make every title a clear statement. Avoid ambiguity (unless the ST is significantly ambiguous): viewers have little time to take in the message, and cannot turn back as they can with a book or a newspaper.
- When a sentence is split over more than one title, end the first one with three suspension points, and begin the next one with three suspension points.
- Do not use telegraphese: viewers rarely have time to work it out.

When timings are short, it is sometimes helpful to have two speakers' dialogue as a double-line title (ideally for question and answer). In such cases, use a dash to introduce each line, and range left, so that the titles are not centred on the screen. For example:

– Where have they gone today?
– To the country

Here is an example of how to split a whole sentence over two or more titles. The text itself conveys the point we are making: 'In such cases, it is extremely important to make each title coherent in itself, unless the speaker is rambling, delirious, or similar, so that the viewer maintains a steady understanding of the dialogue.' This would be effectively subtitled as follows:

Title 1	In such cases...
Title 2	...it is extremely important to make each title coherent in itself...
Title 3	...unless the speaker is rambling, delirious, or similar, so that...
Title 4	...the viewer maintains a steady understanding of the dialogue

ne pas Rompre la compréhension du dialogue

Here is an example of how *not* to do it:

Title 1	In such cases, it is extremely...
Title 2	...important to make each title coherent...
Title 3	...in itself, unless the speaker is rambling, delirious, or similar, so that...
Title 4	...the viewer maintains a steady understanding of the dialogue

The main weakness of this version is that breaks between titles do not always correspond to the structure or the oral phrasing of the sentence. Despite the suspension points, Title 2 looks like the end of the sentence or clause, and Title 3 like the start of one. The result is that the 'unless' clause looks like a clause parenthetically inserted in mid-sentence: the text might seem to be saying 'In itself, unless the speaker is rambling in such a way that the viewer maintains a steady understanding ...'. But the anticipated resolution of this apparent sentence does not materialize, so that the viewer is at best momentarily puzzled.

The maximum number of spaces allowed for a line varies, depending on the equipment used. For the rest of this chapter and the practical we shall take 36 as an example, which is not untypical. This includes letters, spaces between words, and punctuation marks. So, for instance, the following title is exactly 36 spaces long:

> ...it is extremely important to make

Sample subtitling exercise

The ST is from a television interview. It is the start of an explanation of how the interviewee prepares a hide and equipment for catching thrushes, which he will keep and train as decoys for next season's shooting.

Dialogue list
Voilà. Par exemple je... je me fais d'abord une petite cabane, hein. Tout en... broussailles, quoi, voyez. Et je plante des petits arbustes tout le tour. Alors à l'intérieur je me fais des petites... fenestrons. Sous ce... toujours à l'intérieur, je regarde que j'y ai mis sous ces petits arbustes
5 des... des verguettes.

Spotting
Following the recorded text on the dialogue list, mark off convenient sections coinciding, if possible, with pauses and intonational cues in the spoken delivery. Each of these sections will subsequently form the basis of a subtitle. At the end of spotting, the dialogue list will look something like this:

Voilà. Par exemple je... je me fais d'abord une petite cabane, hein. / Tout en... broussailles, quoi, voyez. / Et je plante des petits arbustres tout le tour. / Alors à l'intérieur je me fais des petites... fenestrons. / Sous ce... toujours à l'intérieur, / je regarde que j'y ai mis sous ces petits arbustres
5   des... des verguettes. /

Timing
The sections marked off in spotting are numbered, and the time between the start of one section and the start of the next is measured (with a stop-watch if possible, but the second hand on a watch will do for our purposes). The timing of the subtitles is based on these measurements. *Remember that any pauses in and between sentences are part of the overall time the text lasts.* These pauses are useful allies for the subtitler, because they give extra time for the viewer to digest the titles. The timed list should look like this:

Title 1	6.0 sec	Voilà ... hein.
Title 2	3.5	Tout en ... voyez.
Title 3	3.0	Et je ... le tour.
Title 4	5.0	Alors ... fenestrons.
Title 5	3.5	Sous ce ... intérieur,
Title 6	5.0	je regarde ... verguettes.

[handwritten annotation:] mettre l'emphase sur qqch.

Creating subtitles *[handwritten: des pauses]*
Each of the spottings is translated into English, observing the following constraints:

(i)   No more than two lines can be shown on the screen at once.
(ii)   Lines cannot be longer than 36 spaces.
(iii) The maximum time available for displaying each subtitle is given by the timing measurements above; allow *at least two seconds for a single-line title*, and *at least four seconds for a two-line title*. But do not allow more than six seconds for any title.

Here is a possible TT:

Title 1	6.0 sec	Well, first I get some brushwood...
Title 2	3.5	...and I build myself a little hut
Title 3	3.0	I put small shrubs all round it
Title 4	5.0	Then I put perches under the shrubs and go into the hut
Title 5	3.5	I make little windows in the hut...
Title 6	5.0	...and look out to check I can see the perches under the shrubs

Note that the order of the speaker's sentences has been changed, for the express purpose of subtitling. The TT follows the order in which he originally performed the actions, not the order in which they are mentioned in his narrative. To see why this is so, compare our TT with the following one, which keeps the ST order:

Title 1	6.0 sec	Well, first I get some brushwood...
Title 2	3.5	...and I build myself a little hut
Title 3	3.0	I put small shrubs all round it
Title 4	5.0	Then I go inside, and make little windows in it
Title 5	3.5	I look out through the windows...
Title 6	5.0	...to check that I can see all the perches I've put under the shrubs

As with any subtitled text, the message is given in a series of short bursts, each of which disappears for good after a few seconds. People reading subtitles therefore have to concentrate harder than people reading a printed page, who can see the whole sentence on the page and go at their own pace. Even listeners have an easier job than subtitle readers, because they are helped by the speaker's voice stress and intonation (and body language, if the speaker is visible). These factors create a particular problem in the last sentence of this ST and our second TT. Important new information is fed in retrospectively, in a subordinate clause: although the speaker actually put the perches under the shrubs *before* going into the hut and looking out, he only tells us about it *after* telling us about going inside and looking out. Assimilating this requires a certain mental agility of anyone, but most of all of subtitle readers. Keeping the ST order in the subtitles may lead viewers to panic momentarily and to ask 'What perches? Have I missed something?' While they are sorting that out, they will not register the next subtitle properly, and could end up losing the thread altogether.

That is why we changed the ST order in our first TT. Normally, 'improving' an ST is not necessary or desirable, but it is sometimes a serious option in interpreting, in cross-over between oral and written texts (as here), and in empirical or persuasive texts, where the paramount concern is absolute clarity.

PRACTICAL 5

▶◀ 5.1 Genre and translation

Assignment

(i)   You are producing subtitles for a television documentary featuring the interview from which the following ST is taken. Listen to the recording of the ST. Listen to it again, following it in the printed transcript (the dialogue list). Discuss the strategic decisions that you have to take before starting detailed translation of this ST into sub-titles, and outline and justify the strategy you adopt.

(ii) Use a stopwatch or wristwatch to convert the dialogue list into spot-tings. Remember that pauses are part of the overall time that the text lasts. And remember that a title should not be carried over a cut.

(iii) Translate the text into subtitles, observing a maximum of 36 spaces for each line. Lay your TT out as shown on p. 67.

(iv) Explain the main details of decision you took.

Contextual information

The extract is from the television interview from which the extract on p. 66 is taken. The 'appelants' are decoys, thrushes which have been caught and are then reared and kept in cages. The interviewee uses them to lure other ones, which he hopes to shoot for the pot. He waits in a hide (different from the hut on p. 66) and fires at the thrushes attracted by the decoys. NB A true dialogue list does not contain details of cuts. But, since this is an audio recording, you are given details of the cuts; these are marked by asterisks.

ST

Q Mais alors, dites-moi maintenant : comment se passe une chasse aux grives avec les appelants que vous avez capturés et élevés ?

R *Bien ça se passe que vous prenez encore les cages, vous les mettez par terre, vous vous mettez dans une autre cabane, constituée pour, et
5   vous avez plusieurs pins à droite ou à gauche, **ou en face, simple-ment, selon l'endroit où il[1] est, et vous en avez même derrière, et vous entendez vos bêtes qui chantent. ***Tic tic tic, qui appellent, vous écoutez le s... vous savez où vous avez mis vos cages, « Ah ! tiens, elles chantent de... de là-bas. » Alors vous regardez, vous la voyez
10   sur l'arbre, la bête se pose, vous prenez le fusil, c'est simple, vous leur en f'tez un dedans. Tant vous l'aurez attrapée, tant vous l'avez manquée, hein.

(Adapted from Carton *et al.*, 1983: 54)

*   cut to interviewee
**   cut to clearing in pine wood, with hut
*** cut to interviewee

[1] il: a slip in gender, perhaps because the speaker has in mind the word *cabanon*, commonly used in Provence for a small hut in the country.

⚏ 5.2 Genre and translation

Assignment

(i) You are translating the following song by Georges Brassens (1921–81), to be sung in tribute to him as part of a concert by an English-speaking singer-poet. Listen first to the song, without following the printed text. *Treating it as an oral text*, discuss its genre, content and impact.

(ii) Examine the words of the song, and discuss its salient features *as a written text*.

(iii) Listen to the song again, following it on the text, and discuss the relation between the words and the music.

(iv) Discuss the strategic decisions that you have to take before starting detailed translation of this ST, and outline and justify the strategy you adopt.

(v) Produce a translation of the text that can be sung to Brassens's music, in his style.

(vi) Explain the main decisions of detail you took.

Contextual information

The words of the song are not by Brassens, although the humour is very like his own. The first three verses are by the famous playwright Pierre Corneille (1606–84), and are part of a longer poem addressed to a girl he had fallen in love with. (Note that she was not a marchioness — Marquise is her first name.) As he was getting on in years, she not surprisingly rejected his advances. The poem rebukes her for being so unsympathetic, and reminds her that she too will grow old one day. The last verse was added by the humorist Tristan Bernard (1866–1947). We have modernized the spelling of Corneille's verses.

NB To do this exercise, you do not need to be a musician at all. It is enough just to listen to the song two or three times, marking on the text where the beats come. The melody is simple and easy to remember. Fitting a TT to the music and rhythm is quite straightforward.

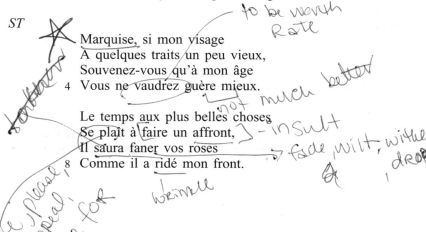

ST

Marquise, si mon visage
A quelques traits un peu vieux,
Souvenez-vous qu'à mon âge
4 Vous ne vaudrez guère mieux.

Le temps aux plus belles choses
Se plaît à faire un affront,
Il saura faner vos roses
8 Comme il a ridé mon front.

Le même cours des planètes
Règle nos jours et nos nuits,
On m'a vu ce que vous êtes,
12   Vous serez ce que je suis.

— Peut-être que je serai vieille,
Répond Marquise, cependant
J'ai vingt-six ans, mon vieux Corneille,
16   Et je t'emmerde en attendant.

5.3   Genre and translation

Assignment

(i)   In partnership with Fréquence Plus and other companies, including
       hotel chains, car-hire firms, etc., Air France is launching a new air
       miles scheme called Fréquence Plus. You have been commissioned
       to translate the pull-out leaflet containing the advertisement and the
       'Résumé des conditions générales', from which the following ST is
       taken. Discuss the strategic decisions that you have to take before
       starting detailed translation of this ST, and outline and justify the
       strategy you adopt.
(ii)   Translate the text into English.
(iii) Explain the main decisions of detail you took.
(iv)   Compare your TT with the published one, which will be given to
       you by your tutor.

Contextual information

The ST is published alongside the application form, but is not part of it.
A note printed in the margin says that it is a 'document non contractuel'.
The extract for translation is the first half of the text.

ST

RESUME DES CONDITIONS GENERALES
applicables à compter du 1er avril 2001

· La participation au programme Fréquence Plus est réservée à toute
  personne physique âgée de 12 ans ou plus, ayant son adresse habituelle
  dans un pays où le programme est applicable, à l'exclusion des personnes
  morales.
5 · L'adhésion à ce programme s'effectue après renvoi à Fréquence Plus
  SA d'une demande d'adhésion dûment remplie (signature du tuteur
  légal pour les mineurs), par tout support disponible agréé par Fréquence
  Plus SA/Air France.
· Fréquence Plus SA se réserve le droit de refuser l'adhésion de toute per-
10 sonne qui ne répondrait pas aux critères pour participer au programme.

- Un numéro d'identification individuel est attribué à tout Adhérent et la participation au programme est effective lors de la première utilisation de ce numéro sur une prestation aérienne donnant droit à des Miles.
- Le Mile est l'unité de calcul du programme Fréquence Plus. Les Miles sont obtenus, selon des barèmes et des conditions détaillés dans les conditions générales et la documentation Fréquence Plus, en utilisant les services d'Air France ou des partenaires de Fréquence Plus du programme.
- Dans le cas où l'Adhérent est également membre d'un autre programme de fidélisation d'Air France ou de l'un de ses partenaires, il ne pourra cumuler à la fois des Miles sur ce programme et sur Fréquence Plus pour un même vol ou une même prestation.
- Les Miles obtenus ont une durée de validité de 36 mois à compter de la date de la prestation réalisée génératrice de Miles ou de Multi-Miles. La péremption des Miles se fait mensuellement. Toutefois, cette durée de validité peut être supérieure dans les cas définis dans les conditions générales et la documentation Fréquence Plus.
- Il est ouvert, pour chaque Adhérent, un compte personnel au crédit duquel sont portés les Miles obtenus. Ce compte, ainsi que les Miles, ne peuvent être cédés, légués ou combinés avec le compte ou les Miles de toute autre personne, participant ou non à ce programme, ou avec tout autre compte dont l'Adhérent pourrait être titulaire.

(Air France/Fréquence Plus 2001)

5.4   Genre and translation

Assignment

(i)   You are translating the word-processed reports on three *tables rondes* held at La jeunesse d'Europe danse en Avignon, a dance festival for young people. The reports and translations are for the EU body which granted a subvention to the festival. The ST below is taken from one of the reports. Discuss the strategic decisions that you have to take before starting detailed translation of this ST, and outline and justify the strategy you adopt.

(ii)   Translate the text into English.

(iii)   Explain the main decisions of detail you took.

(iv)   Compare your TT with the official one, which will be given to you by your tutor.

Contextual information

The festival involved teenage dancers from six countries, and comprised workshops, performances, visits to exhibitions and three *tables rondes*. Each of these was in two parts. The three themes were: 'Le patrimoine culturel européen peut-il être une base de renforcement des liens entre les jeunes ?' (from which the ST is taken), 'La place de l'art dans la vie quotidienne', and 'La danse et l'environnement'. The report on each *table ronde* was written by the professional arts administrator or academic who had chaired it. The three reports differ very greatly in length, layout and style, and are by no means always very polished. The extract given here amounts to half the report. It is printed exactly as in the original.

ST

Ces deux tables rondes ont permis d'intéressants et fructueux échanges entre une quinzaine de jeunes danseuses et danseurs venant de Finlande, Islande, France et Italie.

Après un rapide exposé de l'animatrice sur :

5   1) Ce que pouvait couvrir en France le terme patrimoine avec des domaines : visuels (ex danses, arts plastiques, etc.), gustatifs (culinaires etc.) musicaux qui sont facilement transmissibles sans barrière des langues et les domaines audiovisuels (contes, théâtre, littérature, humour etc.) qui nécessitent la connaissance de la langue ou de la traduction

10   2) La recherche d'un nécessaire équilibre entre :
- d'une part, la connaissance de son patrimoine (individuel ou national) orienté vers une ouverture à la connaissance de l'autre entraînant écoute, tolérance et enrichissement mutuel ;
- et d'autre part la possible « déification » d'un patrimoine ex-

15 acerbé, source possible de nationalisme, d'enfermement et de refus des autres cultures.

Des questions vont, ensuite, servir de point de départ à la réflexion commune :

Le terme patrimoine a-t-il le même sens dans nos différents pays ?

20   Quel sens a ce concept pour de jeunes danseurs européens ? Peut-il être pour vous, entre vous, source de renforcement de liens ? [. . .]

Après avoir essayé de définir, en trois mots, ce qui, pour chacun d'eux, symbolise leur pays respectif, un intéressant échange de vue s'instaure entre d'une part les jeunes françaises et italiennes qui déplorent dans leur

25 pays respectif le poids du patrimoine et de l'histoire tandis que les jeunes européens du Nord (Finlande, Islande) ont beaucoup de mal à imaginer le patrimoine (chez eux on utilise le terme « héritage »), comme un poids, au contraire ils l'assimilent à une richesse culturelle, une fierté. Pays plus « jeunes », pays plus « anciens », les participants sont extrêmement

30 intéressés par ces différences de perception et nous sentons que cela leur procurera sûrement matière à réflexions.

(Angevin 2000)

5.5   Genre and translation

Assignment

(i)   You are translating *Le petit Nicolas* (1960), a set of stories for children aged 8/9 upwards, but also much enjoyed by adults. The stories

all feature le petit Nicolas and his friends and the endless variety of scrapes they manage to get into. Discuss the strategic decisions that you have to take before starting detailed translation of this ST, and outline and justify the strategy you adopt.

(ii) Translate the text into English.

(iii) Explain the main decisions of detail you took.

(iv) Compare your TT with a published one, which will be given you by your tutor.

Contextual information

The ST is from a story called 'Les cow-boys'. It is told by Nicolas, who has invited his friends round to play at cowboys. Rufus is wearing his policeman's outfit, complete with *képi,* handcuffs, and whistle. Eudes is wearing his big brother's scout hat. Alceste is dressed as an Indian, with feathers on his head and a wooden hatchet. Geoffroy is wearing full cowboy gear, complete with cap guns. When this extract starts, they have all just arrived.

ST

On était dans le jardin et maman nous avait dit qu'elle nous appellerait pour le goûter. « Bon, j'ai dit, alors voilà, moi je suis le jeune homme et j'ai un cheval blanc et vous, vous êtes les bandits, mais à la fin c'est moi qui gagne. » Les autres, ils n'étaient pas d'accord, c'est ça qui est em-
5   bêtant, quand on joue tout seul, on ne s'amuse pas et quand on n'est pas tout seul, les autres font des tas de disputes. « Pourquoi est-ce que ce ne serait pas moi le jeune homme, a dit Eudes, et puis, pourquoi je n'aurais pas un cheval blanc, moi aussi ? – Avec une tête comme la tienne, tu peux pas être le jeune homme », a dit Alceste. « Toi, l'Indien, tais-toi ou
10 je te donne un coup de pied dans le croupion ! » a dit Eudes qui est très fort et qui aime bien donner des coups de poing sur le nez des copains et le coup du croupion ça m'a étonné, mais c'est vrai qu'Alceste ressem-blait à un gros poulet. « En tout cas, moi, a dit Rufus, je serai le shérif. – Le shérif ? a dit Geoffroy. Où est-ce que tu as vu un shérif avec un
15 képi, tu me fais rigoler ! » Ça, ça n'a pas plu à Rufus, dont le papa est agent de police. « Mon papa, il a dit, il porte un képi et il ne fait rigoler personne ! – Il ferait rigoler tout le monde s'il s'habillait comme ça au Texas », a dit Geoffroy et Rufus lui a donné une gifle, alors, Geoffroy a sorti un revolver de l'étui et il a dit : « Tu le regretteras, Joe ! » et Rufus
20 lui a donné une autre gifle et Geoffroy est tombé assis par terre en faisant pan ! avec son revolver ; alors Rufus s'est appuyé les mains sur le ventre, et il fait des tas de grimaces et il est tombé en disant : « Tu m'as eu coyote, mais je serai vengé ! »

(Goscinny and Sempé 1960: 17–18)

The formal properties of texts: Introduction

We have suggested that translation is most usefully taken as a challenge to reduce translation loss. The threat of loss is most obvious when the translator confronts general issues of cultural transfer like those discussed in Chapter 3. However, a threat of greater translation loss is actually posed by the formal properties of the ST.

In assessing the formal properties of texts, it is helpful to borrow some fundamental notions from linguistics. Linguistics offers a hierarchically ordered series of discrete levels on which formal properties can be discussed in a systematic way. Of course, although it is essential to *distinguish* between these levels when analysing texts, they do not actually function *separately* from one another: textual features on a given level always have their effect in terms of features on all the other levels.

In any text, there are many points at which it could have been different. Where there is one sound or spelling, there might have been another (compare 'cutting time for tea roses' and 'rutting time for tea cosies', or 'you're naval' and 'your navel'). Where there is one intonation or punctuation mark there might have been another (compare 'What rubbish?' and 'What rubbish!'). The same words might have been spoken in a different order (compare 'She did so' and 'So she did'). Separate sentences might have been linked (compare 'I was bored. I watched TV' with 'I was bored. So I watched TV' or 'I was bored because I watched TV'). Where there is an allusion to the Bible there might have been one to Shakespeare. All these points of detail where a text could have been different – that is, where it could have been *another* text – are what we shall call **textual variables**. These textual variables are what the series of levels defined in linguistics make it possible to identify.

Taking the levels one at a time has two main advantages. First, looking at textual variables on a series of isolated levels makes it easier to see which are important in the ST and which are less important. As we have seen, all ST features inevitably fall prey to translation loss in some respect or other. For example, even if the TT conveys literal meaning exactly, there will at the very least be phonic loss, and very likely also loss in terms of connotations, register, and so on. It is therefore excellent translation strategy to decide in broad terms which category or categories of textual variables are indispensable in a given ST, and which can be ignored.

The other advantage in scanning the text level by level is that a proposed TT can be assessed by isolating and comparing the formal variables of ST and TT. The translator or reviser is thus able to see precisely what textual variables of the ST are absent from the TT, and vice versa. This makes the assessment of translation loss less impressionistic, which in turn permits a more self-aware and methodical way of reducing it.

We suggest six levels of textual variables, hierarchically arranged, in the sense that each level is built on top of the preceding one. Using the term 'hierarchy' is not meant to imply that features on a 'higher' level are by definition more important than those on a 'lower' level: the variables only have their effect in terms of one another, and their relative importance varies from text to text or even utterance to utterance. Other categories and hierarchies could have been adopted, but arguing about alternative frameworks belongs to linguistics, not to translation method. We shall progress 'bottom up', from phonic details to intertextual matters. We find that students are more comfortable with this than with a 'top down' approach. In Chapters 6–8, we shall work our way up through the levels, showing what kinds of textual variable can be found on each, and how they may function in a text. Together, the six levels constitute part of a checklist of questions which the translator can ask of an ST, in order to determine what levels and properties are important in it and most need to be respected in the TT. This method does not imply a plodding or piecemeal approach to translation: applying the checklist quickly becomes automatic and very effective. (For the whole checklist, see above, p. 5.)

6

The formal properties of texts: Phonic/graphic and prosodic issues in translation

Although they are the 'lowest' in the hierarchy, the phonic/graphic and prosodic levels of textual variables are as potentially significant as any other.

THE PHONIC/GRAPHIC LEVEL *lettres et sons*

Taking a text on the **phonic/graphic level** means looking at it as a sequence of sound-segments (or *phonemes*), or as a sequence of letters (or *graphemes*), or as both. Oral texts are normally only looked at in phonic terms. Written texts are always first encountered on the graphic level, but they may need to be looked at in phonic terms as well – in fact, from a translation point of view, they are more often considered phonically than graphically. Although phonemes and graphemes are different things, they are on the same level of textual variables. To help keep this mind, we shall normally refer to the 'phonic/graphic level', whether the text in question is oral or written.

The occasional coincidence apart, no text in one language can reproduce the sequence of sound-segments/letters of a text in another language. This automatically constitutes a source of translation loss. The real question is whether this loss matters at all. The answer, as usual, is that it all depends.

Generally, listeners and readers take little notice of the sounds or shapes of what they hear and read, paying attention primarily to the message of the utterance. The sounds and shapes are usually irrelevant to the message.

People do tend to notice sounds that are accidentally repeated, but even then they attach little importance to them in most texts. Often, however, repetition of sounds is a significant factor, so it is useful to have precise terms in which to analyse it.

Repetition of sounds in words can generally be classified either as alliteration or as assonance. We define **alliteration** as the recurrence of the same sound or sound-cluster at the beginning of words occurring next to or near one another, as in 'two tired toads', 'clever kleptomaniacs' or 'all awful ornithologists'. We define **assonance** as the recurrence, within words occurring next to or near one another, of the same sound or sound-cluster, as in 'a great day's painting' or 'a swift snifter afterwards'. Alliteration and assonance often occur together, as in 'French influence also explains Frederick II's splendid castles in the South of Italy and Sicily'. Terminal sounds that are the same, but are not strictly speaking rhyme, are conveniently defined as assonance; so the five [z] sounds in the following are most simply described as assonance: 'dazzling harmonies of bells and xylophones'. A vital point to remember is that it is the sound, not the spelling, that counts in discussing alliteration and assonance.

In general, the more technical or purely informative the text, the less account is taken of repetitions or other sound patterns, because they hardly ever seem to have any thematic or expressive function. That is true of the sentence about Frederick II's castles (taken from an article on Italian architecture), and it is true of the following sentence from a text on coalmining: 'Testwork has been carried out on screenbowl centrifuges dewatering frothfloated coal.' The alliteration and assonance in these two examples are incidental to the message.

However, many texts are marked by the expressive use of phonic patterns, including rhyme. We shall say that two words **rhyme** where the last stressed vowel, and all the sounds that follow it, are identical and come in the same order, as in 'bream / seem', 'Warwick / euphoric', 'incidentally / mentally', 'morceau / pot', 'cheval / égal', 'verve / serve'. The less purely factual the text, the more likely it is that alliteration, assonance and rhyme will be exploited. The most obvious example is poetry. However, on the phonic/graphic level, the only difference between poetry and many other genres is one of degree: alliteration, assonance and even rhyme are often exploited in fiction, drama, journalism, advertising, polemic, etc.

What are the implications of these observations for translators? As always, the translator must be guided by the purpose of the ST, the purpose of the TT and the function – i.e. the effect – of the phonic feature in its context. In general, the sorts of feature we have been looking at will not have expressive function in a scientific, technical or other purely empirical text, so the translator can happily ignore them: even considerable loss on the phonic/graphic level will not matter. They are sometimes important in advertisements, as in the slogan for Cartier's *So Pretty* perfume:

'Que serait l'audace sans la grace ?' Cartier's English slogan was 'What
is audacity without grace?' – does the translation loss matter here? In
literary and journalistic STs, marked phonic features certainly often do
have thematic and expressive functions – without them, the message would
be less complex and have less impact. Whether these effects are triggered
or not is very much a matter of what the text is for and what the public
is expecting.

Sometimes, even if the ST contains no marked phonic features, a draft
TT will inadvertently contain an obtrusive concentration of sounds. This
might introduce an unwanted comic note, or even make the TT difficult
to read. So, even in written texts, the translator will generally want to
avoid *introducing* tongue-twisters or other phonic features that might
impair the TT's communicative purpose.

The use of phonic echoes and affinities for thematic and expressive
purposes is sometimes called sound-symbolism. It takes two main forms.
In the context, the sounds of given words may evoke other words that are
not present in the text. Or the sound of a given word occurs in one or
more others, and sets up a link between the words, conferring on each of
them connotations of the other(s). The first two lines of Keats's 'To
Autumn' offer examples of both:

①sons des mots → contexte

Season of mists and mellow fruitfulness, ②connection entre
Close bosom-friend of the maturing sun; [...] les mots
(Keats 1958: 273)

The context is crucial. Given the title of the poem and the reference to
fruitfulness, 'mellow' is almost sure to evoke 'yellow', a colour of fruit
and autumn leaves. In its turn, the 'sun' is likely to be a rich yellow,
glowing like a ripe fruit through the autumn haze. These two effects ensure
that the 'mists' are received positively by the reader/listener, and not as
cold, damp and grey. The alliteration in 'mists ... mellow ... maturing'
reinforces the effect, and also gives 'maturing' an intransitive sense as
well as its transitive one: the sun itself is growing mature as the year
advances. And if the sun is maturing (whether in the year or in the day),
it may well be low in the sky; if so, it looks larger when seen through
mist, like a swelling fruit. The [m] in 'bosom' links this word, too, with
the other three; so the mellow fruits are perhaps reminiscent of milk-filled
breasts, as if the season, sun and earth affectionately unite in maternal
bountifulness. This suggestion is itself reinforced by the alliteration and
assonance in 'fruitfulness ... friend', and by the alliteration and assonance on [s] throughout the two lines, which associates all these key words
still more closely with one another. – les mêmes sens

Not many translators earn their living translating poetry. But in respect
of sound-symbolism – as of many other things – poetry offers very clear
examples of two vital factors which all translators do need to bear in

mind. The Keats example is useful for this very reason. Practically none of the images and associations we saw in those two lines derive from literal meaning alone – that is why perceiving and reacting to sound-symbolism is bound to be subjective. All of them are reinforced or even created by phonic features. Yet those phonic features are objectively present in the text. This points to the first factor that needs to be remembered: unlike many other sorts of symbol, those in 'sound-symbolism' do not have a single, unchanging meaning. In fact, none of the phonic features in the lines from Keats has any *intrinsic* meaning or expressive power at all. Such expressiveness as they have derives from the context – and that is the second vital factor. In a different context, the same features would almost certainly have a different effect. The *sounds* of the words have their effect in terms of the literal and connotative *meanings* of the words. So, without the title, 'mellow' might very well not evoke 'yellow'. Nor is there anything intrinsically mellow, maternal or mature about the sound [m]: the smell in a pig-yard might be described as 'the mingling mias-mata from the slime and muck'. And, in [fr], there is as much potential for frightful friction as for fruitfulness and friendship.

To take a French example, the sound [s] does not in itself suggest the horrifying menace of snakes, or misty dreaminess, or choking and suffo-cation. Yet it does suggest the first of these at the end of Racine's *Andromaque*, where the hallucinating Oreste sees the Furies advancing on him and cries: 'Pour qui sont ces serpents qui sifflent sur vos têtes ?' And it carries the other connotations in Baudelaire's 'Harmonie du soir'. The first occurs at the very start of the poem:

> Voici venir les temps où vibrant sur sa tige
> Chaque fleur s'évapore ainsi qu'un encensoir.

The second occurs at a turning-point in the text, where the mood briefly changes to one of anguish:

> Le soleil s'est noyé dans son sang qui se fige.

In all three cases, [s] draws most of its suggestive power from the *literal and connotative meanings* of the words it occurs in, and of the words associated with them in the context.

Clearly, before starting to translate, a translator confronted with sound-symbolism has to decide how it is produced, what its function is, and how it relates to the purpose of the text. The aim will be to convey as much of the ST message as possible. Even if it is essential to this message that the TT include sound-symbolism, it is almost certain that the TL sounds involved will be *different* from the ST ones: trying to reproduce phonic patterns in the TT usually entails too much loss in respect of literal and connotative meaning. The translator's question therefore has to be: is what

Les types de sons

matters the *specific sounds* in the ST's alliteration, assonance, etc. (as in the case of the snakes), or is it rather *the fact that there is* alliteration, assonance, etc.? Fortunately, the latter is generally the case, and it is usually possible to compensate for the loss of given ST phonic details by replacing them with TL ones that are different but have a comparable effect.

These points are perhaps obvious, but it does no harm to be reminded of them, because student translators often get themselves into difficulties by assuming that they have to *replicate* ST sounds in the TT. In reality, the translator is only likely to want to try replicating ST sounds when they are onomatopoeic. Onomatopoeia must not be confused with alliteration and assonance. An **onomatopoeia** is a word whose phonic form imitates a sound – 'splash', 'bang', 'cuckoo', etc. In translating onomatopoeia, there will virtually always be some phonic translation loss. This is usually inconsequential, as for instance in translating 'ploc' by 'plop', or even 'plouf' by 'splash'. It can be more significant if, as often happens, the ST onomatopoeic word does not have a one-to-one TL counterpart, as in the following:

considérer le
p. o.s.

ST	TT
squeak	cric-crac (a floorboard), couic (a mouse), craquement (a shoe), grincement (a hinge), etc.
siffler	hiss, whistle, wheeze, whizz, etc.
floc	plop, splosh, splash, etc.

As these examples show, some onomatopoeic words are purely interjections, while others can be nouns or verbs as well as interjections. Thus French 'plouf' and 'cric-crac' double as nouns, and their English counterparts, 'splash' and 'squeak/creak', are even more versatile (interjection, noun or verb). Where such onomatopoeic counterparts exist, translation loss is generally limited to the phonic/graphic level. Where they do not, there is a danger of significant loss on the grammatical level.

We can illustrate this with a translation from English into French. It is a bitterly cold night in the Canadian forest. One of the great trees suddenly gives out a single 'crack like a revolver-shot'. This has been translated as 'un craquement sec comme un coup de revolver' (Vinay and Darbelnet 1958: 298). The onomatopoeic ST 'crack' is a noun which can also function as an interjection, but French 'crac' can only occur as an interjection. Translating the ST as 'un *crac* comme un coup de revolver' would entail little phonic/graphic loss, but it would incur considerable loss on the grammatical level. In fact, unlike 'crack', this TT would not both denote and imitate the noise, but only imitate it: it would be more like a vivid, informal oral text than a written one. It is presumably to avoid this change in tone that the translators have used the noun 'craquement'. *— pour "modifier" le mot*

la signifiance
spécifiquement

But this choice brings problems of its own. 'Craquement' is certainly onomatopoeic, but it has a much wider range of reference than ST 'crack', embracing 'crackle', 'creak' and 'squeak' as well. This semantic loss is compensated for by the addition of 'sec', which has two functions. First, in respect of literal meaning, it specifies what kind of 'craquement' this is. And phonically, it adds another [k] sound to those in 'craquement', thus suggesting the sharp crispness of the noise. This is a skilful piece of compensation. But the recurrence of [k] here has a disadvantage as well. It interferes with the literal meaning by phonically suggesting a multiple or progressive cracking rather than a single crack: the reader may thus think of something like a branch creaking before falling – very different from what is in the ST. This example typifies a common translation risk: a single thematic clue in the TT combining with sound-symbolism to distort the ST message with unwanted nuances.

As for rhyme, similar considerations apply as to alliteration and assonance. Only very rarely will it be desirable or possible to use the ST rhyme sounds in the TT. In fact, there can be no hard and fast rule regarding rhyme in translation. Each TT requires its own strategic decision. Often, producing a rhyming TT means an unacceptable sacrifice of literal and connotative meaning, and it is best not to try. Translators often compensate for this loss by using different sorts of recurrent sound, such as assonance, alliteration or half-rhymes, and perhaps gratefully accepting the odd true rhyme if it presents itself and is not inappropriate. With some sorts of ST (especially comic or sarcastic ones), where the precise nuances of meaning are less important than the phonic mockery, it is often easier, and even desirable, to stock the TT with rhymes and echoes that are different from those of the ST, and perhaps differently distributed, but have a similar effect.   *l'effet*

So far, our examples of textual variables on the phonic/graphic level have concerned the *sounds* of words, because the *shapes* are less commonly a source of textual effects on this level. However, written texts often do depend to some extent on their visual layout. Advertisements, publicity material and websites make frequent use of visual effects on the phonic/graphic level. Instruction leaflets are often laid out almost in tabular form, with a lot of short sentences introduced with bullet points. Legal texts, too, often list the relevant articles of law one under the other.

le visuel

There can be problems of layout if the text includes a picture and the TT takes up more space than the ST, or if the TT has long words in places where the ST has short ones. Mathieu Guidère analyses a revealing example from Lancôme's slogan for 'Poème' perfume: 'Tu es le grand soleil qui me monte à la tête.' The centre of the picture is filled with a front view of a woman down to just below shoulder level. The bottle of perfume is superimposed on her, towards the bottom right. The slogan begins near the left, slants gently down, then curves up again as it passes under the bottle with the words 'le grand', and continues up the

right-hand edge, slightly sinuously touching her hair with its final words
('monte à la tête'). The size of the lettering gets smaller with each word,
from 16-point to 8-point, imitating the increasingly subtlety of the perfume
as it rises.

There is a particularly serious problem here for translators into Arabic,
because Arabic reads from right to left. As Lancôme want to use the same
picture and layout, the message is forced to work its way down the image
instead of up, and the print is going to get progressively bigger, not smaller.
So, whatever the intrinsic linguistic problems of putting 'Tu es le grand
soleil qui me monte à la tête' into Arabic, a TT reference to 'rising' is
going to look pretty silly, given that the slogan is descending *from* head
level. The Arabic translator is forced by graphic constraints to produce a
completely different text. Here is a schematic representation of the ST
and TT layouts:

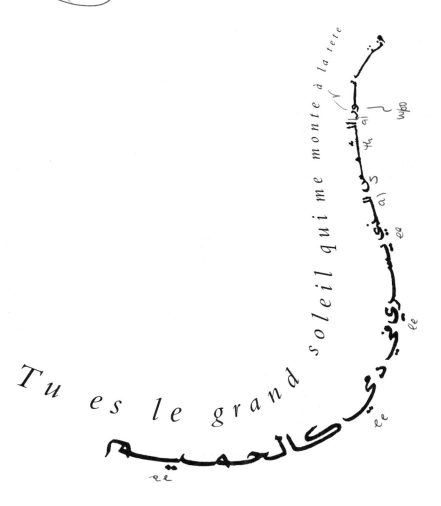

Guidère comments:

> Si l'on considère la version arabe, la construction métaphorique est tout autre bien que reprenant la même référence au « soleil ». Le contexte n'est plus celui de l'enivrement mais de la passion : « *Tu es la lumière du soleil qui coule dans mon sang* » (trad. littérale). A la jouissance cérébrale symbolisée par « la tête » en français est substituée l'image ambivalente et charnelle d'une expérience où se mêlent plaisir (*lumière*) et douleur (*sang*). Ainsi, la relation métaphorique initialement instaurée entre le slogan et l'image se trouve pervertie.
>
> (Guidère 2000: 238; cf. 231–4)

The particular graphic problem posed by Arabic does not arise for English, of course. But the example illustrates a type of graphic issue that often does cause difficulties if the TT will not fit into the same space. In this example, the implications of the ST play on words present a real challenge to the translator into English, and can probably only be rendered through compensation, at greater length. This is something to try out for the practical, when you will be able to compare your TT with the published one.

THE PROSODIC LEVEL

On the **prosodic level**, utterances count as 'metrically' structured stretches. 'Metrical' here covers three sorts of thing. First, in a given utterance, some syllables will conventionally always be accented more than others; on top of this standard accentuation, voice stress and emphasis will be used for greater clarity and expressiveness. Second, clarity and expressiveness also depend on variations in vowel pitch and voice modulation. And third, the speed of vocal delivery also varies, for similar reasons. On the prosodic level, therefore, groups of syllables may form *contrastive* patterns, (for example, short, fast, staccato sections alternating with long, slow, smooth ones), or *recurrent* ones, or both. Prosodic features have a crucial role in any text. Go back to the start of this paragraph, and try reading it in a monotone and without any variations in stress. This is very difficult to do, because it is so unnatural. If you do succeed, the text becomes virtually incomprehensible to a listener.

For the translator, there are four factors to be borne in mind when considering the prosodic level. The first is that English and French are as different from one another on the prosodic level as on the phonic/graphic level. This is vividly illustrated by listening to a French person speaking in the next room, or on the radio with the tuning not quite on the station, so that it is not quite possible to distinguish the words. This brings the prosodic features to the foreground. It only takes a few seconds to realize that the tempi, rhythms and melodic undulations sound very different from

les inflections

those of English. It is virtually impossible to produce a TT that both sounds natural and reproduces the prosodic characteristics of the ST. Just occasionally, it is worth aiming for similar rhythms in the TT to those of the ST. For instance, if part of the ST's expressive effect stems from imitative rhythms – galloping horses, breaking waves, dripping water, etc. – there would be significant translation loss on the prosodic level if the TT failed to use similar rhythms to similar effect.

However, prosodic translation loss far more commonly arises from a failure to heed one or more of the other three factors. For example, it is vital to recognize the nature and function of ST intonation and stress. This is relatively straightforward in the case of oral texts. Even in written texts, either the grammatical structure or the context will usually show what the intonation is and what its communicative purpose is. Take the following two sentences:

Il parle aussi un français impeccable [e.g. as well as excellent Spanish].

Lui aussi parle un français impeccable [e.g. like you].

It is impossible to confuse these two sentences. In each, the grammatical structure engenders a specific prosodic profile – intonation and stress pattern – and a specific meaning.

Following from this factor is the third: the need to select an intonation and a stress pattern which ensure that the TT sentence has the same communicative purpose as its ST counterpart. The main thing is to avoid ambiguity. If the genre or style of the TT precludes using italics to mark the stress, a judicious comma or cohesion marker may do the trick. Here, for discussion, are some possible renderings of the two sentences:

Il parle aussi un français impeccable.	He speaks perfect *French* as well. He speaks perfect French, as well. And he also speaks perfect French.
Lui aussi parle un français impeccable.	*He* speaks perfect French as well. He, too, speaks perfect French.

The fourth factor arises from the third, and is the one that needs closest attention. Even where the TL expression does not seem grammatically or prosodically problematic, the translator must be sure not to *introduce* prosodic features that are inappropriate to the message content. Perhaps the commonest cases of significant translation loss on the prosodic level arise when a grammatical choice in the TT implies a stress pattern and an intonation that lead the reader/listener to expect a different sort of message from the one that actually materializes. This often happens when the translator chooses an inappropriate connector. We can illustrate this with examples from the translation of Marcel Pagnol's *Jean de Florette*.

(*Contextual information.* The story is set in the Provençal countryside. Ugolin has come to call on his new neighbours from the city, a hunchback called Jean, his attractive wife and their little girl. He is already somewhat in awe of these people. This morning, they have just taken delivery of a load of concrete pipes and wire netting. Ugolin is worried about what Jean is planning: he secretly wants to acquire his neighbour's property, and does not want to see him settle in permanently. Here, he is trying to find out what's going on, without revealing his intentions.)

ST	TT
« J'ai vu passer un beau charge-ment qui venait chez vous. Vous allez refaire la clôture ?	'I saw a big load on the way to you. Are you going to mend the fence?'
– Eh oui ; une clôture un peu 5 spéciale : elle doit descendre à 0,60 m sous terre.	'Oh yes; a rather special fence – it's going to go 0.60 meters underground.'
– Ha ! ha ! dit Ugolin. Vous avez peur que les lapins viennent manger vos légumes ? »	'Ha ha!' said Ugolin. 'You're afraid the rabbits are going to come and eat your vegetables?'
10 Le bossu, l'index levé, prit un air mystérieux pour dire :	The hunchback raised a finger, assumed a mysterious air, and said:
« Vous brûlez ! Vous vous trompez seulement sur la direction des lapins ! » . . .	'You're getting very warm! You're only wrong about the direction of the rabbits!' [. . .]
15 Ugolin pensait :	Ugolin thought:
« La direction des lapins ? Qu'est-ce que ça veut dire ? En tout cas il a dit que les tuyaux, c'est un grand secret. Et cette 20 femme qui sourit toujours, c'est sûr qu'elle se fout de moi. Et cette petite qui me regarde de loin comme si j'étais une bête féroce... Finalement, je n'y 25 comprends plus rien, et ils sont trop malins pour moi... »	'"The direction of the rabbits"? What's he trying to say? In any case he said the pipes were a great secret. And this woman who's always smiling, I'm sure she doesn't give a damn for me. And the litle girl who keeps away from me as if I were a ferocious beast . . . And on top of that I don't understand anything, they're too smart for me . . .'
(Pagnol 1988: 133)	(Pagnol 1989: 89)

There is plenty to be said about the TT, but we will mention just three things. First, in line 7 of the ST, 'Ha ! ha !' is not laughter; it is the joyous exclamation of someone who has just found the answer to a riddle: 'Ha ! ha ! j'ai trouvé !' ('Aha! Got it!'). But the TT, even with only one exclamation mark, turns Ugolin's interjection into scornful laughter. The intonation of the TT thus becomes that of the *paysan* mocking the ignorant townie. Prosodic features are hard to represent in print, of course, but the two alternatives correspond more or less to the following:

Aha! Got it! You're worried the rabbits'll get at your vegetables, aren't you?

Ha! Ha! You're not worried the rabbits'll get at your vegetables, are you?

The first is closer to the ST both in message content and prosodically. The sneering tone of the second changes the relationship between Jean and Ugolin, and is a less convincing preparation for the final paragraph of the extract, which furnishes our other two examples.

First, Ugolin's 'En tout cas' does not mean 'In any case'. This TT connector triggers a particular prosodic line for the whole sentence. In English, when 'In any case' comes at the start of a sentence it normally follows an affirmation, and announces another affirmation supporting the first, as in: 'He said it wasn't to keep the rabbits out. In any case, there *aren't* any round here.' The emphatic tone in effect confirms the first statement, usually in order to convince the listener that it is true. Here, however, 'In any case' comes straight after a question, 'What's he trying to say?', thus turning these words into more of a statement than a question. In terms of communicative purpose, this interpretation of the TT is perfectly plausible, especially as 'What's he trying to say?' sounds like an expression of scornful dismissiveness (in effect, the TT Ugolin is saying: 'What's he on about? The man's a fool! And anyway, . . .'). Revealingly, a back-translation would give something like 'Mais qu'est-ce qu'il raconte, celui-là ?', or perhaps even 'Il raconte des bêtises, celui-là' – in practice, a sneering affirmation that is very different from the ST Ugolin's panic-stricken question.

Clearly, 'In any case', coming on top of 'What's he trying to say?', triggers a TT prosodic line (intonation and accentuation) that implies an Ugolin confident in his intellectual superiority. But this clashes with the message content and the context, especially the rest of this paragraph. At best, the clash is disconcerting; at worst, readers will think they have misunderstood and go back to the start. A better translation would be: '"The direction of the rabbits"? What's he getting at? And he said the pipes were a great secret . . .' The suspension points are intended to show that the intonation is one of puzzlement and disquiet; italicizing 'secret' might make this even clearer.

There is a similar clash between intonation and message content in the last sentence. 'And on top of that' does not do what 'Finalement' does in the ST. 'And on top of that' is typically used in English to announce the last or greatest in a set of unpleasant experiences (cf. 'the last straw', 'to crown it all', etc.). The peevish tone of the TT expression is no more appropriate than its meaning. In the TT, what Ugolin is saying amounts to: 'I don't understand, I don't understand – and on top of that I don't understand.' A closer translation would be: 'I can't make head nor tail of it. They're too clever for me.'

We shall return to the translation of connectors in Chapter 8.

Rudiments of French and English versification

A special set of features on the prosodic level are those found in verse, which present specific translation challenges. Our aim in the following short introduction to the rudiments of French and English versification is to give students a foundation for discerning and interpreting the conventional patterns in French verse, and for making an informed choice between English metres if the strategic decision is to produce a verse TT. We shall look only at the metrical side of versification. But remember that tempo and melodic pitch are also vital prosodic textual variables requiring as much attention in verse translation as in prose. We shall not consider other aspects of verse, such as types of stanza, or the phonic question of rhyme. For fuller information on these and on metrical questions, see Lewis (1982) and Hollander (1981).

French

A line of verse in French is defined in terms of the number of syllables it contains. The pattern of stresses may vary greatly within that framework. The commonest line-lengths in traditional verse have an even number of syllables: they are the alexandrine (twelve syllables), the decasyllable (ten) and the octosyllable (eight).

From the sixteenth to the late nineteenth century, the alexandrine was the staple of French verse. It is the line of the great playwrights and lyric poets, and is still commonly used today. Until the mid-nineteenth century, it nearly always had a natural pause, or caesura, after the sixth syllable. (Though modern, Lancôme's 'Poème' slogan is just such an alexandrine.) Since the mid-nineteenth century, the caesura or caesuras in the alexandrine have often been positioned more flexibly. The octosyllable is the second most common traditional line. It has no fixed caesura. It is found in odes and lyrical ballads of all kinds, including folk songs, ballads and humorous verse. The decasyllable has never had a fixed caesura. With a 5/5 division it lends itself to light, song-like use.

Lines with an odd number of syllables are much less common in traditional verse. They are more fluid, since it is impossible to divide them into equal halves. They lend themselves to light, popular or playful verse, but they can also be emotionally highly charged.

In determining the number of syllables in a line, it is vital to remember the status of the mute e (or *e atone*, in French). The mute e is an e which is written, but either not pronounced (as in *joi(e), sav(e)nt, fin(e)*) or pronounced very slightly (as in *le, petit, genou*). In standard speech, the mute e is very often not sounded even in words like *petit* or *genou*. In traditional verse, the mute e is pronounced in the interior of a line, but only if it is *immediately preceded and followed by pronounced consonants*. This is illustrated in the following examples. The bold letters represent pronounced consonants immediately adjacent to a mute e; (e) represents a mute e that is not pronounced.

l'ho**mm**e vaincu = 4 syllables.
elle **h**ait = 3 syllables (NB The aspirate h counts as a pronounced consonant, and is often actually sounded as [h] in verse).
ell(e) est = 2 syllables.
tu jou(e)**r**as = 3 syllables.
ils voi(e)nt = 2 syllables.
ils travail**l**ent **s**ouvent = 6 syllables.
ils travail**l**ent en vain = 6 syllables (NB Liaison is more strictly observed in verse).
ils voi(e)nt en vain = 4 syllables.

The rigorous application of this rule in traditional verse explains why song lyrics so often contain apostrophes to show where the singer must *break* the rule to fit the words to the music. Note also that *sung* verse is different from spoken verse in that a mute e *at the end of the line* is also pronounced (even after a preceding vowel) unless otherwise indicated. Thus each of the following lines (from a satirical song sung after the French defeat in 1870) has six syllables:

L'pèr', la mèr' Badingue,
A deux sous tout l'paquet,
L'pèr', la mèr' Badingue,
Et le p'tit Badinguet !

For practical purposes, the following simple system is an adequate way of notating stress in French verse (these are the first four lines of Baudelaire's 'Correspondances'; naturally, they could in some places be accented differently, depending on the expressive effect desired):

La natur(e) est un **templ**(e) / où de viva**nts** piliers / = 3+3 / 4+2 /
Laissent par**f**ois sortir / de confuses parol(e)s ; / = 1+3+2 / 3+3 /
L'homm(e) y pass(e) / à tra**v**ers des forêts de symbol(e)s / = 1+2 / 3+3+3 /
Qui l'obser/vent avec des rega**r**ds familiers. / = 3 / 6+3 /.

In this notation, the following symbols are used:

- [/] denotes a caesura or end-of-line pause, however slight.
- Syllables in bold type are stressed (however slightly), those followed by a caesura or end-of-line pause more so than the others.
- A digit immediately before [/] denotes a group containing that number of syllables and ending with a main stress followed by a pause, or apparent pause, however slight.
- A digit immediately before [+] denotes a group containing that number of syllables and ending with a secondary stress, with no pause after it.

Occasionally, a group actually ends with a pronounced mute e, which is always unstressed. This feature usually has expressive effect, the nature of which depends on the context. Such cases can be notated thus:

Mais **par**le : / de son **sort** / qui t'as ren**du** l'**arbitr(e) ?** / = 2(+1) / 3 / 1+5 /

In reading French verse, then, there is no need to look for some rigid pattern of feet that has to be imposed on the text. The pattern of stresses in the line virtually always coincides with the 'natural' stresses the words have in prose. The reader should therefore read the verse as the sense dictates, while taking due account of the rules concerning the mute e. Observing these rules will automatically have certain rhythmic consequences and mean highlighting certain words: that is, the versification will have specific thematic and expressive functions. These functions are special effects on the prosodic level, and the translator simply has to be as aware of them as of every other feature of the ST. If the verse is in rhyme, the phonic/graphic functions of the rhymes will also be affected by these prosodic features.

The foregoing applies to texts in traditional, regular, verse. The very fact that a text is in regular verse is usually significant, marking the text as belonging to a particular genre. This in itself is a factor that will weigh in deciding a strategy.

If a text is in *free verse, this* fact is similarly strategically important. Apart from that, all the student translator needs to remember is to read the text as the sense demands, while taking due account of the phonic/graphic and prosodic effects of the line-ends.

English
English metre is syllable-and-stress metre. That is, the line is defined in terms of feet. A line of traditional verse consists of a fixed number of particular feet. For example:

The **cur**/few **tolls**/ the **knell**/ of **par**/ting **day**/

This line has five feet; that is, it is a pentameter. In this particular case, each foot consists of an unstressed syllable followed by a stressed one. This is known as an *iamb, or iambic foot. A line* consisting of five iambs is an iambic pentameter. It is the most common English line, found in the work of the great playwrights and poets. The commonest other feet are:

trochee (adj. *trochaic*):	**When** the/ **pie** was/ **opened**/
dactyl (adj. *dactylic*):	**Merrily**/ **chat**ting and/ **clat**tering/
anapest (adj. *anapestic*):	And made **ci**/der in**side**/ her in**side**/

Most poems do not have a regular beat throughout. This would be intolerably dreary. Even limericks are very rarely exclusively anapestic or dactylic. The opening lines of Keats's 'To Autumn', quoted on p. 79, are examples of typical variations on the basic iambic pentameter. These lines still count as iambic pentameters, because they do have five feet, they are predominantly iambic, and the rest of the poem has these qualities.

One other sort of English metre is worth mentioning, strong-stress metre. This is different from syllable-and-stress metre, in that only the stresses count in describing the line, the number of weak syllables being variable. Much modern verse uses this metre, often in combination with syllable-and-stress metre.

In translating verse, the important thing is to decide what the *function* of the verse is, and the relation between it and the purpose of the text. Is the verse simply decorative? Does it have thematic and/or expressive effect? What is the effect of its regularity or irregularity? Would there be significant translation loss in writing a prose TT? (And, of course, similar questions have to be asked on the phonic/graphic level.) Only when these questions have been answered can a reasoned decision be taken either to translate into prose or to couch the TT in an appropriate verse-form. The introduction to versification given above will help in deciding what, if any, this TL verse-form is to be.

PRACTICAL 6

6.1 Phonic/graphic and prosodic issues

Assignment
Taking each ST–TT pair in turn,

(i)   See first of all if you can discern any salient phonic or prosodic features in the ST, and whether they have an expressive function. Say what the function is, how it is achieved, and how well it accords with the purpose of the ST. Whatever your findings (i.e. whether or not there are salient features, etc.), discuss their strategic implications for translation of the STs.

(ii)   See if you can discern any salient phonic or prosodic features in the TT, and whether they have an expressive function. If you do see a function, say whether it is similar to that of the ST phonic and prosodic features, and how well it accords with the purpose of the TT. If you do not, say why the TT phonic and prosodic features have no expressive function.

(iii) Where you think you can improve the TT in respect of phonic and prosodic features, give your own revised version and say why your revision is better.

(iv)   If you think the TT is significantly defective in any other respect, revise it and say briefly why your revision is better.

Contextual information

The texts are from a leaflet supplied with Azzaro Eau belle toiletries. All texts are *sic*.

ST (i)

L'EAU DE TOILETTE
Bien plus qu'une simple Eau
Fraîche, c'est un véritable PARFUM
DE FRAICHEUR qui raconte une
5   escapade olfactive riche et
savoureuse, aux couleurs turquoises
et orangées. C'est une belle harmonie florale hespéridée construite
sur un fond de sous-bois, tendre et
10 généreux ; Départ hespéridé
pétillant, cœur floral rayonnant,
fond miellé et tendrement boisé.
    Existe en vaporisateur 30 ml,
vaporisateurs et flacons 50 ml et
15 100 ml et vaporisateur 200 ml.

TT (i)

EAU DE TOILETTE
Much more than a mere Eau de
Toilette, EAU BELLE is a true
'PARFUM DE FRAICHEUR' a
delightful, rich olfactive experience, in pastel hues of turquoise
and orange. A wonderful floral cit-
rus blend that plays against a background of soft, generous woody
notes: sparkling hesperidian top
notes, wild floral heart, soft honey
bed tenderly woody.
    The line includes a 30 ml spray
and 50 ml and 100 ml sprays and
bottles and 200 ml spray.

ST (ii)

L'EAU SANS ALCOOL
Il existe aujourd'hui, un nouveau
geste de parfumage mis au point par
les Parfums AZZARO. C'est une
5   formulation très tendre, sans alcool,
tout spécialement étudiée pour les
peaux sensibles. Enrichie d'agents
hydratants et satinants, cette eau
sans alcool permet un parfumage
10 doux et sûr, même en plein soleil.

TT (ii)

SUN MIST
Today, AZZARO introduces a new
fragrance interpretation with an
ultra-gentle, alcohol-free formula,
especially suited for sensitive
skins.
    Enriched with moisturizing and
softening ingredients, this alcohol-
free fragrance mist can be worn
safely, even in the hot midday sun.

6.2 Phonic/graphic and prosodic issues

Assignment
  (i) You are translating for publication in the UK the novel from which
       the following ST is taken. The ST describes a huge shanty town.
       A major feature of the extract is its cumulative style, most notably
       on the phonic/graphic and prosodic levels, and in the repetitions of
       grammatical structures. Discuss the strategic decisions that you have
       to take before starting detailed translation of this ST, and outline
       and justify the strategy you adopt.
 (ii) Translate the text into English.
(iii) Explain the main decisions of detail you took. Concentrate on gram-
       matical, phonic/graphic and prosodic issues and their interaction,
       but do not neglect other important decisions.

Contextual information
The passage is from Patrick Grainville's *Les Flamboyants* (1976). The
mad Tokor, king of an African country, has taken his European guest,
William, to visit the town of Le Mourmako. They drive to the top of a
hill, from which they look down onto the town, described as a 'chancre
ignoble et sublime'. William is gripped by its vastness, and recoils at the
stench that rises from the town. (Note that, although the passage is narrated
from William's point of view, he is not the narrator.)

ST
Le Mourmako était une bidonville unique au monde de par ses dimensions.
Il s'étendait sur plusieurs kilomètres en long et en large. Ses pittoresques
frappaient, ses complications ténébreuses, ses dédales illimitées, ses invis-
ibles recoins. Il couvrait une surface énorme, irrégulière, composée de
5 buttes et de grandes cuves. L'ensemble offrait à l'œil l'ondulation d'une
souillure sombre et vaste de gadoue et de matières amalgamées. Le sol du
Mourmako au lieu d'être rouge ou jaune comme la plupart des paysages du
royaume était noir et gluant. Une humidité poisse baignait l'entassement
des constructions disparates qui semblaient avoir poussé au hasard, en vrac,
10 dans des postures anarchiques et biscornues à même les renflements de sombre mélasse. Les abris misérables et saugrenus se collaient dans la boue un
peu comme ces coquillages ou ces grandes algues endeuillées qu'incrustent
les enfants aux flancs de leurs châteaux de sable. Le Mourmako était planté,
roulé dans la prédominance de la fange.

  (P. Grainville, *Les Flamboyants*, © Editions du Seuil, 1976: 77)

6.3 Phonic/graphic and prosodic issues

Assignment
  (i) You are translating the following text for a bilingual anthology
       of First World War French writers killed in action. Like the author

of this text, many of these writers will have been killed before they
had a chance to fulfil their potential. Your aim is to give the reader
a clear idea of what qualities were lost when these men died. Your
readership will include some people who read French, but more who
do not. Discuss the strategic decisions that you have to take before
starting detailed translation of this ST, and outline and justify the
strategy you adopt.

(ii)   Translate the text into English.
(iii) Discuss the main decisions of detail you took.

Contextual information

The poem is by Marc de Larreguy de Civrieux, who was killed in action
in 1916, aged twenty-one. It is one of two satirical poems purporting to
be written by an ugly monkey in the trenches of Argonne to a parrot in
Paris. In both, the soldiers are seen as 'dehumanized' by their experiences
and thereby, ironically, more human and humane than the armchair strat-
egists parroting patriotic slogans in Paris. This poem is a sarcastic attack
on Maurice Barrès. Barrès was a right-wing jingoist, whose sabre-rattling
Germanophobia and predictions of imminent victory were given daily
space in the *Echo de Paris*. From 1914 to 1918, this newspaper typified
the fervour-whipping, conscience-salving ignorance (or avoidance) of the
facts of life in the trenches which reassured civilians but outraged most
soldiers. 'On les aura' was a great patriotic slogan of the war. The poem
contains allusions to three books by Barrès: *Sous l'œil des barbares*, *Du
sang, de la volupté et de la mort* (in which he expresses his admiration
for violence in Spanish culture) and *Colette Baudoche*. Colette is a patriotic French girl in post-1870 occupied Alsace, who refuses to marry a
German. The poem's remaining allusion is to Bayard (d. 1524), the 'cheva-
lier sans peur et sans reproche'; this satirizes Barrès's cult of the dead
and the soil, these two things being in his view the essence of *patrie*.

ST

L'EPITRE AU PERROQUET

As-tu lu le journal, Jacko, mon vieux Jacko ?
Il me semble aujourd'hui t'entendre qui jacasse
    – De la façon la plus cocasse –
    Tous les « en-tête » rococos
5   De la gazette de l'« Echo » :
« Crr… Crr… on les aurra… Crr… Rrr… Victoire prroche… »
    Et tu rêves que tu bamboches
    Avec quelques tripes de Boches !
    Te voici donc l'« alter ego »
10   De ton grand maître, l'Hidalgo,
    (Toujours « sans peur et sans reproche »)

Qui – « loin de l'œil des Wisigoths » –
Ecrit, pour tous les bons gogos,
Au nom de Maurice... Baudoche !
15   Crois-le, je suis fier de connaître
Un perroquet aussi savant
Qui peut répéter à son Maître :
« Nous les tenons ! » et « En avant ! »
Car nous, les Singes des grands Bois,
20   Dans notre Argonne, loin des Hommes,
Nous les oublions et nous sommes
Bien plus sauvages qu'autrefois !
« Le hareng toujours se sent dans la caque »,
A dit un bipède écrivain :
25 Vouloir imiter l'homme est ridicule et vain
A moins que l'on ne soit perroquet ou chauvin.
...Et j'aime mieux rester :

Ton fidèle

Macaque.
(Larreguy 1926: 43–4)

▣ 6.4 Phonic/graphic and prosodic issues

Assignment
  (i)   You are translating the following song from the finale of a TV docu-
        mentary. The TT will be displayed as subtitles as the song is sung.
        You will be working from the printed text. You are not asked neces-
        sarily to produce a singable TT, but you are required to produce a
        TT that not only reflects the overall meaning and impact of the song
        as sung, but does also give an idea of its formal qualities. Discuss
        the strategic decisions that you have to make before starting detailed
        translation of this ST. (One factor you will have to consider is the
        relation between the printed text, the musical setting and the perfor-
        mance: are there any differences between the text as you would read
        it and the text as sung?)
 (ii)   Translate the text into English.
(iii)   Explain the main decisions of detail you took.
 (iv)   After discussion of your TT, compare it with the published sub-
        titles, which will be given to you by your tutor. Where you think
        they are defective, revise them and explain your revisions.

Contextual information
The printed text is a poem by René-Guy Cadou (1920–51), a village
schoolmaster in the Loire-Atlantique. His poetry is generally nature poetry
and love poetry, simple, domestic, sometimes verging on the sentimental.

Jealous of his independence, he refused to join any clique or compromise his talent by writing Resistance or political poetry during the Second World War. This poem was written at the end of the war.

The text is sung by Gilles Servat to his own setting. He is a great admirer of Cadou. He has long been a militant campaigner for greater cultural and political autonomy for Brittany, and for the full integration of the Loire-Atlantique into Brittany. At the height of the campaign against the proposed siting of a nuclear power station at Plogoff, in Finisterre, he used to sing this song at gigs and social gatherings, getting the audience to join in.

The film is one of a militant series entitled *How to be Celtic*. It examines the fortunes of Breton language and culture, notably music and song, during the twentieth century. It relates the struggle to affirm Breton culture and identity to the rise in support for the Front de la libération bretonne. It shows violent scenes of political demonstrations as well as the effort in schools and universities to save the Breton language.

ST

Liberté couleur des feuilles
Liberté la belle joue
Jeune fille qui dénoues
4   Tes cheveux blonds sur le seuil
Flamme neige épaule nue
Arc-en-ciel de la rosée
Haut visage pavoisé
8   De cent regards inconnus
Oiseau la plume légère
Seins jaillis odeur de pain
Blanche vague de la main
12   A tâtons dans la lumière
La plus pauvre du village
La plus belle sous les coups
Toi qui fais chanter les fous
16   Et qui fais pleurer les sages
Liberté je t'ai nommée
Pour que nous vivions ensemble
Tu me vêts et tu ressembles
20   Au portrait de mon aimée
(Cadou 1972: 67–8)

7

The formal properties of texts: Grammatical and sentential issues in translation

We saw in Chapter 6 that the alliteration and assonance of 'Season of mists and mellow fruitfulness' trigger effects over and above the literal meaning of this phrase. We were considering the alliteration and assonance as features on the phonic/graphic level. But, like all utterances, this one can also be considered on the other five levels of textual variables. The extra meanings, for instance, are features on the *grammatical* level, while part of the effect of Keats's phrase derives from features on the *sentential* level. These are the levels we look at in the present chapter.

THE GRAMMATICAL LEVEL

(handwritten annotation: ① words - formation, etc. ② syntax - arranging words)

There are two features on the **grammatical level**: (1) words, and their formation by affixation, inflection, derivation and compounding; (2) syntax, the arrangement of words into phrases and sentences. It is on the grammatical level that translation loss is generally most immediately obvious, whenever grammatical transposition occurs. Loss on this level is very common, so we shall only give a few examples here. The course as a whole yields scores more, and Chapters 16–19 will be devoted to four specific areas in which grammatical translation loss is an especial threat. As ever, the question is not whether there is translation loss, but what it consists in and whether it matters.

Words

Everybody is familiar with dictionaries. They list the practical totality of the words in a given language. This totality is known as the **lexis** of a language (adj. **lexical**). However, meanings are not found exclusively in the words individually listed in the dictionary. Any text shows that the combination of words creates meanings that they do not have in isolation, and even meanings that are not wholly predictable from the literal senses of the words combined.

In translation, lexical loss is very common, but it is just one kind of translation loss among many. It can occur for all sorts of reasons. It very often arises from the fact that exact synonymy between SL words and TL words is relatively rare. The translator is usually obliged to choose between either more specific or less specific TL words. A few examples among thousands:

Less specific	*More specific*
mes filles	my girls, my daughters
la conscience	consciousness, conscience
hacher	to chop, to mince
gun	canon, fusil, pistolet, revolver
nut	noix, noisette, amande, etc.
sly	rusé, sournois, narquois, etc.

We shall look at this important issue in detail in Chapter 9. Another common source of lexical translation loss is the fact that, in any text, words have connotations on top of their literal meaning. The lines from Keats are a good example (see p. 79). It is difficult, and usually impossible, to find TL words that will convey an accurate literal meaning *and* produce appropriate connotations. We shall look at these questions in more detail in Chapter 10.

Grammatical arrangement

Lexical issues are a particular category of grammatical issue, so it is not surprising that some of them are most conveniently examined under the heading of grammatical arrangement. Under this heading, we subsume two types of grammatical structure: (1) patterns affecting individual words – affixation/inflection, compounding and derivation; (2) **syntax** (adj. **syntactic**), the patterns whereby words are linked to form more or less complex phrases and sentences. In both, what concerns the translator is the fact that the structural patterns differ from language to language.

Take 'étudiante' in the following example (a woman is recalling her past love of jazz):

ST	TT
Etudiante, je l'adorais.	As a student, I loved it.

The TT keeps the core notion of 'me a student', but it loses a detail, omitting the ST reference to gender. This is because French grammar demands a feminine ending here, but English grammar does not allow one. Yet, at the same time, it is practically obligatory to *add* detail not explicit in the literal meaning of 'étudiante' – '{when I was/because I was/in my capacity as} a student', etc., depending on the context. Here, too, the deciding factor is a difference in grammatical structure between French and English. French grammar allows a noun to stand on its own at the start of a sentence, without an article or any qualifying phrase (such as 'en tant que', 'étant', '{puisque/quand} j'étais', etc.). The context is enough to suggest what kind of link there is between 'étudiante' and 'je l'adorais', without any explicit syntactic connection. But this is not often possible in English, which generally uses a syntactic connection ('{As/being/when I was}', etc.) to make explicit a qualification that is implicit in the French context. Usually, the context will show which qualification to choose; but even if it does not, added detail there will have to be.

Many other structural differences between the languages have semantic consequences. For instance, English more readily adds -ly to words to form adverbs than French does -ment, particularly in cases where English has two adverbs in juxtaposition. Compare the following:

ST	TT
Ce détail est *d'une importance décisive*.	This detail is *crucially important*.
Il parle *avec une lenteur exaspérante*.	He speaks *infuriatingly slowly*.

In each case, there is a different nuance between the English and the French. The English adverbs give an impression of the importance actively striking people as crucial, and the slow speech actively infuriating people. The French nouns suggest more that the importance and slowness have been analysed and then categorized as crucial and infuriating. The different grammatical structures have different semantic effects.

Compounding, too, differs from language to language. German is capable of long compounds, English less so. French is a more analytical language, in that the relations between the elements in a compound expression tend to be marked explicitly, through either syntax (generally prepositions) or inflection, or both. English compounds in particular are potentially ambiguous. For instance, a bodyguard guards the body, but a mudguard guards *against* the mud.

In the following example, only knowledge of the topic makes it possible to say whether the English expression refers to a display of liquid crystals, a liquid display of crystals, or a display that is liquid and crystal: 'Flüssigkristallanzeige = liquid crystal display = affichage à cristaux liquides.' The French expression is less ambiguous, thanks to the preposition and the plural inflections.

Grammatical differences are especially clear in differences in verb systems between languages, which can require special care in translating. Two obvious differences between French and English are the tense/aspect systems and ways of constructing passive expressions. Thus, there are at least thirteen ways of translating 'he was injured' into French:

Tenses	*Quasi-passive reflexives*
il était blessé [state]	N/A
il était blessé [habitual action]	il se blessait/se faisait blesser
il a été blessé	il s'est {blessé/fait blesser}
il fut blessé	il se {blessa/fit blesser}
il avait été blessé	il s'était {blessé/fait blesser}

Not to mention the past anterior, or constructions with 'se voir' ('il s'est vu blesser' etc.) . . .

The pluperfect calls for comment. It is sometimes best translated as a preterite in English. This is because French is usually more rigorous than English in marking the distinction between successive stages in the past. The paradigm here is Panoramix's immortal explanation to Obélix, printed on the endpapers of every *Astérix* book. Obélix has asked Panoramix for a cup of magic potion, and this is his reply:

ST	*TT*
Je t'*ai dit* mille fois que tu *étais tombé* dedans étant petit [our italics].	I'*ve told* you a thousand times, you *fell* in when you were little.

Panoramix *has explained* to Obélix about this in the past, but Obélix fell in *before* these explanations, i.e. further back in the past. Hence the pluperfect. But in this context, as so often, a pluperfect would sound unnatural in English: 'I've told you, you'd fallen in when you were little.' This is why 'il *avait été* blessé' is most idiomatically translated as 'he *was* injured' in the following example: 'En ce qui concerne nos remarques de la semaine dernière concernant la méforme de Zidane, on nous a très aimablement rappelé qu'il avait été blessé en début de saison.'

There are nuances in French quasi-passive reflexive structures which can be hard to convey in English. 'Il s'est blessé' usually translates as 'he was injured', but is sometimes closer to 'he got injured'. 'Il s'est fait blesser' is close to 'il s'est blessé', but it can have a nuance of being to some extent responsible for what happened ('he got himself injured'). The problem is that it does not *always* have this nuance. This is partly because *il s'est + past participle* often cannot be used as a quasi-passive. It depends on the verb. The following example refers to a friend who was walking along the footway when a car swerved out of control and hit her: 'Elle s'est fait écraser par une voiture.' Here, the construction simply draws attention to the unfortunate fact that it was she, and not anyone else, who was walking along the footway – her only responsibility was to have chosen, unwittingly, to be in the wrong place at the wrong time. 'Elle a été écrasée par une voiture' would not convey this tragic irony, and 'elle s'est écrasée' is impossible in this context. If this kind of nuance is important in the ST, it may have to be conveyed through compensation.

While it is true that French has a choice between several ways of saying 'he was injured', English often has a choice of verb forms where French has none, e.g.

J'écoute.	I listen, I'm listening.
J'ai écouté.	I listened, I've listened.
J'écoutais. > *imparfait*	I listened, I was listening, I would listen, I used to listen.

These are standard differences between the languages. They certainly require the translator to be awake, but they only present a problem where there is a significant ST nuance that TL verb forms cannot convey on their own. This typically happens when the ST either switches between tenses unavailable in the TL, or departs from established SL practice in some way. We saw a good example on p. 45, where a powerful effect was produced by switches between past historic and perfect, and by the startling use of a perfect instead of a pluperfect; this effect could only be conveyed in English through compensation.

Sometimes the 'departures' from established practice have themselves become established convention, as in the so-called *imparfait d'ouverture* and *imparfait pittoresque*. It is, for instance, quite common to see a biographical text begin with an imperfect where the 'rules' require a past historic or a perfect, as in 'Le 5 janvier 1906, je naissais à Paris'. There is a nuance of announcement or momentousness in such imperfects which the translator will hope is not important enough to be captured in the TT. The English verb system on its own cannot replicate it, so the only recourse would be compensation. The *imparfait pittoresque* is more of a challenge. It is often used in journalism. If judiciously mixed with the more usual narrative tenses (past historic and perfect), it can create a dynamic variety in aspect which, again, English cannot convey through its verb system alone. Here is an example from a report on a rugby match (cases of the *imparfait pittoresque* are in bold type):

> En première mi-temps, les avants **gagnaient** un ballon dans les 22 mètres gallois. Patterson **lançait** son premier centre qui **prêtait** le ballon à Irwin, deuxième centre. Celui-ci ne le lui rendit qu'après avoir marqué le premier essai irlandais ! Ollie Campbell **transformait**.

These imperfects are like a running commentary (cf. 'he's racing down the wing – he's tackled by Smith – he's looking for someone to pass to – Jones is there in support', etc.), but in the past. The past historic stands out among the imperfects as marking an abrupt and indisputable conclusion to a series of events which are seen as cumulatively blurring into one another in a dramatic build-up. The reversion to the imperfect in 'Campbell transformait' then restores the exciting continuous aspect: though it happened in the past, this is effectively unfolding before your very eyes, here and now. Neither the build-up, nor the contrast, nor the continuousness can be produced in English through verb forms alone ('the forwards were winning a ball in the Welsh 22. Patterson was releasing', etc.).

With many texts (such as your average rugby report), losing these effects will not matter enough for it to be worth trying to compensate for the loss. But the loss often is serious enough to require compensation. For the sake of argument, we shall suppose that the alternation of tenses in our rugby report does produce an effect that needs to come over in the translation. Here is a TT which conveys the drama through other means:

> In the first half, the forwards won a ball in the Welsh 22. Patterson released his inside centre, who fed Irwin. No way was the outside centre parting with the ball till he'd scored the first try. Ollie Campbell converted.

In the TT, the third sentence stops the action and describes Irwin's attitude and intentions. This exegetic element creates suspense and anticipation, which compensates to some extent for the loss of the ST continuous aspect. There is no explicit reference to Irwin actually scoring the hoped-for try. It only becomes clear that he has scored when we read 'Campbell converted'. This abrupt jump in time conveys something of the effect of the abrupt switch to the past historic in the ST, and something of the surprise of the retrospective 'après avoir marqué'; but it does it by different means, through compensation.

It would take a whole book to cover translation between different verb systems. We will just briefly mention one other area of difference between French and English, the subjunctive. In British English, the subjunctive is more or less defunct, and its use in English is in any case largely different from French practice. Translators therefore need to be especially alert to its ~~implications in French~~ — not so much in its standard canonic uses ('{je veux/il faut/il est inadmissible} que' etc.) as in cases where the speaker has a genuine choice between subjunctive and indicative. Here are some examples for discussion:

[*Subjunctive expresses desire or will*] Il a fait signe qu'on le serve.	He {motioned/signalled} them to serve/He nodded for them to start serving/He indicated he was ready to be served, etc.
[*Indicative has declarative function*] Il a fait signe qu'il comprenait.	He {indicated/signalled/nodded} that he understood/He nodded {his understanding/in comprehension}, etc.
[*Subjunctive expresses desire, or highlights speaker's reaction*] L'essentiel, c'est que nous soyons d'accord.	The main thing is {for us to/that we should} agree.
[*Indicative has declarative function*] L'essentiel, c'est que nous sommes d'accord.	The main thing is we agree/We agree, and that's the main thing.
[*Subjunctive highlights speaker's reaction*] Ce qui me déroute, vois-tu, c'est qu'un homme intelligent comme toi ait trouvé ça naturel.	What floors me is how someone as intelligent as you are {can/could} have thought it was natural.
[*Indicative has declarative function*] Ce qui déroute et démoralise nombre d'immigrés en quête de travail, c'est que leurs qualifications n'ont pas la même définition aux yeux de ceux qui leur offrent des emplois.	A lot of immigrants looking for work are disconcerted and demoralized by the fact that their qualifications aren't rated {the same/as highly} by their prospective employers.

Obviously, translation loss on the grammatical level is universal and inevitable. Translators therefore tend to give priority to the *mot juste* and to constructing idiomatic TL sentences, ignoring changes in grammatical structure or economy. As long as *significant* loss is compensated for, there is no need to fret over this. Of course, exceptions may be made where the translator has chosen to colour the TT with exoticism. More often, the ST may have salient textual properties resulting from the manipulation of grammatical structure. This is a common feature in literary or critical texts. The translator has always to decide how distinctive the grammatical structures are, what their function is, and what the aim of the ST is. Only then can a decision be taken about how distinctive the TT's grammar should be. A typical issue is that of syntactic simplicity versus syntactic complexity. Often (but not necessarily), syntactic simplicity coincides with short sentences, and complexity with long ones. There is a good example of syntactic simplicity in the ST in Practical 2.2. Turn back to it, and you will see that some of the notable translation losses in TT (i) occur on the grammatical level; this is something to discuss in class.

With STs that are literary, journalistic, rhetorical, etc., the translator has first to decide what the *function* of the grammatical structures is. Only then can a decision be taken whether, for instance, to divide long ST sentences into shorter TT ones, or merge short ST ones into longer TT ones. Take the first 18 lines of the ST in Practical 5.4. They are grammatically incoherent. But the structure, length and complexity of these lines do not seem to have a purpose or even to be deliberate, so there is no need to feel obliged to respect the grammatical non sequiturs in the TT. In some sorts of text, however, the translator has little choice, and must usually adhere strictly to the norms governing such texts in the TL. This is especially true of scientific and legal texts. In such cases, TL grammar will certainly demand grammatical transpositions, but the imperative priorities are to respect the structural and intellectual integrity of the ST message and to observe the TL conventions for formulating such messages. Here is an example for discussion. It is taken from a European Council act concerning the transmission of personal data by Europol. It is not clear which of the texts, if either, is the ST. Most administrative EU texts, however, are more marked by French convention than by English, German or Italian. (Certainly, about 45 per cent of official Commission documents are produced in French, most of the others in English. Most, however, are produced in both languages (and others) at each stage of drafting – good news for translators, if expensive for the Commission.) Which text is a translation of which is not the issue here, however; the point is that they exemplify French and English conventions for the genre.

French text	English text
Le directeur informe le conseil d'administration et l'autorité de contrôle commune dans les meilleurs délais de toute décision 5 de transmission de données à caractère personnel effectuée au titre de l'article 2, paragraphe 1, point b), et des motifs de cette décision. Sur demande, il transmet 10 au conseil d'administration et à l'autorité de contrôle commune d'autres informations, telles que	The Director shall inform the Management Board and the Joint Supervisory Body without undue delay of any decision to transmit personal data taken under Article 2 (1) (b) and of the reasons for that decision. On request he shall transmit to the Management Board and the Joint Supervisory Body further information, such as the basis for his assessment that, given the circumstances of the

les éléments sur lesquels il s'est
fondé pour apprécier le caractère
15 adéquat du niveau de protection
des données offert par le ou les
Etat(s) tiers ou la ou les instance(s)
non liée(s) à l'Union européenne
destinataire(s), dans les circon-
20 stances de la transmission et
compte tenu de ses objectifs, du
type de données à transmettre et
des fins de la transmission.

transmission and in view of its
objectives, the type of data to be
transmitted and the purpose for
which the data were transmitted,
the level of data protection
afforded by the recipient third
State(s) or non-European Union-
related body or bodies was
adequate.

Apart from grammatical and genre issues, these texts also serve to introduce the sentential level of textual variables. This is something to discuss
in the practical, after reading the remainder of this chapter.

THE SENTENTIAL LEVEL

We can use the lines from 'To Autumn' to show how different grammatical arrangements create different assumptions in the listener or reader
as regards the communicative purpose of an utterance.

> Season of mists and mellow fruitfulness,
> Close bosom-friend of the maturing sun; [. . .]

Keats's lines are partly an address to Autumn and partly an exclamation
about it: the very structure of the utterances leads the listener/reader to
expect an expression of wonderment and enthusiasm. A different grammatical arrangement, however, would most likely announce a different
communicative purpose. For instance:

> Autumn is a season of mists and mellow fruitfulness.
> Indeed, it is a close bosom-friend of the maturing sun.

This structure tells us that we are about to read an informative text – even
though, in the event, phonic and lexical features do give the utterances
something more than simply informative value. In each version, the
grammatical arrangement marks the utterances as having a particular
communicative purpose, whatever overtones may turn out to be involved.
When, as here, the *communicative purpose* of a given grammatical arrangement is studied, rather than the grammatical arrangement in its own right,
the utterance is studied on the **sentential level**. On this level are considered sentences. A **sentence** is defined as a complete, self-contained and
ready-made vehicle for communication: nothing needs to be added before

it can be uttered and understood in concrete situations. The starter's command 'Go!' is a sentence. So is 'In your dreams' as an expression of mocking dismissiveness. Note that, in this definition, a sentence does not necessarily contain a verb.

Any text counts on the sentential level as a succession of sentences, each with a built-in communicative purpose. This purpose is usually conveyed by one or more of three features: (1) prosodic features, such as intonation or stress (e.g. the rising pitch that signals a question in French and English); (2) grammatical features, such as sequential focus (e.g. 'On this level are considered sentences', which puts emphasis on 'sentences'); (3) **illocutionary particles** (e.g. the question-forming particle 'n'est-ce pas', or the particle 'hélas', which qualifies an utterance as an expression of regret); illocutionary particles do not fit into syntax proper, but simply mark the sentence as having a particular communicative purpose, i.e. they tell the listener/reader how to take the utterance.

The sentential level of spoken language is extremely rich, fine shades of intonation and stress distinguishing sentences with subtly different nuances. It is possible to take the same words, in the same order, and turn them into quite different sentences, with different communicative purposes, purely through manipulating features on the prosodic level – most notably, varying intonation and stress. Such refinements largely disappear in written texts, because the only ways of conveying intonation and stress in writing are punctuation and typography. These offer far fewer alternatives than the rich nuances of speech. Try saying 'That's the salt' in the four ways described below, and listen to the intonation and to where the stresses come and how strong they are. Then compare the result with the attempts at achieving the same result in written transcription. Both the descriptions and the transcriptions are crude, compared with the subtleties of speech.

Intonation	Communicative purpose	Transcription
Falling	Statement	That's the salt.
Falling + stress on 'salt'	Impatient or aggressive statement	That's the *salt.*
Rising	Question	That's the salt?
Fall-rise	Amazed or sarcastic question	That's the *salt*?!

Further effects can be achieved by a combination of prosodic features, word order and illocutionary particles: 'Is that the salt?', 'That's the salt, isn't it?', 'Surely that's the salt?', 'The salt, please.', 'The salt, dammit!' Each of these formulations could be spoken in a wide variety of ways, to express surprise, enthusiasm, weariness, anger, etc. If, in context, punctuation and typography cannot clearly produce the desired impact, the writer has to add an explicit indication of how the sentence is spoken ('she exclaimed in surprise', 'she sneered', etc.).

In translating both oral and written texts, then, the sentential level needs as much care as any other. Illocutionary particles and sequential focus are easier to represent in written texts than prosodic features are; but how to translate them still cannot be taken for granted. For instance, the impact of 'bien' as an illocutionary particle is not always easy to put into English; compare the following alternative TTs for a simple French sentence:

ST	*TT*
Je t'avais bien dit de rester chez toi.	I *told* you to stay at home.
	I did tell you to stay at home.
	Didn't I *tell* you to stay at home?

Which of these, or other, alternatives is chosen, and whether the prosodic features need be marked with italics or punctuation, will depend on the context.

Illocutionary particles and sequential focus are generally accompanied by appropriate prosodic features, notably intonation and stress, as in the 'bien' example. The translator therefore has to make sure not to introduce *inappropriate* prosodic features in the TT – for good examples of this, see the discussion of the Pagnol TT on pp. 86–8. As regards sequential focus, it must be remembered that French and English differ in how and when they vary word order, and how they combine it with prosodic features. The general question of sequential focus in language, or 'theme and rheme', is too complex and controversial for our needs. There is an excellent discussion of it in Baker (1992: 119–79). Ayres-Bennett and Carruthers (2001: 248–92) give a good introduction specifically to French word order. What we are going to do here is simply look at some translation implications of the fact that what is expressed in French through sequential focus, perhaps in combination with illocutionary particles, is often most idiomatically expressed in English through voice stress and intonation alone.

The six French sentences below are good examples of this. In an oral English TT, each of them can be satisfactorily translated as 'I'm not picking it up', the speaker choosing from the vast prosodic range of English to make the communicative purpose clear. In a written TT, however, while some of this impact may be conveyed with italics and punctuation marks, it will be much vaguer. In any case, italics, capitals and exclamation marks soon become tiresome. The effect may in some cases be clearer if an illocutionary particle or a different grammatical arrangement is used. If this is too cumbersome for the context, the only solution is to insert an explicit indication of how the words are spoken. Here are the sentences. Try reading them out to achieve the stated communicative purpose:

Written sentence	*Communicative purpose*
Je ne le ramasse pas.	Statement.
Je ne le ramasse pas?	Question.
C'est pas moi qui vais le ramasser.	Belligerent statement.
Je ne le ramasse donc pas.	Firm statement: negative intent.
Je ne vais tout de même pas le ramasser.	Indignant statement: negative intent.
C'est pas moi qui dois le ramasser.	Relieved statement.

The challenge is how to convey in a written TT the intonation, stress and emotive impact corresponding to each ST sentence. Here, for performance, discussion and improvement in class, are some possible renderings of the French sentences:

Italics + punctuation only	*Italics + punctuation + illocutionary particles + grammatical rearrangement*
I'm not picking it up.	N/A
I'm not picking it up?	Am I not picking it up?/Don't I pick it up?/{Shall/Do} I leave it there?
I'm not picking it up.	{*I'm* not/No way am *I*} picking it up.
I'm *not* picking it *up*.	So I'm just not picking it up.
I'm not picking it *up*!!	I'm not picking *that* up!/Come off it, I'm not picking it *up*!
I'm not picking it *up*.	I'm not the one who's {picking/got to pick} it up.

Since English relies more than French does on prosodic factors alone to create the sentential function, it is common to read sentences like the last one in this letter from a woman reader to a newspaper:

To those many thousands of us who have no interest in sport, the television schedules at the present time are grossly unfair and discriminatory. How would the male half of the population feel if, during the fashion show season, three channels were given over to women prancing up and down the catwalk and endless chat about them and their clothes? No, I wouldn't watch them either.

The writer knows what intonation and stress are required in the last sentence, and relies on the reader to supply it. This usually works in English, even though there is very often a potential ambiguity in the written sentence. In this example, however, the ambiguity is real. How should we read the sentence? There are two possibilities in this context:

No, I wouldn't watch *them*, either. [i.e. she'd watch neither sport nor fashion]

No, *I* wouldn't watch them either. [i.e. she wouldn't watch fashion any more than men would]

This particular type of ambiguity is rare in French (although French-speakers are as capable of misleading writing as the rest of us). Sequential focus and grammatical arrangement are essential adjuncts to prosodic features in creating clarity and emphasis:

[She would watch neither] {Elles non plus, je ne les/Ça non plus, je ne le} regarderais pas.

[She wouldn't watch the fashion any more than men would] Moi non plus, je ne {les regarderais pas/regarderais pas ça}.

In a different context, there would even be a third possibility, as in: 'I'd hate hearing about them, I wouldn't read about them, and I wouldn't *watch* them either' ('Je détesterais qu'on en parle, je ne lirais rien les concernant, je ne les regarderais pas non plus').

Here is a beauty, a statement by an Orangeman quoted out of context in a newspaper:

I am not going to condemn violence because Gerry Adams never condemns it.

There are at least three different possible readings of this sentence. Here they are, each with a French version in which grammatical arrangement prevents ambiguity:

I'm not going to condemn violence because G.A. never condemns it, [but for some other reason, e.g. I'm against it on principle].

Si je condamne la violence, ce n'est pas parce que G.A. ne la condamne jamais, [mais bien parce que je m'y oppose par principe].

The reason I'm not going to condemn violence is that G.A. never condemns it.

Si je ne condamne pas la violence, c'est parce que G.A. ne la condamne jamais.

Just because G.A. never condemns violence, that doesn't mean *I'm* going to.	Ce n'est pas parce que G.A. ne condamne jamais la violence que je la condamnerais moi-même.

A final typical example, which speaks for itself:

> The Queen has said that Britain will join a successful European single currency during a private dinner at Buckingham Palace.

We have spent time on these examples to show two things. First, that it is easy to overlook the possibility of using prosodic features in an English TT to do what grammatical arrangement does in the ST. As we have seen, this will not always work, but it is often a clearer and more idiomatic solution than copying the ST sentence structure; this would be the case in translating either of the French sentences about fashion shows. Second, even where copying the ST sentence structure produces an idiomatic English sentence, it can easily be misleading. Compare these TTs with likely back-translations:

ST	TT	Back-translation
C'est pas moi qui vais le ramasser.	It's not me who's going to pick it up.	Ce n'est pas moi qui dois {le ramasser/aller le chercher}.
Je ne vais tout de même pas le ramasser.	All the same, I'm not going to pick it up.	Ça ne fait rien, je ne le ramasse pas.

As regards sequential focus, a final small but important point to bear in mind is that when an adjective is placed before its noun in French, this can be for several reasons. Usually it is to put greater focus on the noun, making it more of the centre of attention than it would be with the adjective in the orthodox place. Sometimes it also avoids prosodic anticlimax, French preferring not to finish clauses or sentences with a long syntactic unit followed by a short one. Sometimes it also avoids ambiguity, especially if the noun is a compound one. Compare these pairs of sentences:

Adjective before	Adjective after
Il y a aussi ces assourdissantes U.L.M. qui polluent nos soirées. [The microlights are certainly noisy, but there is extra focus on them: they are relatively unpredictable new information in the context.]	Il y a aussi ces U.L.M. assourdissantes qui polluent nos soirées. [Focus on the noise; the microlights are to some extent taken for granted, as being relatively predictable information in the context.]
De grêles arbres à fruits se découpent sur le ciel. [Focus on	Des arbres à fruits grêles se découpent sur le ciel. [Focus on

the trees; and it is the trees that are spindly.]

Cet ouvrage fait naître une singulière réflexion sur les rapports qu'entretiennent l'artiste et son public. [Focus on the reflection: the book is unusually successful in making you think about artist and public.]

the spindliness; and is it the fruit that is spindly???]

Cet ouvrage fait naître une réflexion singulière sur les rapports qu'entretiennent l'artiste et son public. [Focus on 'singulière': the book makes you think in the most peculiar way about artist and public.]

PRACTICAL 7

7.1 Grammatical and sentential issues

Assignment

In class discussion, compare the French and English Europol texts on pp. 104–5. To prepare for the discussion, make notes on salient grammatical similarities and differences between the texts (including constraints that seem to be imposed by the genre), and on any sentential differences between the texts, notably in respect of sequential focus.

7.2 Grammatical and sentential issues

Assignment

(i)   The following ST is from the memoirs of a retired Paris police chief, Roger Le Taillanter, which you are translating for a general readership. Discuss the strategic decisions that you have to take before starting detailed translation of this ST, and outline and justify the strategy you adopt. Pay careful attention to grammatical and sentential issues, but do not neglect other important factors.
(ii) Translate the text into French.
(iii) Discuss the main decisions of detail you took.

Contextual information

This extract is from a chapter devoted to a notorious case which started in April 1967, and involved a lone hold-up man, dubbed 'Le Solitaire' by the press, who committed over twenty hold-ups at small post offices. The first three times, he wore a beige raincoat and a grey trilby. The extract reproduced here refers to the fourth and fifth hold-ups. A Simca was a make of car. The year-long case is recounted in full, in some 5,000 words, and is narrated throughout in the present tense.

ST

« Le Solitaire » commence à construire sa légende. Le 1er juin, il remet
ça à Nanterre, dans le bureau auxiliaire de la cité Marcellin-Berthelot. Un
seul détail change : l'agresseur porte une casquette. Sous la menace de
son arme, il s'empare de 7 450 francs et prend la fuite sans problème.
5 J'ai beau actionner toutes mes vieilles connaissances du milieu : rien. A
croire que le Solitaire est un pur esprit. Plusieurs groupes d'inspecteurs
sont sur le coup. Chou blanc. Pas la moindre amorce de piste.

6 juillet. On le tient ! Notre homme a attaqué, à 15 heures, la poste de
l'avenue Wilson, à Cachan. Fantaisie de sa part : il portait une blouse
10 bleue et des lunettes. Mais on a pu relever le numéro minéralogique de
la Simca 1000 à bord de laquelle il a pris la fuite, après avoir raflé
10 000 francs. On retrouve bientôt la voiture avec, à l'intérieur, la blouse
et les lunettes. Stupeur : elle appartient à un gardien de la paix retraité.
Or, c'est bien connu, les policiers en uniforme ont aussi en dotation des
15 blouses bleues. L'ancien flicard est aussitôt appréhendé et placé en garde
à vue. Le temps qu'on s'aperçoive qu'il avait déclaré le vol de sa voiture
bien avant le hold-up de Cachan... Le Solitaire court toujours, et me fait
même un beau pied de nez en venant attaquer une seconde fois ce même
bureau de poste, le 24 octobre.

(Le Taillanter 1990: 82–3)

7.3 Grammatical and sentential issues

Assignment
   (i)   The following ST is from André Gide's *L'Immoraliste* (1902). You
         have been commissioned to produce a new translation for a modern
         foreign classics collection. Discuss the strategic decisions that you
         have to take before starting detailed translation of this ST, and
         outline and justify the strategy you adopt. Pay careful attention to
         grammatical and sentential issues, but do not neglect other impor-
         tant factors. You are only translating the second paragraph, but
         remember that the content and expression of the first one are impor-
         tant strategic factors.
  (ii)   Translate the second paragraph of the text into English.
 (iii)   Explain the main decisions of detail you took.
 (iv)   Compare your TT with the published one, which will be given to
         you by your tutor.

Contextual information
Michel, the narrator, has grown up surrounded by books, learned six
ancient languages, and made an early reputation as an ancient historian.
He marries at the age of 25, 'n'ayant presque rien regardé que des
ruines ou des livres, et ne connaissant rien de la vie'. He nearly dies of

tuberculosis, and develops an overwhelming urge to 'live', henceforth scorning scholarship, books and the past, and pursuing physical pleasures. At the point where this passage comes, it is July, he is living on his well-farmed and admirably productive estate in Normandy, his wife Marceline is pregnant, and he has taken to riding through his fields in the mornings with a friend. Ironically, he has been asked to give a course of lectures. He has decided to stir up the academic world and write his lectures on the Goths of the fourth century: in their admirable barbarism, he sees the very opposite of all that Greece and Rome represent. He thinks – mistakenly, if the style of this passage is anything to go by – that this choice of subject is tantamount to a rejection of his bookish past, which was characterized, as he puts it, by 'la culture tuant la vie'. The first paragraph is itself useful contextual information.

ST

Je rentrais ivre d'air, étourdi de vitesse, les membres engourdis un peu d'une voluptueuse lassitude, l'esprit plein de santé, d'appétit, de fraîcheur. Marceline approuvait, encourageait ma fantaisie. En rentrant, encore tout guêtré, j'apportais vers le lit où elle s'attardait à m'attendre, une odeur
5 de feuilles mouillées qui lui plaisait, me disait-elle. Et elle m'écoutait raconter notre course, l'éveil des champs, le recommencement du travail… Elle prenait autant de joie, semblait-il, à me sentir vivre, qu'à vivre. – Bientôt de cette joie aussi j'abusai ; nos promenades s'allongèrent, et parfois je ne rentrais plus que vers midi.
10 Cependant je réservais de mon mieux la fin du jour et la soirée à la préparation de mon cours. Mon travail avançait ; j'en étais satisfait et ne considérais pas comme impossible qu'il valût la peine plus tard de réunir mes leçons en volume. Par une sorte de réaction naturelle, tandis que ma vie s'ordonnait, se réglait et que je me plaisais autour de moi à régler et
15 à ordonner toutes choses, je m'éprenais de plus en plus de l'éthique fruste des Goths, et, tandis qu'au long de mon cours je m'occupais, avec une hardiesse que l'on me reprocha suffisamment dans la suite, d'exalter l'in-culture et d'en dresser l'apologie, je m'ingéniais laborieusement à dominer sinon à supprimer tout ce qui la pouvait rappeler autour de moi comme
20 en moi-même.

(Gide 1958: 417–18)

8

The formal properties of texts: Discourse and intertextual issues in translation

In the last chapter, we briefly discussed a grammatical rearrangement of the two lines from 'To Autumn':

> Autumn is a season of mists and mellow fruitfulness.
> Indeed, it is a close bosom-friend of the maturing sun.

We saw that, on the sentential level, this arrangement marks the text as informative, rather than as an expression of excitement. Now, part of this sentential effect derives from the adverbial 'Indeed' and the pronoun 'it', which explicitly link the two sentences. 'Indeed, it' announces that the second sentence is going to confirm and amplify the first, conveying additional information about Autumn. The linking of one sentence to another is the most significant feature found on the discourse level.

THE DISCOURSE LEVEL

The textual variables considered on the **discourse level** are those that distinguish a cohesive and coherent textual flow from a random sequence of unrelated utterances. Strictly speaking, this level is concerned with inter-sentential relations (relations between sentences) and with relations between larger units, such as paragraphs, chapters, stanzas, and so on. Accordingly, for the most part, we shall be concentrating on intersentential relations. But before looking at the translation issues these raise, we should point out that it is often useful also to consider relations between *parts* of sentences on the discourse level, as if the parts were sentences in their own right. For instance, the rearranged lines from 'To Autumn' could easily have been written as one sentence, whether in verse or prose, as in the following:

Autumn is a season of mists and mellow fruitfulness: indeed, it is a close bosom-friend of the maturing sun.

pause, ou continuer l'idée

Connexion

Here, the colon acts as a connector between the two statements, with 'indeed' indicating the kind of direction the second one will go in. We shall see similar examples below.

It is useful to distinguish between two aspects of discourse: cohesion and coherence. Following Halliday and Hasan (1976), we define **cohesion** as the transparent linking of sentences (and larger sections of text) by explicit discourse connectors like 'then', 'so', 'however', and so on. These act as signposts pointing out the thread of discourse running through the text. **Coherence** is a more difficult matter than cohesion, because, by definition, it is not explicitly marked in a text: it is a tacit, but discernible, thematic or emotional development running through the text. We can illustrate the difference with a simple example:

and?

Cohérence *dans la phrase*

I was getting hungry. I went downstairs. I knew the kitchen was on the ground floor. I was pretty sure the kitchen must be on the ground floor. I didn't expect to find the kitchen so easily. I made myself a sandwich.

I was getting hungry. *So* I went downstairs. *Well* . . . I knew the kitchen was on the ground floor. *I mean,* I was pretty sure *it* must be *there. Still,* I didn't expect to find *it* so easily. *Anyway,* I made myself a sandwich.

transitions *pas formel*

The first text is given a degree of cohesion by the repetitions, although there are no intersentential connectors as such. But it is coherent, thanks to the underlying chronological narrative structure. In the second text, a train of thought is restored by inserting connectors (printed in italics). These act as cohesion markers, setting up a transparent intersentential structure. Some of the cohesion markers link the sentences by explaining or commenting on the speaker's actions: 'So', 'Well', 'I mean', 'Still', 'Anyway'. Others are instances of **grammatical anaphora** – that is, the replacement of previously used words and phrases by expressions referring back to them; here, the anaphoric elements are 'it' (replacing 'the kitchen') and 'there' (replacing 'on the ground floor').

The sentential and discourse levels are by definition closely related. In the Keats example, the intersentential elements 'Indeed' and 'it' are also what mark the text as informative. In the kitchen example too, many of the intersentential connectors also function on the sentential level; rather like illocutionary particles, they give each utterance a particular tone and tell the listener how to take it – 'So', 'Well', 'I mean', 'Still', 'Anyway'. For example, the two versions of the third sentence will almost certainly be spoken differently, because, on the sentential level, they have different functions: the first announces a new fact out of the blue, while in the second, 'Well' marks the sentence as explaining or justifying the decision to go downstairs. 'Well' therefore has both a sentential and a discourse function here. Punctuation can have a similar double function, as in this heading to a magazine article:

La Porte d'or
Anse de toutes les promesses, elle n'a été découverte qu'au milieu du XVIIIᵉ siècle. Chercheurs d'or, enfants de Kerouac, gays... Depuis toujours, une Californie particulière s'y est lovée : celle qui aime la vie. Et qui laisse vivre.

Orthodox punctuation would have a comma (or nothing at all) before 'et qui laisse vivre'. The full stop reinforces the cohesive function of 'Et', by highlighting it. So it has a discourse function. But it also has a sentential function, because it tells the reader that this sentence beginning with 'Et' is intended to be emphatic.

This is a common technique in journalism and advertising. Here is an example from an advertisement. We quote the first and last paragraphs. Between the two, the text give details of the new car (it is the fruit of long development, reveals the future of motoring, etc.):

CERTAINS HOMMES EVOLUENT PLUS SUREMENT QUE D'AUTRES

Vérité première, l'évolution concerne la vie, conjugaison plusieurs fois millénaire du hasard et de la nécessité. Pourtant, pas de hasards chez Volvo, seulement l'impérieuse nécessité d'être toujours en accord avec notre idéal : évoluer plus loin, donc évoluer plus sûr. [. . .]
    Pour évoluer plus fort, plus sûrement, plus longtemps. Comme ceux, rares et privilégiés, à qui cette voiture s'adresse.

The colon in the first paragraph has a discourse function, doing duty for either a relative clause (e.g. 'notre idéal, qui est d'évoluer') or a conjunction (e.g. 'c'est-à-dire', 'à savoir'). But it also has what amounts to a sentential function, marking the final two phrases for emphasis. These two phrases could indeed easily have been printed as separate sentences, or even separate paragraphs.

The closing paragraph begins in just that way. The first sentence seems to be in a void; it is not even followed by a main verb (e.g. 'Pour évoluer

plus fort [. . .], achetez donc une Volvo'). In the context of the advertisement as a whole, the paragraph break itself has both a discourse
function, announcing the paragraph as a summing-up of the text, and a
sentential function, marking the sentence as emphatic. The full stop after
'longtemps' has a similar dual function, stressing the connector 'comme'
and announcing an emphatic sentence.

Many connectors can be used to join short sentences together to make
longer ones. Conjunctions such as 'so', 'and' or 'but' are simple examples. This is another way in which intersentential and sentential functions
are often close in practice, even though they are distinguishable in analysis.
For instance, 'I was getting hungry, so I went downstairs' will probably
have a different communicative impact from 'I was getting hungry. So I
went downstairs'. Similar considerations apply to **rhetorical anaphora** –
that is, the repetition of a word or words at the start of successive or
closely associated clauses or phrases. Typically, this occurs at the start of
sentences, as in the opening of another car advertisement, this time a
SEAT:

> Imaginez une voiture familiale dessinée par l'homme qui a conçu la
> Maserati Bora, la Lotus Esprit.
>   Imaginez qu'elle soit protégée par une cellule de sécurité construite
> par l'un des plus éminents carrossiers européens.
>   Imaginez qu'elle soit propulsée par un moteur dont le nom est respecté
> dans le monde entier.
>   Imaginez pour finir un constructeur prêt à briser toutes les règles
> établies pour construire une telle voiture.

Rhetorical anaphora is common in political speeches, advertising, journalism and literary texts. For our purposes, we shall assume that it can
also occur within single sentences, and still have a discourse function.
The SEAT text could easily be printed as a single sentence, with semi-
colons instead of full stops, without damaging the discourse function of
the rhetorical anaphora. By the same token, the penultimate sentence
of the Volvo text has as strong an anaphorical structure as if it were
split into three sentences: 'Pour évoluer plus fort. Plus sûrement. Plus
longtemps.' It is certainly important to watch out for quasi-anaphorical
repetitions within sentences, because they generally have just as powerful
a discourse function as when they occur at the start.

Normally, translators will try to preserve an anaphorical structure in the
TT. But TL grammar sometimes makes this difficult. There are spectacular examples in Jo-Ann Léon's *Poèmes d'un amour inutile*. These are
very simple, down-to-earth texts, but translating them is not so simple.
Take the poem called 'Toi'. This consists of sixteen couplets with the
same structure, all starting 'Toi, tu ne m'aimes pas', then a seventeenth
with a surprise twist. Here are the first two, and the last one:

> Toi, tu ne m'aimes pas,
> Moi qui connais la douce chaleur de ton corps.
>
> Toi, tu ne m'aimes pas,
> Moi qui sens ta bouche brûlante mordre ma bouche. [. . .]
>
> > Toi tu m'aimeras,
> > Moi qui ne suis plus là.
>
> > > > > (Léon 1989: 16–17)

Even in the 'Toi' lines, there is a sentential problem: how to give sufficient emphasis to 'you'. But the 'Moi qui' lines are a bigger problem,
because 'I who' is hardly a serious option. The structure is much more
common in French than in English (cf. e.g. 'Vous qui êtes épicier, vous
devez le savoir' > '*You're* a grocer, you should know'; 'Qu'est-ce que
tu en dis, toi qui es mécanicien?' > 'What do you think – *you're* a
mechanic?'). One possibility would be to start all the 'Moi qui' lines with
'But I'. But this would spoil the stark opposition of 'Toi' and 'Moi' at
the start of every line. Alternatively, 'but' could be placed at the end of
the 'Toi' lines ('You don't love me, but / I know the soft sweet warmth
of your body'); even then, though, the conjunction would give the wrong
impression – something like 'but I know something you don't know' or
'but I don't care, because. . .' . Perhaps it would do less damage to reverse
the lines. Here are some alternatives for discussion:

> I know the soft sweet warmth of your body, but
> You don't love me. [. . .]
>
> > You will love me, but
> > I've gone.
>
> I know the soft sweet warmth of your body, but you
> Don't love me. [. . .]
>
> > You will love me, but I
> > Have gone.
>
> I know the soft sweet warmth of your body, and
> You don't love me. [. . .]
>
> > You will love me, and
> > I have gone.

The last arrangement probably comes closest to conveying the ST effects.
   Common though it is, rhetorical anaphora is a special case. The presence
or absence of explicit discourse connectors is a more common translation

issue. We can illustrate it clearly with an extract from Voltaire's *Zadig* (1747) and John Butt's translation. (*Contextual information*. Zadig comes upon an Egyptian beating his girlfriend. Zadig protests, and the Egyptian, taking him for her lover, vows to punish him.)

> En disant ces paroles, il laisse la dame qu'il tenait d'une main par les cheveux, et, prenant sa lance, il veut en percer l'étranger. Celui-ci, qui était de sang-froid, évita aisément le coup d'un furieux. Il se saisit de la lance près du fer dont elle est armée. L'un veut la retirer, l'autre l'ar-
> 5   racher. Elle se brise entre leurs mains. L'Egyptien tire son épée ; Zadig s'arme de la sienne. Ils s'attaquent l'un l'autre. Celui-ci porte cent coups précipités ; celui-là les pare avec adresse. La dame, assise sur un gazon, rajuste sa coiffure et les regarde.
>
> (Voltaire 1960: 24)

For the most part, cohesion is marked by grammatical anaphora, in the shape of pronouns. The most striking thing is the relative absence of conjunctions. This is typical of the quick-fire, laconic matter-of-factness of Voltaire's style in *Zadig*. Successive events are registered without comment, as if they have not yet been interpreted and sorted into a meaningful whole. This, allied to the rapid movement, creates an impression of disorder and unintelligibility. We are left to sort out the relations between events for ourselves. This technique actually has an important function in *Zadig*. It is not unlike Camus's technique in *L'Etranger*. It puts us, the readers, into a position like Zadig's. The whole story traces his attempts to make sense of an apparently baffling, absurd universe. Our surprised reactions to the dearth of explanatory connectors, and our constant sense-making as we cope with this dearth, are analogous to Zadig's own interpretive activity in the story. Voltaire's strategy is a risky one; it may not even be deliberate. But the fact remains that it is a major feature of the text. It therefore demands careful attention from the translator. Here is John Butt's translation (the italics are ours):

> With those words, he let go the lady, whom he was holding by the hair, and tried to stab the stranger with his lance. Zadig, whose temper was cool, had no difficulty in avoiding an angry man's attack, *and* seized the lance by its iron tip. *While* the one tried to snatch it away *and* the
> 5   other tried to get possession of it, the lance broke in their hands. *At that*, the Egyptian drew his sword; Zadig did likewise, *and* they fell upon each other. The former dealt a hundred violent blows, *which* the latter skilfully parried. *Meanwhile* the lady sat down on the grass, tidied her hair, and watched them.
>
> (Voltaire 1964: 53)

Confining comment to the italicized expressions, we can say that the translator has greatly streamlined the jerky ST, filling in the gaps with connectors that between them have three effects. Some of them implicitly explain events (e.g. Zadig's coolness explains *why* he could seize the lance; and they drew their swords *because* the lance broke). Others link separate actions into seamless complex single ones, making a succession of events into a coherent episode (e.g. one trying to snatch and the other trying to get possession are parts of a single process; their falling upon each other is the culmination of the joint sword-drawing; and parrying the blows is inseparable from dealing them). Finally, above all, instead of doing as Voltaire does, and leaving the reader to observe the events and work out their significance, the TT makes the links and the irony explicit. Obviously there *are* links – it takes two to make a fight, after all. But the point is that we should work them out, not be fed them on a spoon. The TT spoils this vital effect, most of all perhaps with that unfortunate 'Meanwhile'.

We are not suggesting that translators should slavishly copy ST cohesion structures. Languages differ in this respect as in many others. English often prefers coordination where French prefers subordination. An English text as devoid of coordination as *Zadig* would be almost unreadable. But then, for a French text, *Zadig* is surprisingly lacking in subordination as well as in coordination. The point is to ask what the *function* of the ST discourse structure is. If its nature and function are completely unexceptional in terms of SL practice, then translators normally aim to produce a TT with equally typical TL structures and effects (unless a degree of exoticism is part of the strategy). But if ST discourse function is exceptional, as in *Zadig* (and *L'Etranger* – cf. Practical 2.2), this may well imply a need for similarly exceptional discourse features in the TT.

Clearly, then, translators should never forget that languages have different expectations in respect of cohesion and coherence. It is more common in French than in English for texts to be explicitly structured with connectors ('or', 'donc', 'ainsi', 'en effet', 'par ailleurs', 'en revanche', etc.) that signpost the logical relationship between sentences. An English TT using explicit connectors to reproduce all those found in a French ST will often sound unidiomatic or pedantic. This piece of dialogue is a simple example:

ST	TT
– On retrouve ces qualités chez Hugo.	'You find these qualities in Hugo.'
– C'est bien à Hugo que je pensais.	'I was *thinking* of Hugo.'

The 'bien' is part connector and part illocutionary particle. But even taking it purely as a connector, it would probably be rendered in an oral TT by voice stress and intonation, not with a connector. In a written TT, it might well be rendered with a connector: 'I was indeed thinking of Hugo.' A halfway house is 'Yes, I was thinking of Hugo'. The decision will be influenced by the genre of the ST. In a play or a novel, italics would probably be used rather than the connector. But in e.g. an academic text, 'indeed' will be more likely than 'Yes' or the italics.

Here is another example, from a bilingual leaflet enclosed with a tube of whitening toothpaste:

ST	TT
Le désir de retrouver la blancheur naturelle des dents est normal et les dentifrices classiques ne sont pas tous aptes à déloger ces 5 colorations inesthétiques.	The desire to regain the natural whiteness of one's teeth is normal and traditional toothpastes are not all able to dislodge this unsightly staining.
En revanche, ces taches sont facilement éliminées par l'usage régulier d'un dentifrice blan- chissant aux vertus nettoyantes et 10 polissantes.	On the other hand, these stains can easily be removed through the regular use of a whitening tooth- paste with cleaning and polishing properties.

The standard dictionary suggestion for 'en revanche', 'on the other hand', is not logically right here, and it triggers the wrong prosodic expectations (cf. the examples on pp. 86–8). The best rendering in this text is prob- ably just 'but': 'But these stains can be removed' – there is not much point in striving to capture the subtleties of 'en revanche' in a leaflet that no one is going to read anyway. A closer approximation would be some- thing like 'What one can do, though, is remove these stains [. . .]'. In other contexts, 'en revanche' might need to be translated in other ways, as in the following (the author is talking about metaphor, and quotes the clichéd image of a village 'blotti au creux du vallon'):

Que perdrait le village à être seulement 'situé' au creux du vallon ? Le mot 'blotti' ne nous donne aucun renseignement complémentaire. En revanche, il transporte le lecteur [. . .] dans l'âme supposée du village.

(Robbe-Grillet 1963: 49)

'En revanche' often calls for the verb 'do' used as an auxiliary, which would work well in this context: '{What it does do is/But it does} carry the reader [. . .]'.

As these examples show, even in cases where SL and TL do both habit- ually use discourse connectors, this can be a weak spot in translation. This is because some cohesion markers can be *faux amis*, or require gram- matical transposition in the TT. We have already seen examples on pp. 86–8, where translating 'En tout cas' as 'In any case' and 'Finalement' as 'And on top of that' made the TT incoherent. Other examples are easily found. Take this question to a colleague who was not at the office yesterday:

ST	TT
– Vous n'étiez pas là hier ?	'Weren't you in yesterday?'
– En effet, j'étais souffrant.	'{No/That's right,} I wasn't feeling well.'

Here, translating 'En effet' as 'In effect' or 'In fact' would be near-nonsensical. 'En effet', like 'effectivement', is usually a confirmatory connector.

Another common way of signalling explicit cohesion is grammatical anaphora. However, rules of anaphora differ from language to language. Normally, translators follow TL anaphorical practice rather than SL practice. Translating from French, this is vividly illustrated by 'dont'. Very often, this translates as 'whose', 'of whom' or 'of which', but preserving ST anaphora can easily result in unidiomatic calque. Compare the following alternative TTs:

ST	TT
Des ouvrages exigeants dont ils savent qu'ils ne les vendront pas.	(i) Difficult works about which they know they won't sell them. (ii) Difficult works (that) they know they won't sell.
Un vieux bouquin dont j'avais hésité jusque-là à aborder la lecture.	(i) An old book {the reading of which/whose reading} I'd hitherto been reluctant to start. (ii) An old book I'd hitherto been reluctant to embark on.
Les véhicules dont les sièges peuvent être rabattus.	(i) Models whose seats can be folded forward. (ii) Models with seats that fold forward.

Even where SL and TL rules for anaphora as such are not different, other grammatical factors can be a trap. A common one is the implications of gender. Here are two examples from another of the reports referred to in Practical 5.4.

ST	TT
Pour peu que l'on soit prêt à le saisir, l'art est présent dans la vie quotidienne. Elle est une source d'inspiration intarisssable.	Provided we are ready to see it, art is present in everyday life. Everyday life is an inexhaustible source of inspiration.

If 'Elle' were rendered as 'It' here, the reference would unambiguously be to 'art'. But 'Elle' refers to 'la vie quotidienne'. The obvious way round this is to translate 'Elle' as 'Everyday life'. This kind of repetition is a common way of avoiding misleading anaphora, and is more usual in English than in French. If the repeated expression is felt to be too long (as it may be here), an alternative is to merge the sentences and use a relative pronoun: 'everyday life, which'. The only drawback to that solution here is that 'which' might itself be ambiguous: does it refer to 'everyday life', or to 'art is present in everyday life'? It has to be said that the ST sentence itself is a bit unorthodox. A single sentence with a relative clause would be more usual – 'la vie quotidienne, qui est': there would be no ambiguity there, because of the clear grammatical distinction between 'qui' and 'ce qui'.

The second example is even odder:

ST	TT
Une différence nette a été ressentie entre l'art « officiel », celui des musées, par exemple, et l'art au quotidien. Bien plus : il serait l'expression de cette différence.	A clear difference was sensed between 'official' art, for example museum art, and art in the everyday. Indeed, it was mooted that art is the expression of that difference.

Translating 'il' as 'it' is impossible: in e.g. 'it was said to be the expression of that difference', 'it' refers to 'difference', which is nonsense. This confusion is impossible in French, because 'il' cannot refer to feminine 'différence'. But there is a different confusion in the ST. Does 'il' refer to 'l'art officiel' or 'l'art au quotidien'? If it is to the second, one would have expected 'celui-ci'; but that would not have made much sense. Only an exchange of e-mails with the author confirmed that 'il' actually refers to 'l'Art en général'. The poorly drafted ST certainly needs clarification in the TT, and the only way to do it seems to be to repeat 'art'. Even then, the idea is a bit obscure, but further exegesis would be beyond the translator's remit, unless the author agreed to it. (Sometimes authors actually ask the translator to rectify an ST mistake or obscurity in the TT.)

On the discourse level, then, translators have to ask three simple but important questions. Assuming that the ST is coherent, are the connective elements explicit (e.g. cohesion markers, or sequential focus acting as a connector) or implicit (e.g. prosodic features, or narrative chronology)? What is the thematic and expressive function of the connective elements? And what, in context, is the most accurate and idiomatic TL way of marking a given intersentential relation – should it be explicit or implicit, and does it require grammatical transposition?

As for relations between larger units on the discourse level (paragraphs, chapters, etc.), these are generally less problematic than intersentential relations. As usual, the translator must first ask what the function of such features is in the ST. If they have no marked purpose, but simply reflect SL conventions, altering them to match TL conventions is unproblematic. Commercial considerations may also come into play: for instance, a publisher may be afraid that a text full of long paragraphs or unusually short ones would not sell. On the other hand, if the division into paragraphs does have a thematic or emotive function, the translator should hesitate before significantly altering it. It is undeniable that the first Camus TT in Practical 2.2 sabotages the ST effect to some extent by bringing the paragraphing into line with what the translator presumably thought was normal TL practice in the 1940s: the text is domesticated and made expressively weaker, much as *Zadig* is by the addition of all those connectors. A more recent example is *Harry Potter à l'école des sorciers,* the translation of J.K. Rowling's *Harry Potter and the Philosopher's Stone*: the TT is quite often paragraphed more orthodoxly, more 'logically', and consequently less vividly, than the ST. In some genres, there can be no question of the translator *choosing* whether or not to alter ST paragraphing: in texts having the force of law, for instance, the ST structure generally has to be observed, however inelegant or difficult this makes the text for a non-specialist.

THE INTERTEXTUAL LEVEL

No text, and no part of any text, exists in total isolation from others. Even the most innovative texts and turns of phrase form part of a whole body of speaking and writing by which their originality or unoriginality is measured. We shall give the term **intertextual level** to the level of textual variables on which texts are viewed as bearing significant external relations to other texts in a given culture or cultures.

There are two main sorts of intertextual relation that particularly concern translators. The most common is that of genre membership. An instruction manual, for example, will or will not be typical of a certain sort of instruction manual in the SL culture; a play will or will not be typical of a certain sort of play, and so on. So before translating an ST, the translator must judge how typical it is of its genre. If it is utterly typical of an established SL genre, it may be necessary to produce a similarly unoriginal TT. This will be relatively straightforward in the case of, say, scientific abstracts or thrillers. It can prove tricky where there is no TL genre corresponding to that of the ST. And, whatever its genre, the more innovative the ST is, the more the translator may feel impelled to formulate a TT that is equally innovative in the TL. Alternatively, if accuracy of content is the chief priority, it may be necessary to sacrifice any stylistic originality the ST may have. This will usually be the case with scientific or technical texts. There are scientific or academic texts, however (e.g. Jacques

Lacan's writings), where style and thematic content form an indissoluble whole. In such cases, translation cannot do justice to the ST without trying to emulate its innovative nature.

A variation on genre membership is imitation, which may shade into parody. The translator must be alert to this, and also be able to produce the TL style appropriate to the genre parodied. From entertainment to satire, parody can have many purposes and effects. It is found in advertising, and is common in journalism and literary texts. Some texts imitate or parody a whole range of genres. An example is Pascal Lainé's *La Dentellière*. For important thematic reasons, this novel parodies romantic pulp fiction, property ads, the *nouveau roman* and the travel brochure. Translating a parody of a type of text that is also found in the target culture is relatively straightforward; it is trickier when the parodied style is specific to the source culture.

Parody brings us to the second category of intertextual relation, that of quotation or allusion. These are very widespread in many kinds of text. A recent article on the Yves Saint Laurent dressmaking archive was entitled 'Les robes au bois dormant' (cf. 'La belle au bois dormant'). There are several examples in Practical 6.3. In the Volvo text on p. 116, the first sentence contains an allusion to Jacques Monod's famous book on evolution, *Le Hasard et la nécessité*. Assuming the reader spots it, the allusion is doubtless intended to touch Volvo with some of Monod's stature and authority. A different effect is produced in the following example taken, with the published TT, from a recent lingerie catalogue:

ST	TT
En écru soyeux, en noir distingué et en blanc nacré, une romantique dentelle Textronic aux éclats mats et brillants sublime les modèles confortables et raffinés pour que la séduction soit à son comble... Et, pour qu'il vous prenne dans ses bras, qu'il vous parle tout bas, la ligne s'habille en... rose !	Available in silky ecru, elegant black and pearlized white, this sophisticated, easy-to-wear range features romantic Textronic lace with matt and lustrous detailing for that supremely seductive touch ... For added powers of attraction – it comes in pink!

No, it is not a parody, although it could have come straight out of *La Dentellière*. The first challenge is to spot the quotation, from Edith Piaf's 'La vie en rose': 'Quand il me prend dans ses bras, / Qu'il me parle tout bas, / Je vois la vie en rose.' The second is to decide what to do with it. Should the translator borrow the familiar TL translation of the quoted text, if there is one? In this case there is not. Even if there were, the point with this kind of text is not to capture every last nuance in a virtuoso display of compensation, but to take the essential details and wrap them in a fragrant cloud of exegetic puff. This is what the translator has done.

There is another example in Lancôme's Poême advertisement that we looked at on pp. 82–3: 'Tu es le grand soleil qui me monte à la tête.' Not only is this an alexandrine, it is also the penultimate line of one of the best love poems by one of France's best-known love poets, Paul Eluard's 'Je t'aime'. The poem ends: 'Tu es le grand soleil qui me monte à la tête / Quand je suis sûr de moi.' For readers who recognize the allusion, the connotation of self-confidence is added to the semantic complexity of the line. However, even if the translator sees the allusion, and even if there is an existing translation of the poem, the chances are that there is no single line in the TT that corresponds to the ST line, because successful poetry translation often requires wholesale compensation of all kinds.

Sometimes, however, the quotation is very familiar in the TL culture. If so, there will have to be special reasons for departing from it. Take Dante's 'Lasciate ogni speranza, voi ch'entrate', the sign over the entrance to Hell. The translator would seem to be making a special point if this appeared as e.g. 'Give up all hope, those people who are coming in' and not 'Abandon all hope, {ye/you} who enter here'. Again, however, the translator has to be sure that it really is a quotation – and to decide which version to use if there is more than one. Some English translations are literal; in others, the Italian is rearranged to make an iambic pentameter: 'Abandon hope, all ye who enter here.'

There is a good illustration of these questions in Christiane Rochefort's novel *La Porte du fond*. The first part is headed 'Vous qui entrez'. As we saw on p. 118, this construction is common in French, more so than in English. French readers thus may or may not feel that 'vous qui entrez' is from Dante; the possibility could easily not even occur to them. In an English TT, however, 'You who enter' is so marked stylistically that it would immediately come across as the Dante. What is the translator to do? Perhaps provisionally draft the heading as something like 'The people coming in' or 'Those of you who are coming in'. It soon becomes clear, however, that the novel concerns hellish events, the narrator's repeated sexual abuse by her father. Eventually, on p. 69, the narrator tells us that she once pinned a notice, in capitals, above her parents' bedroom door: 'VOUS QUI ENTREZ / PERDEZ TOUTE ESPERANCE'. And later, she quotes chilling words of her father's: 'perds l'espérance ma petite' (p. 206). For French readers who suspected that the heading may be a Dante quotation, those suspicions are now confirmed, and the text has acquired a new dimension. For those who did not, p. 69 comes as a surprise, but the text still acquires a new dimension. The translator, however, is in a more difficult position. If the heading is translated 'You who enter', it looks like Dante and probably gives the game away on the first page (it certainly will if the TT has 'Ye who enter'); the further descent into hell on p. 69 is somewhat fudged. But if the TT has 'The people coming in' or 'Those of you who are coming in', a vital cohesive element is lost. There is bound to be a loss; the translator has to decide which one is less unacceptable.

Sometimes, an ST quotation that is full of resonances for the SL reader would be completely lost on the TL reader. In such cases, the translator may either leave it out altogether, or simply translate it literally, or, if it has an important function in the ST, use some form of compensation. We saw a good example in Ponge's 'Bords de mer', on p. 45.

When ST intertextual features are wholly or mostly a matter of culture-specific allusion, translation problems can become acute. In *L'Express* of 29 June 2000 there is an article entitled 'Ivry, libertaire chéri'. The title contains an allusion to the sixth verse of *La Marseillaise*: 'Liberté, Liberté chérie, / Combats avec tes défenseurs.' This is entirely appropriate, since 15,000 *communards* are buried in Ivry cemetery, and Maurice Thorez, leader of the French Communists from 1930 till 1964, was the *député* for Ivry. Then in the second paragraph of the article we read: 'Même le lilas et la rose s'accrochent dans les jardins pentus de la rue René-Villar.' This is an allusion to Aragon's famous proto-Resistance poem, 'Les lilas et les roses'. Aragon was a leading Communist, and is perhaps the best-known of all the Resistance poets. Add to all this the fact that an iconic book of Resistance poems by Pierre Emmanuel was entitled *Combats avec tes défenseurs*, and you see that there is a whole nexus of allusions in these few phrases which are clear to many or most French readers, but would be completely lost on English-speaking readers. If the translator decided that these allusions matter (as, to some extent, they surely do), the only hope would be exegetic additions. 'Liberty is in the very blood of Ivry' might be added at the start of an appropriate paragraph. The allusion to lilacs and roses might be discreetly explained: 'There are even lilacs and roses, legendary emblems of wartime French resistance, growing in the hillside gardens of the rue René-Villar.'

There is a further problem with allusions. An allusion is normally something deliberate, but we often see allusions where none was intended. An accidental allusion may be more accurately called an echo. Whatever one calls it, when readers or listeners respond to intertextual features of this sort, they are real factors in the meaning and impact of the text. We know, for example, that Keats was not alluding to Donovan's 'They call me mellow yellow' in 'To Autumn'; but, for many modern readers, Donovan's line will be a major intertext in their response to 'mellow' when they first encounter Keats's poem. Conversely, when Donovan first sang his song, many listeners will immediately have recalled Keats. What we do *not* know is whether Keats was alluding to Thomson's 'roving mists', or to Wordsworth's 'mellow Autumn charged with bounteous fruit'; and we do not know whether his readers in 1820 responded to these and other echoes and allusions. But, for readers who do hear these possible echoes and allusions, they are part of the richness of Keats's lines.

Intertextual questions like these are a good illustration of why, in Chapter 2, we were reluctant to accept the notion of 'equivalent effect': any text will have different resonances – even different meanings – for different people and for different generations. This is truer of literary than of scientific or technical texts, but it is a crucial factor that translators cannot ignore in assessing the relevance of intertextual features. And, as ever, the translator must also be careful to avoid unintentionally *introducing* inappropriate intertextual features. Translating the sentence from the article on Ivry, a subconscious echo could easily lead the translator to write 'You can gather lilacs and roses in the hillside gardens': but an allusion to Ivor Novello is the last thing you want here.

PRACTICAL 8

8.1 Discourse issues

Assignment
(i)   For a forthcoming book on attitudes to Communism in post-1945 Europe, you are translating the article from which the following ST is taken. Discuss the strategic decisions that you have to take before starting detailed translation of this ST, and outline and justify the strategy you adopt.
(ii)   Translate the text, including the title, into English.
(iii) Explain the main decisions of detail you took.

Contextual information
The article, a hostile survey of Communist sympathy among French intellectuals, appeared in a right-wing newspaper in 1990. By this time, the Communist monopoly on power in the Soviet Union and most of the former Iron Curtain countries had been broken, and the Berlin Wall had been pulled down. The ST is the opening paragraph of the article. 'PC' is often used instead of the more correct 'PCF'.

ST

BREVE HISTOIRE DES COMPAGNONS DE DEROUTE

Imperturbable, le PC à la fin de la semaine dernière a poursuivi son parcours bizarre et ses discours irréels. Sans importance : le public n'attache guère d'intérêt à ces débats qu'il sait truqués. Seuls les media expédient encore leurs spécialistes patentés. Il faut se faire une raison : le PC ennuie.
5   Or, il s'agit d'un phénomène neuf. Pendant plus d'un demi-siècle, ceux qu'on désignait du terme de « compagnons de route », ont répercuté les thèmes, les émotions, les colères du PC. Ils ont sans complexe jeté l'anathème sur tel ou tel, condamné sans appel l'action d'un homme politique, l'œuvre d'un écrivain, etc. Ils siégeaient dans les maisons d'édition,
10   les radios, la télévision des années 60–70. Surtout, ils signaient des manifestes vibrants que la plupart des grands journaux reproduisaient avec complaisance.

Qui étaient-ils ? D'où tenaient-ils leur puissance ? Comment ont-ils pu conserver aussi longtemps une telle influence ? Comment ont-ils pu écrire
15 autant de sottises sans voir se dresser en face d'eux une barricade faite de bon sens et d'ironie ?

(*Le Figaro* 27 September 1990)

8.2 Discourse issues

Assignment
  (i) The supposition for this assignment is that you might be asked to translate for publication in the United Kingdom the work from which the ST on p. 130 is taken. Concentrating mainly on discourse and sentential issues, discuss the strategic decisions that you would have to take before starting detailed translation of this ST, and outline and justify the strategy you would adopt. (Remember to look for discourse features within sentences as well as for intersentential features.)
  (ii) In the light of your findings in (i), analyse the TT printed opposite the ST. Where you think the translation can be improved, give your own revised TT and explain your decisions.

Contextual information
The text is taken from General de Gaulle's war memoirs. It is the first part of a radio speech he broadcast to the nation four days after the Liberation of Paris in August 1944. It is thus a written transcript of an oral text, and you are translating it as part of a written text (the war memoirs). The 'vaillants combattants' (line 12) are the *Forces françaises de l'intérieur*, the combined armed units of the Resistance.

Turn to p. 130

ST

Il y a quatre jours que les Allemands qui tenaient Paris ont capitulé devant les Français. Il y a quatre jours que Paris est libéré.

Une joie immense, une puissante fierté ont déferlé sur la Nation. Bien plus, le monde entier a tressailli quand il a su que Paris émergeait de
5 l'abîme et que sa lumière allait, de nouveau, briller.

La France rend témoignage à tous ceux dont les services ont contribué à la victoire de Paris ; au peuple parisien d'abord qui, dans le secret des âmes, n'a jamais, non jamais, accepté la défaite et l'humiliation ; aux braves gens, hommes et femmes, qui ont longuement et activement mené
10 ici la résistance à l'oppresseur avant d'aider à sa déroute ; aux soldats de France qui l'ont battu et réduit sur place, guerriers venus d'Afrique après cent combats, vaillants combattants groupés à l'improviste dans les unités de l'intérieur ; par-dessus tout et par-dessus tous, à ceux et celles qui ont donné leur vie pour la Patrie sur les champs de bataille ou aux poteaux
15 d'exécution.

Mais la France rend également hommage aux braves et bonnes armées alliées et à leurs chefs dont l'offensive irrésistible a permis la libération de Paris et rend certaine celle de tout le territoire en écrasant avec nous la force allemande.
20 A mesure que reflue l'abominable marée, la Nation respire avec délices l'air de la victoire et de la liberté. Une merveilleuse unité se révèle dans ses profondeurs. La Nation sent que l'avenir lui offre désormais, non plus seulement l'espoir, mais la certitude d'être bel et bien une nation victo-rieuse, la perspective d'un ardent renouveau, la possibilité de reparaître
25 dans le monde, au rang où elle fut toujours, c'est-à-dire au rang des plus grands.

Mais la Nation sent aussi quelle distance sépare encore le point où elle en est de celui qu'elle veut et peut atteindre. Elle mesure la nécessité de faire en sorte que l'ennemi soit complètement, irrémédiablement battu et
30 que la part française dans le triomphe final soit la plus large possible. Elle mesure l'étendue des ravages qu'elle a subis dans sa terre et dans sa chair. Elle mesure les difficultés extrêmes de ravitaillement, de transports, d'armement, d'équipement, où elle se trouve, et qui contrarient l'effort de combat et l'effort de production de ses territoires libérés.

(De Gaulle 1956: 711–12)

TT

Four days ago the Germans who held Paris capitulated to the French. Four days ago Paris was liberated.

An immense joy and a powerful pride spread through the nation. More, a tremor shook the whole world when they heard that Paris was rising
5 from ruin and that her light was going to shine again.

France is grateful to all who contributed to the victory of Paris; to the people of Paris first of all who in their secret hearts never, never accepted defeat and humiliation; to the brave people, men and women, who opposed and resisted the oppressor long and actively before helping to rout him;
10 to the soldiers of France who beat and defeated him here, warriors from Africa with a hundred battles behind them or warriors organized on the spur of the moment into units of the French Forces of the Interior; and, above all, to those who gave their lives for their country on the battle-field or who were executed.

15 France equally pays homage to the good and courageous Allied armies and their leaders whose irresistible offensive made the liberation of Paris possible: and which make the liberation of all the territory and the crushing of German strength a certainty.

As the abominable tide recedes, the nation sniffs the air of victory and
20 freedom with delight. A marvellous unity is visible. The nation feels that the future offers, not merely the hope but the certainty of being, at last, a victorious nation; the prospect of an ardent regeneration and gives France the chance of reappearing in the world in her old place, that is to say amongst the greatest.

25 But the nation also knows that a great distance still separates it from the point it is at and the point which it wants to, and can, reach. It appreciates the necessity of seeing that the enemy is completely and irremediably beaten and that the French role in the final triumph should be as great as possible. It knows what ravages it has suffered both materially and in
30 human terms. It appreciates the extreme difficulty of feeding the population, arranging transport, arms and equipment; difficulties which hamper the war effort and the productivity of the liberated territory.

(De Gaulle 1959: 412–13)

9

Literal meaning and translation issues

Having reviewed translation issues typically encountered on the six levels of textual variables, we now return to the grammatical level. In this chapter, we are going to look in more detail at major features of translation loss threatened by literal meaning.

Translation is concerned with meaning. However, the term 'meaning' is elastic and indeterminate, especially when applied to a whole text. This is true even of literal (or 'cognitive' or 'denotative') meanings – that is, those that are fully supported by ordinary semantic conventions, such as the convention that 'door' refers to a panel that closes an entrance in a building or a vehicle. In the case of words, it is this literal meaning that is given in dictionary definitions. Yet even the dictionary definition of a word has its problems. This is because it imposes a rigidity of meaning that words often do not show in context. In any case, many words have more than one literal meaning, and the situation and/or context in which the word occurs will rule out one meaning or another. So if someone introduces a 25-year-old woman as 'ma belle-mère', you will assume they mean 'my stepmother', not 'my mother-in-law'.

Sometimes, utterances made up of expressions with apparently identical literal meanings can have different meanings. Compare 'She's not in the same league as Germaine Greer' and 'She's in a different league from Germaine Greer'. The component parts of each utterance have identical literal meanings: she = she; in = in; not the same as = different from; league = league. Yet the sentences generally have opposite meanings:

she's not in the same league as = she's not as good as
she's in a different league from = she's better than

The implication is that a good dictionary should include both expressions as discrete items, having different literal meanings. But if a dictionary listed all such nuances, it would run into several volumes. In any case, dictionaries very often differ from one another in defining literal meanings, especially of words denoting abstractions. As an example for class discussion, here are the *Collins* and the *Shorter Oxford* definitions of 'anticlimax':

Collins
1 a disappointing or ineffective conclusion to a series of events, etc. **2** a sudden change from a serious subject to one that is disappointing or ludicrous. **3** *Rhetoric.* a descent in discourse from the significant or important to the trivial, inconsequential, etc.

Shorter Oxford
a trivial conclusion to something significant or impressive, esp. where a climax was expected.

We shall return to these definitions, in discussing possible translations of 'anticlimax'.

Given the influence of situation and context, and the differences between dictionaries, it is hard to pin down the precise literal meanings in any text of any complexity. The more literary the text, the more this is so; but it is true even of informative texts. These are crucial factors on the grammatical level. What we want to do now is raise awareness of the translation implications of these factors. We shall do this in terms of three degrees of semantic equivalence – that is, how close given expressions are to having identical literal meanings. Some expressions will be examined out of context, because this is how most literal meanings are defined in dictionaries. The very uncertainty inherent in this will show how important context and situation are to understanding and translating any individual expression.

SYNONYMY

Literal meaning is a matter of categories into which a language divides the totality of experience. Thus, the literal meaning of the word 'pencil' consists in the fact that all over the world there are similar objects that are included in the category of 'pencil' – and all sorts of other objects that are excluded from it. To define a literal meaning is to specify the range covered by a word or phrase in such a way that it is clear what items are included in that range or category and what items are excluded. It is helpful to represent semantic equivalence visually. We shall use circles to give a rough depiction of semantic equivalence. So, for instance, the expressions 'my mother's father' and 'my maternal grandfather' can be represented as two separate circles. The two ranges of literal meaning, however, coincide perfectly: that is, in every specific instance, 'my mother's father' and 'my maternal grandfather' include and exclude exactly the same referents. This can be visualized as drawing two circles of exactly the same size, sliding them on top of each other and seeing that they cover one another exactly, as in the figure below:

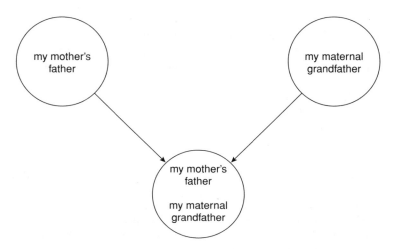

This exemplifies the strongest form of semantic equivalence, full **synonymy**: the two expressions are **synonyms** of one another, having exactly the same range of literal meaning.

For practical purposes, we shall take it that comparisons of literal meaning can also be made between different languages. For example, in most contexts 'mother' and 'mère' cover exactly the same range, and are therefore fully synonymous, as in this figure:

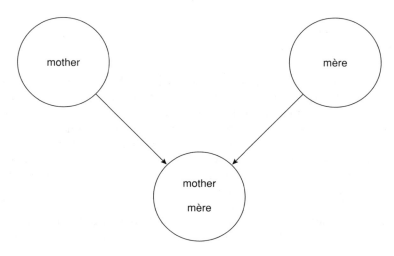

In terms exclusively of literal meaning, synonymy rarely if ever causes translation problems. Things are not so simple when it comes to connotations, as we shall see in Chapter 10. And of course, in literary contexts especially, phonic or prosodic factors can also sometimes make using a TL synonym problematic.

HYPERONYMY–HYPONYMY

Connotations etc. aside, the unfortunate fact is that even the nearest semantic equivalent for translating the literal meaning of an ST expression usually falls short of being a full TL synonym. To return to an earlier example, depending on situation or context, 'belle-mère' has to be translated either as 'mother-in-law' or as 'stepmother'. The French expression is wider and more general than either of the English ones. This can be shown as:

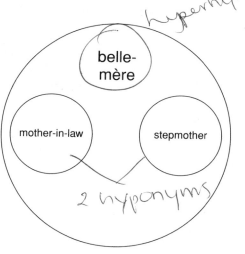

The relationship between 'belle-mère' and each of the English expressions is known as **hyperonymy–hyponymy**. An expression with a wider, more general, range of literal meaning is a **hyperonym** (or 'superordinate') of one with a narrower and less general literal meaning. Conversely, the narrower one is a **hyponym** of the wider one. So 'belle-mère' is a hyperonym of 'mother-in-law' and 'stepmother', and they are both hyponyms of the French expression. (The key to the difference between the terms lies in the prefixes: *hyper-* = over, as in 'hyperactive'; *hypo-* = under, as in 'hypodermic').

If, as is most often the case, no full TL synonym for a given ST expression can be found, the translator has to look for an acceptable TL hyperonym or hyponym. In fact, translators do this automatically, in response (ideally) to context. Thus 'mother-in-law' *must* be translated as 'belle-mère', a hyperonym. Conversely, translating from French into English, 'belle-mère' necessarily translates as *either* 'mother-in-law' *or* 'stepmother'. Each of the English expressions is narrower in literal meaning, and is therefore an example of translating an SL hyperonym with a TL hyponym.

For a spectacular example of hyperonymy–hyponymy, see p. 100, where there are at least thirteen French hyponyms of 'he was injured'.

GENERALIZING TRANSLATION AND PARTICULARIZING TRANSLATION

Translating by a hyperonym results in a TT expression with a wider literal meaning than the ST expression. TT 'ma belle-mère' is more general than ST 'my stepmother', omitting particulars given by the ST (viz, that she is married to my father but is not my mother). We shall call this **generalizing translation, or generalization** for short.

Translating by a hyponym results in a TT expression with a narrower literal meaning than the ST expression. TT 'my mother-in-law' gives particulars not present in ST 'ma belle-mère' (viz, I am married to a son or daughter of hers). We shall call this **particularizing translation, or particularization** for short.

Generalization and particularization both entail a degree of translation loss on the grammatical level: detail is added to, or omitted from, the ST message. Where convenient, we shall refer to this mode of translation loss as lexical loss. Lexical loss often does not matter very much. Translating by a hyperonym or a hyponym is entirely unremarkable, unless it is unnecessary, inappropriate or misleading.

A generalizing translation is acceptable if there is no suitable TL alternative and if the omitted detail is either unimportant or is implied in the TT context. For example, to denote the panel that closes an entrance, French distinguishes between 'porte' (e.g. in a building) and 'portière' (e.g. in a car or train); these can only be translated into English with the hyperonym 'door', but this lexical loss is virtually never going to matter. Similarly, English distinguishes between 'moths' and 'butterflies', but these can only translated into French as 'papillons'. Normally, the context will make it clear which is referred to. If not, then a particularization may be needed (e.g. 'moths' > 'phalènes', if these fit the context), or some form of compensation (e.g. an exegetic reference to the rapid wingbeats of the moth).

A particularizing translation is acceptable if there is no suitable TL alternative and if the added detail does not clash with the overall context of ST or TT. Thus 'on fait une promenade ?' has to be translated in one of many ways: '{are we going/shall we go/does anyone go/is someone going/are they going} for a {walk/ride/drive/sail}?', etc. It is impossible not to particularize 'on fait' and 'promenade'. Luckily, the situation or context will usually make it clear which hyponym to use. Likewise, translating Molière's title '*L'Ecole des femmes*' as '*The School for Wives*' rather than '*The School for Women*' accords better with the content of the play. And there will have been no hesitation over translating 'étude' as 'design' rather than 'study' in the following sentence from a text on electronic equipment:

ST

Le CNES a confié à ESD l'étude et la réalisation des sous-ensembles détection et datation chargés de mesurer le temps d'arrivée au satellite de signaux laser provenant de plusieurs stations.

(Dassault 1987a: 57)

TT

The French CNES has placed an order with ESD for the design and manufacture of the detection and datation [*sic*] subassemblies for measuring the times of arrival at the satellite of laser signals from several stations.

(Dassault 1987b: 57)

A generalizing or particularizing translation will only be *un*acceptable if the TL does offer a suitable alternative, or if omitting or adding the detail creates a clash with the overall context of ST or TT. For instance, in the Dassault TT, the phrase 'times of arrival' denotes the times *at which* the signals arrive – a back-translation would inescapably give 'heure(s) d'arrivée'. In this context, 'time' is thus a hyperonym of 'temps' and 'heure'. This is a good example of the role of context in governing literal meaning: if the TT had e.g. 'transit time', the irrelevant idea of 'what time they arrive' would never occur to the reader. (In a different context, 'heure' could itself be a hyperonym of 'hour' and 'time'.) As it is, 'time' is an unnecessary and misleading generalizing translation.

Similarly, even racy French narratives of battle often use 'fusant' or 'percutant' instead of the hyperonym 'obus'. In most narrative contexts, the generalization 'shell' would certainly be sufficient – specifying 'time-shell' or 'percussion-fuse shell' would be needlessly ponderous. But in translating a bomb-disposal manual, a generalizing translation of 'fusant' as 'shell' would be unacceptable, incurring potentially lethal translation loss.

As for the dangers lurking in particularization, here is an example from the opening paragraph of Victor Serge's *L'affaire Toulaév* and the published TT. The relevant words are highlighted in bold type. (*Contextual information.* The novel is a study of, among other things, the poverty and drabness of existence in the Soviet Union of 1939.)

ST
Kostia méditait depuis plusieurs
semaines l'achat d'une paire de
chaussures quand une subite
fantaisie dont il s'étonna lui-même
5 brouilla tous ses calculs. En se
privant de cigarettes, de cinéma
et, un jour sur deux, du repas de
midi, il économiserait dans les six
semaines les cent quarante roubles
10 nécessaires à l'acquisition d'assez
bonnes **bottines** que l'aimable
vendeuse d'un magasin d'articles
d'occasion promettait de lui
réserver « en douce ». [*Three
15 weeks later*] Kostia alla voir, pour
le plaisir, ses futures **chaussures**,
mi-cachées dans l'obscurité d'un
rayon, derrière de vieux samovars
en cuivre, un amoncellement
20 d'étuis à jumelles, une théière
chinoise, une boîte de coquillages
sur laquelle se détachait en bleu
céleste le golfe de Naples... Des
bottes royales, en cuir souple,
25 tenaient le premier plan du rayon :
quatre cents roubles, dites ! Des
hommes en paletots fatigués s'en
pourléchaient les babines.
– Soyez tranquille, dit la petite
30 vendeuse à Kostia, vos **bottines**
sont là, ne craignez rien...
(Serge 1967: 659)

TT
For several weeks Kostia had
been thinking about buying a pair
of **shoes**. But then a sudden
impulse, which surprised even
himself, upset all his calculations.
By going without cigarettes, films,
and lunch every other day, he
would need six weeks to save up
the one hundred and forty roubles
which was the price of a fairly
good pair of **shoes** that the
salesgirl in a second-hand shop
had kindly promised to set aside
for him 'on the q.t.' [. . .] he gave
himself the pleasure of going to
see the **shoes** that would one day
be his. He found them half hidden
on a dark shelf, behind several old
copper samovars, a pile of opera-
glass cases, a Chinese teapot, and
a shell box with a sky-blue Bay
of Naples. A magnificent pair of
boots, of the softest leather, had
the place of honour on the shelf –
four hundred roubles, imagine!
Men in threadbare overcoats
licked their lips over them. 'Don't
worry,' the little salesgirl said to
him. 'Your **boots** are still here,
don't worry . . .'
(Serge 1968: 9)

'Chaussures' is a hyperonym embracing many types of footwear, from
sandals to shoes and boots. It is commonly used in situations where an
English-speaker would refer specifically to 'shoes', 'sandals', etc. The
closest TL semantic equivalent to 'une paire de chaussures' would be
something like 'some footwear'. But 'footwear' is used much less often
in English than 'chaussures' is in French. 'Shoes' excludes boots, sandals,
etc., so it is a hyponym of 'chaussures', a particularization that in most
contexts – as here – is natural and acceptable.

'Bottines' is likewise a hyponym of 'chaussures'. This is men's footwear,
so 'bootees' will not do, and 'ankle-boots' are usually worn by women.
In this case, 'shoes' is a *generalizing* translation of 'bottines', inasmuch

as 'shoe' is often loosely used to denote any outdoor footwear that is not as heavy as a boot, or comes less far up the leg. But as long as the specific nature of Kostia's footwear is not significant in the text, the lexical loss is unimportant.

Rendering the second instance of 'chaussures' (in 'futures chaussures') as 'shoes' is acceptable, and consistent with the TT so far. So is rendering 'bottes' – yet another hyponym of 'chaussures' – as 'boots'. But 'bottes' sets a trap for the translator. What is the function of these boots in the ST context? They are described as 'royales' – 'fit for a king'. So, like the Chinese teapot and the picture of the Bay of Naples, they are redolent of an opulent, splendid, exotic pre-1917 world that Kostia and the others can only dream of. At 400 roubles, their price is astronomical – even saving 140 roubles for his 'bottines' is going to take Kostia six weeks of deprivation. Translating 'bottes *royales*' in this context simply as '*magnificent boots*' therefore loses some of the ST impact, but there is skilful compensation in 'of the softest leather' (instead of e.g. the more prosaic 'a magnificent pair of soft leather boots') and 'the place of honour'. So far, then, the TT hyponyms and hyperonym are consistent with the ST and with one another, and incur fairly insignificant lexical translation loss.

Then disaster strikes. When the shopgirl says 'vos bottines sont là', it is clear to the ST reader that she is referring to the ones she has set aside for Kostia. But in the TT she says 'Your boots are still here'. 'Boots' is a particularization of 'chaussures', but a generalization of 'bottines'. Inescapably, 'boots' looks as if it refers to the magnificent boots, partly because of its position immediately after the two sentences concerning them, and partly because the footwear Kostia is saving for has previously only been referred to as 'shoes'. Baffled, the TT reader wonders: have I missed something? Better go back and read the paragraph again . . .

This is a good example of the need to make sure that the choice of hyperonyms and hyponyms does not clash with the overall ST or TT context. *In itself*, generalizing or particularizing translation is unremarkable, in fact almost inevitable. But it is vital to look beyond individual words and sentences towards the text as a whole, so as to avoid this kind of needless obscurity or contradiction. It is not a case of avoiding a generalization or a particularization, but of picking the right one. As it happens, in 'opera-glass', the Serge TT contains just such an instance, where the choice of hyponym is determined by the context, accords perfectly with it, and helps to compensate for lexical translation loss a line or two later. We will return to this example in the next chapter, as an illustration of connotative meaning.

PARTIALLY OVERLAPPING TRANSLATION

There is a third degree of semantic equivalence. We can illustrate it from the italicized phrase in the following sentence: 'Il y a *un étudiant de ma belle-mère* qui arrive demain.' As we have seen, 'belle-mère' can only be translated with a particularizing translation, 'mother-in-law' or 'step-mother' – English is obliged to specify detail where French is not. Conversely, the only plausible translation of 'étudiant' (masc.) is 'student'; this is a generalization, omitting the specific detail of the student's gender and the fact that he is a tertiary level student. And translating French 'étudiante' (fem.) as 'student' would be a generalization for the same reasons. In these two cases, French is obliged to specify detail where English is not.

However 'un étudiant de ma belle-mère' is translated, the TT combines particularization and generalization. This can be visualized as two partially overlapping circles as shown in the figure:

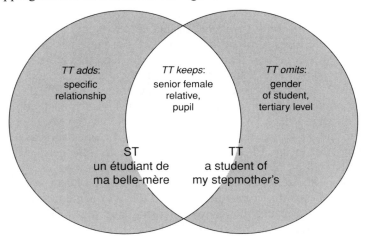

The unshaded area, where the circles overlap, represents the material the ST and TT have in common. The shaded areas represent what is added and what is omitted in the TT. This is another category of degree in the translation of literal meaning. We shall call it **partially overlapping translation**, or **partial overlap** for short. Partial overlap is almost unavoidable in whole sentences, and usual in phrases. It is common even in single words. Sometimes this is because of differences in grammatical structure between SL and TL; sometimes it is because of purely semantic differences, the TL having no synonym, hyperonym or hyponym for the SL word.

Look again at the example on p. 99: 'Etudiante, je l'adorais' > 'As a student, I loved it'. The TT certainly *keeps* the core notion of 'me a student'. But 'student' unavoidably generalizes, *omitting* the ST reference to gender. Yet, at the same time, it is practically obligatory to particularize here, *adding* detail not explicit in the literal meaning of 'étudiante' – '{when I was/because I was/in my capacity as} a student', etc. So any plausible translation of 'étudiante' in this sentence is bound to be a partial overlap, a combination of generalization and particularization.

This partial overlap (a semantic phenomenon) results entirely from non-lexical differences in grammatical structure between French and English.

For an example in which the only issue is lexis, take the *Oxford-Hachette* dictionary's suggestion (in the English–French section) of 'déception' as a translation of 'anticlimax'. Significantly, under 'déception' in the French–English section, the same dictionary does not give 'anticlimax', but only 'disappointment'. The fact is that there is no single French word which covers exactly the same semantic range as 'anticlimax'. The asymmetry between the two halves of the bilingual dictionary signals the likelihood of partially overlapping translation. And indeed, in terms of literal meaning, 'anticlimax' arguably does not denote 'disappointment' so much as 'sudden outcome falling short of what was anticipated'. The *Shorter Oxford* definition of 'anticlimax' thus seems closer to actual usage than the Collins (see above, p. 133). An anticlimax may be frustrating, trivial or comic, but it is always incongruous. That is, a turn of events is relatively *objectively judged* to fall short of what was expected. 'Déception' is different, in that a turn of events is relatively *subjectively reacted to* as falling short of what was desired or hoped for. So whereas 'anticlimax' implies expectation and rational assessment, 'déception' implies hope and emotional response.

Translating 'anticlimax' as 'déception' thus seems to be at best a case of partial overlap: the TT *keeps* the core element of 'turn of events falls short of what was expected', but it *adds* a nuance of 'relatively emotional reaction to the event as regrettable', and *omits* the nuance of 'relatively unemotional assessment of the event as incongruous'.

A partial overlap will be acceptable or unacceptable for the same reasons as apply to particularizing and generalizing translation. What is added must not clash with the ST or TT context; what is omitted must be either insignificant or recoverable from the TT context, if necessary through some form of compensation.

OF CONTEXTS AND DICTIONARIES

One reason we spent time over 'chaussures' and 'anticlimax' was to make students aware of the potential translation pitfalls even in something as seemingly straightforward as literal meaning. Another was to encourage an attitude of constructive suspicion towards all dictionaries, monolingual as well as bilingual. Dictionaries are indispensable, but if the translator is not prepared to pause and think about the literal meanings and translations given in them, or about how the context influences the meanings, needless mistakes are going to be made. Our analyses are intended to equip students to find the best translation for an expression, not the right label for it.

This priority can be confirmed by actually taking a bit more time to show the very difficulty of finding the right label. Take the earlier example of 'he was injured' (p. 100). Any French translation of this phrase is bound to be a particularization, because of the difference in tense-system between English and French. But what about the verb 'injure' itself? Is it synonymous with e.g. 'wound' or 'hurt', or are there nuances of literal meaning between these words? And is any of them synonymous with 'blesser'? If not, then 'blesser' is a hyperonym of 'injure', 'wound' and 'hurt'. In that case, while 'il a été', etc. are certainly particularizations, 'blessé' is a generalization, so that the phrase as a whole is a partially overlapping translation of 'he was injured'. And of course matters are complicated still further by the possibility of using a quasi-passive construction with 'se faire' – see the discussion of this on pp. 100–1.

But does finding the right labels for these nuances matter? Not in itself, no. These analyses are a means, not an end. Doing them helps to develop the ability to work out as nearly as possible, and pretty quickly, what the ST and the draft TT are saying. It does this partly by exposing the limitations of dictionaries. As we saw on p. 133, monolingual dictionaries often disagree among themselves over literal meanings. If you look up 'anticlimax' in the *Collins* and the *Shorter Oxford*, you find *significantly* different definitions. There is thus normally an element of subjectivity in defining the literal meaning of an abstract term – and often even concrete ones. As it happens, there is little variation between monolingual French dictionaries in definitions of 'déception', but this is an exception rather than the rule. Bilingual dictionaries, too, often suggest very different translations for given words or phrases. Thus, unlike the *Oxford-Hachette*, neither the *Harrap* nor the *Collins-Robert* gives 'déception' for 'anticlimax', but a number of suggestions which – depending on how you define 'anticlimax' in the first place – are either particularizations or partial overlaps. In the light of this uncertainty, it is vital to remember that, except in the case of highly specific technical terms, *no dictionary can cover all the possibilities for translating a given expression*. What all this means in practice is that translators often need to check meanings in more than one source, and with friends and colleagues – but also that the final decision is their own responsibility.

The reason why dictionaries disagree over literal meanings and do not cover all possible translations for a given expression is that literal meaning is ultimately conditioned by the context in which the expression occurs. Even where the possibilities are limited, it is the context that determines, say, which particularization is best. So for instance 'un soldat blessé' is 'a wounded soldier', but 'un passager blessé' (in a road accident) is 'injured' or 'hurt', as is a footballer. But if the soldier is 'blessé' in a regimental football match, then of course he is 'injured' or 'hurt'. Or take this phrase from a newspaper headline about the severe flooding in the Somme in 2001: 'les sinistrés de la Somme'. The noun 'sinistré' specifically denotes the victim of a natural disaster. (It is a hyponym of 'victime'.)

But the apparent synonym 'disaster victim' (as given in the bilingual dictionaries) does not sound right here, perhaps because 'Somme disaster victims' could as well denote the victims of a rail crash or an explosion in a coal mine. 'Somme natural disaster victims' is unidiomatic. More idiomatic in an English headline would be a particularization: 'Somme flood victims'. A different context would imply a different particularization – 'Corrèze landslide victims', 'Japanese earthquake victims', etc.

To sum up. On the grammatical level, literal meaning is obviously of fundamental importance in translation. Yet context and subjectivity tinge even this most basic of givens with uncertainty. Thinking about the literal meaning of a given expression forces the translator to become aware as precisely as possible of what is being said. And of *where* it is being said: there are many reasons – e.g. the need for grammatical transposition or compensation or a particular style in the TT – why literal meaning might be conveyed through different parts of speech and in different places from those of the ST. Ironically, then, analysing the literal meaning of individual words and expressions obliges the translator to consider the text as a whole, which is an essential prerequisite for effective reading of any kind, including translation. Sometimes, the resulting TT will be so free that there is only an overall general correspondence in message content between it and the ST, precise details of literal meaning being either lost or drastically redistributed throughout the TT. There is a good example in TT (ii) in Practical 6.1: look again at this, and discuss it in class, focusing on the most striking instances of generalization, particularization and partial overlap, and on whether – and why – any ST literal meanings have been lost altogether.

PRACTICAL 9

9.1 Literal meaning and translation

Assignment
(i)   Taking all or part of the following ST (your tutor will say which), make a detailed analysis of examples of synonymous, generalizing, particularizing and partially overlapping translation in the TT.
(ii) Where possible, give a revised TT that is a better translation, and explain your decisions.

Contextual information
This is the beginning of *La Force de l'âge*, Simone de Beauvoir's autobiography. The first volume covered her childhood, adolescence and undergraduate career. The second begins with her renting a flat from her grandmother. The translation was first published in 1962.

ST

Ce qui me grisa lorsque je rentrai à Paris, en septembre 1929, ce fut d'abord ma liberté. J'y avais rêvé dès l'enfance, quand je jouais avec ma sœur à « la grande jeune fille ». Etudiante, j'ai dit avec quelle passion je l'appelai. Soudain, je l'avais ; à chacun de mes gestes je m'émerveillais
5 de ma légèreté. Le matin, dès que j'ouvrais les yeux, je m'ébrouais, je jubilais. Aux environs de mes douze ans, j'avais souffert de ne pas posséder à la maison un coin à moi. Lisant dans *Mon journal* l'histoire d'une collégienne anglaise, j'avais contemplé avec nostalgie le chromo qui représentait sa chambre : un pupitre, un divan, des rayons couverts de
10 livres ; entre ces murs aux couleurs vives, elle travaillait, lisait, buvait du thé, sans témoin : comme je l'enviai ! J'avais entrevu pour la première fois une existence plus favorisée que la mienne. Voilà qu'enfin moi aussi j'étais chez moi ! Ma grand-mère avait débarrassé son salon de tous ses fauteuils, guéridons, bibelots.

(S. de Beauvoir, *La Force de l'age,*
© Editions GALLIMARD, 1960: 16)

TT

The most intoxicating aspect of my return to Paris in September 1929 was the freedom I now possessed. I had dreamed of it since childhood, when I played with my sister at being a 'grown-up' girl. I have recorded elsewhere my passionate longing for it as a student. Now, suddenly, it
5   was mine. I was astonished to find an effortless buoyancy in all my movements. From the moment I opened my eyes every morning I was lost in a transport of delight. When I was about twelve I had suffered through not having a private retreat of my own at home. Leafing through *Mon Journal* I had found a story about an English schoolgirl, and gazed envi-
10   ously at the coloured illustration portraying her room. There was a desk, and a divan, and shelves filled with books. Here, within these gaily painted walls, she read and worked and drank tea, with no one watching her – how envious I felt! For the first time ever I had glimpsed a more fortunate way of life than my own. And now, at long last, I too had a room
15   to myself. My grandmother had stripped her drawing room of all its armchairs, occasional tables and knick-knacks.

(Beauvoir 1965: 11)

9.2   Literal meaning and translation

Assignment
  (i)   You are translating for publication in the English-speaking world the publication from which the following ST is taken. Discuss the strategic decisions that you have to take before starting detailed translation of this ST, and outline and justify the strategy you adopt.
 (ii)   Translate the text into English.
(iii)   Discuss the main decisions of detail you took, concentrating on cases of synonymous, generalizing, particularizing and partially overlapping translation.
 (iv)   Compare your TT with the published translation, which will be given to you by your tutor.

Contextual information

The text is from a publicity brochure outlining the activities, achievements and policies of the electronics firm Electronique Serge Dassault (ESD). It is taken from the section on the firm's 'Espace' division. CNES = Centre national d'études spatiales; ARGOS = Advanced Research and Global Observation Satellite; LASSO = Laser Synchronization from Stationary Orbit.

ST

ARGOS

Dans le cadre du programme franco-américain ARGOS, ESD a conçu et produit, à la demande du CNES, un système de localisation et de collecte de données relatives à l'environnement (météorologie, océanographie, vulcanologie, hydrologie, pollution, etc.). Ce système comporte des équipements embarqués sur satellite, des stations d'orbitographie et des balises pour utilisateurs.

Depuis sa mise en place, en 1978, le système ARGOS a totalisé plus de 150 000 heures de fonctionnement sans défaillance, démontrant la fiabilité des matériels embarqués.

LASSO

ESD participe au programme LASSO de l'Agence Spatiale Européenne : il est destiné à permettre la synchronisation des horloges atomiques distantes de plusieurs milliers de kilomètres et équipées de stations laser.

(Dassault 1987a: 57)

10

Connotative meaning and translation issues

Literal meaning is only one aspect of verbal meaning. The meaning of a text comprises a number of different layers: referential content, emotional colouring, cultural, social and personal associations, and so on. Features that are significant on the intertextual level nearly always illustrate this fact, because they import apparently extraneous associations into the text. This many-layered nature of meaning is a crucial lexical translation issue.

Whether within a single language or as between two languages, synonyms are usually different in their overall semantic effects – compare 'viper' and 'adder', 'peewit' and 'lapwing', 'nymphéa' and 'lune d'eau', 'perce-neige' and 'snowdrop', 'gooseberry' and 'groseille à maquereau', etc. Each of these has overtones which differentiate it from its synonym. We shall call such overtones **connotative meanings** (or **connotations**) – that is, associations which, over and above the literal meaning of an expression, form part of its overall meaning. Still more than literal meanings, connotative meanings are reminders that extra-textual factors – part of the *situation* in which the text is produced and read or heard – are crucial to the existence and communicative power of texts.

Connotative meanings are many and varied, and it is common for a single piece of text, or even a single expression, to combine more than one kind into a single overall effect. However, it is useful at this learning stage to distinguish six major types of connotative meaning (some of them adapted from Leech 1974: 26). Learning to identify these sharpens awareness of the presence and significance of connotations both in STs and in TTs. Note that, by definition, we are only concerned here with socially widespread connotations, not personal ones. Translators do not normally let personal connotations influence a TT if they can help it.

ALLUSIVE MEANING

An **allusive meaning** occurs when an expression evokes a saying or quotation in such a way that the meaning of the saying or quotation becomes part of the overall meaning of the expression. An obvious example of allusive meaning is the allusion to Aragon's proto-Resistance poem 'Les lilas et les roses' in the Ivry text on p. 127. In this case, the allusive meaning is the general one of 'Communist's love of France and determination to resist oppression'. Like most allusive meanings, this one is culture-specific. As we suggested on p. 127, it can probably only be rendered with some kind of exegetic compensation. This is generally the case with culture-specific allusive meanings. Take the title of Morvan Lebesque's polemical book defending Breton identity against French centralism, *Comment peut-on être Breton ?* The French reader immediately picks up the allusion to Letter XXX of Montesquieu's *Lettres persanes*, in which a Persian living in Paris is writing about a social gathering he has been to:

> Mais si quelqu'un, par hasard, apprenait à la compagnie que j'étais Persan, j'entendais aussitôt autour de moi un bourdonnement : Ah ! ah ! Monsieur est Persan ? C'est une chose bien extraordinaire ! Comment peut-on être Persan ?
>
> (Montesquieu 1960: 69).

'Comment peut-on être Persan ?' has acquired proverbial status as the expression of patronizing, uncomprehending insularity, and this is the allusive meaning in Lebesque's title. Perhaps a combination of tone and affective meaning (see below) would compensate for the absence of a suitable English allusion – something like '*Breton? Gosh, What's That?*' or '*Breton? How Quaint!*'

Another book title using allusive meaning is Julien Green's *Mille chemins ouverts*, his memoir of the Great War. The allusion is to Act 1 Scene 2 of Racine's *Phèdre*, in which Œnone, the loyal, misguided servant, says to her mistress: 'Mon âme chez les morts descendra la première. / Mille chemins ouverts y conduisent toujours.' The allusive meaning is 'how easy it is to die', an appropriate way of referring to the trenches of the First World War. It is tempting to translate with something like '*Roads to Hell*'. The danger here is that of *unwanted* allusions, in this case the proverb 'The road to hell is paved with good intentions' (cf. 'L'enfer est pavé de bonnes intentions'), which would place intentions, rather than hell, at the centre of the allusion. If this is unsuitable, a quite different title will have to be found; this is actually common with book titles, which are often built round intertextual allusions.

We saw a good example of using compensation to translate allusive meaning on p. 45. We quote it again here, because it also illustrates another type of connotative meaning:

| [La mer] ne sort jamais de ses bornes qu'un peu, met *elle-même* un frein à la fureur de ses flots. (Ponge 1965: 66; Ponge's italics) | [The sea] never oversteps its bounds by much, and needs no God to help it bridle its wild waves. |

The allusion to the Almighty (cf. *Athalie*: 'Celui qui met un frein à la fureur des flots / Sait aussi des méchants arrêter les complots') is clear to the French reader. It is lost if '*elle-même*' is translated as 'itself'. Hence the explicit reference to God. In this case, the change also accords with the other connotative meaning in the ST, the hostile attitude to religion. We shall look at this in the next section.

ATTITUDINAL MEANING

Attitudinal meaning is that part of the overall meaning of an expression which consists of some widespread *attitude to the referent*. The expression does not merely denote the referent in a neutral way, but also hints at some attitude to it. For instance, in appropriate contexts, 'the police', 'the filth' and 'the Old Bill' are synonyms in terms of referential content, but they have different overall meanings. These attitudes are not part of the literal meaning of the expressions, but it is impossible to ignore them in responding to the expressions. It is therefore important not to overlook them when translating. Translating 'la flicaille' as 'the police' accurately renders the literal meaning of the ST, but fails to render the hostile attitude connoted by 'la flicaille' ('the filth', 'the pigs'). Conversely, the translator must be careful not to introduce significant connotations that are absent from the ST and clash with the TT context, as in translating 'le curé' as 'the sky-pilot'.

There is a common variety of attitudinal meaning that is well illustrated by the example from Ponge's 'Bords de mer'. Here, the hostile attitude is not to the sea, but to religion – not to the referent of '*elle-même*' ('la mer'), but to the referent of the *connotation*, viz, the religious mindset which claims that it is God that tames the wild waves. This is a good example of how a single expression may combine more than one type of connotative meaning: Ponge's allusive meaning contains within itself an attitudinal meaning.

ASSOCIATIVE MEANING

Attitudinal meaning often also occurs with associative meaning, although the two are analytically distinct. **Associative meaning** is that part of the overall meaning of an expression which consists of expectations that are

– rightly or wrongly – widely *associated with the referent* of the expression. Although 'Ivry' is a proper name, we can say for translation purposes that it has an associative meaning of 'Maurice Thorez and Communism'. A good example of a common noun with an almost universal associative meaning is 'nurse'. Most people automatically associate 'nurse' with 'woman'. This unconscious association is so widespread that the term 'male nurse' has had to be coined to counteract its effect: 'he is a nurse' sounds odd, even today. A related French example is 'maïeuticien', a male midwife. Presumably this word was coined because 'sage-homme' would have clashed strongly and comically with the literal and associative meanings of the 'femme' component in 'sage-femme'.

'Nurse' is another example of an expression that combines two types of connotation. As well as the associative meaning of 'woman', it has a widespread *attitudinal* meaning of 'trust', 'gratitude' and 'affection' – feelings which most people have for these generally gentle, caring people. Similarly, given its hostile attitudinal meaning, 'la flicaille' is also certain to have an associative meaning of something like 'brutality' or 'racism', depending on context.

For a good example of translation problems raised by associative meaning, we can turn back to the extract from Serge's *L'Affaire Toulaév* on p. 138: 'Des bottes royales, en cuir souple, tenaient le premier plan du rayon.' The literal meaning of 'royales' here is 'princely' or 'fit for a king', and that of 'tenaient le premier plan du rayon' is 'occupied the front of the shelf'. In the context of a poverty-stricken post-Revolution republic, the 'royales' acquires the associative meaning of 'aristocratic luxury from a bygone age': the boots are such as might have been worn by a strutting tsar. This connotation in turn confers one on 'tenaient le premier plan', which acquires the associative meaning of 'lording it in the forefront of attention'.

This is actually a clear illustration of the complexity of lexical effects: the impact of 'tenaient le premier plan' is not just a matter of associative meaning, but partly also of *literal* meaning. Connotative meaning cannot exist without literal meaning. In this example, there are two hyponyms of 'premier plan' that are relevant to the context: 'foreground' and 'first rank'. The reason that 'royales' triggers such a strong associative meaning of 'lording it' is that these literal meanings of 'premier plan', especially 'first rank', lend themselves to this connotation. If 'premier plan' did *not* have these literal meanings, then 'royales' would trigger a less aristocratic associative meaning, such as 'flaunting themselves'. And there is even more to it than that: the associative meaning of 'tenaient le premier plan' is probably also partly triggered by an echo of the expression 'tenir le haut du pavé'. We shall return to this shortly, in discussing collocative meaning.

This kind of semantic complexity can usually only be conveyed by compensation. We saw on p. 139 how the published TT of *L'Affaire Toulaév* does just this. Now we are in a position to see more clearly how the compensation works. An appropriate choice of hyponym (a matter of *literal* meaning) in the nearby context contributes to restoring the ST's *connotative* force. 'Jumelles' is a hyperonym of 'binoculars' and 'opera glasses'. The associative meaning of 'binoculars' is perhaps 'the military' (or 'birdwatching'), whereas that of 'opera glasses' is 'high-society theatre-going', which helps to convey the connotation of aristocrats flaunting their wealth. Both the ST and the TT thus clearly show how literal meaning and connotative meaning can be distinguished for analysis, but actually work together in producing the overall semantic impact.

COLLOCATIVE MEANING

Collocative meaning is given to an expression over and above its literal meaning by *the meaning of some other expression with which it collocates to form a commonly used phrase*. Some collocative meanings are so strong that they hardly need triggering by context. For example, 'chauvinism' (literally, 'fanatical patriotism') can hardly be used today without evoking its collocative partner 'male', and has virtually become a synonym of 'male sexism'. Likewise, 'intercourse' (literally, 'mutual dealings') nowadays practically always evokes 'sexual', and is virtually synonymous with 'coitus'.

Other collocative meanings need to be activated by the context. There is a good example in the last sentence of the Grainville ST in Practical 6.2: 'Le Mourmako était planté, roulé, dans la prédominance de la fange.' The connotations of abandonment and injustice in 'planté, roulé, dans' are partly collocative meanings. In the context of deprivation, 'planté' ('firmly implanted/rooted', etc.) evokes 'planter là', as in 'on nous a plantés là' ('walked out on/ditched/dumped'), and 'roulé + dans' ('rolled + in') evokes 'rouler quelqu'un dans le farine' ('to {do/cheat} someone'). Our TT tries to convey these things by compensation: 'Le Mourmako was *well and truly dumped* in the all-smothering mire.' The italicized expressions share between them both the literal and the connotative meanings of 'planté' and 'roulé' in this context.

Note that 'well and truly' only works here because it most often (though not always) collocates with expressions denoting negative experiences. Collocative meanings are important for the translator, not only because they contribute to the overall meaning of the ST, but also because of the need to avoid unwanted collocative clashes in the TT. These are often produced by failure to spot the need for a communicative translation:

ST	*TT*
Elle nourrissait un serpent dans son sein.	She harboured a snake in her breast (cf. snake in the grass?; Cleopatra's asp?) vs She harboured a viper in her bosom.
Jolie comme un cœur.	Pretty as a heart (cf. playing cards? anatomy?) vs Pretty as a picture.

Collocative clashes can also arise if the wrong choice of hyponym triggers an inappropriate associative meaning:

ST	*TT*
Une cave humide.	A humid cellar (cf. the sticky heat of summer?) vs A damp cellar.
Une gifle sonore.	A sonorous slap (cf. a resonant bass?) vs A loud/resounding slap.

Even within a single language, collocative meanings can sabotage a message very effectively. The prime reason for the coinage 'maïeuticien' was doubtless that 'sage-homme' would have had a disastrous collocative meaning of 'woman', making the male midwives into imitation women.

Collocative meaning is often inseparable from other sorts of connotation, in particular allusive meaning. To return once more to the 'bottes royales' example, we saw that the context gives 'tenaient le premier plan' an associative meaning of 'lording it in the forefront of attention'. But the same context activates a further connotation, a combination of allusive and collocative meaning. An echo of the figurative expression 'tenir le haut du pavé' is triggered by 'royales', which sensitizes the reader to the element of 'first rank' in 'premier plan'. 'Tenir le haut du pavé' nowadays has the figurative meaning of 'occuper le premier rang', and does itself have a nuance of the rich lording it over hoi polloi (the original reference is to walking along the higher, drier part of the roadway, not down in the gutter). This allusive meaning thus reinforces the complex connotations of the sentence: the boots are a throwback to a bygone age of splendour, but one which it is illicit to want to recapture, because it was the age of the rich lording it over the poor and keeping the best things for themselves. But the allusive meaning only fully works because 'tenaient' evokes its collocative partner 'le haut du pavé'. In most other contexts, of course, this would not happen, because 'tenir' regularly collocates with many other expressions. The example is in fact another good illustration of the role of context in triggering connotative meanings; the operative factors in this complex case are the occurrence of 'royales' as part of the motif of post-Revolution poverty, and the semantic kinship between 'le premier plan' and 'le haut'.

REFLECTED MEANING

In the example from Grainville's *Les Flamboyants*, the connotations of abandonment and injustice in 'planté, roulé, dans' are partly collocative meanings, as we have seen. These are reinforced by reflected meanings. **Reflected meaning** is the meaning given to an expression over and above its literal meaning by the fact that *its form calls to mind the completely different meaning of an expression that sounds, or is spelled, the same, or nearly the same*. In 'planté', the meaning 'dumped' is actually a combination of collocative and reflected meanings, triggered by the implied collocation 'planté là'. In 'roulé, dans' the context triggers the collocative meaning of 'rouler dans la farine', but it also thereby gives 'roulé' a reflected meaning of 'fiddled/duped' (as in 'il m'a roulé/tu t'es fait rouler', etc.).

Reflected meanings do not usually occur spontaneously to the listener or reader. When an expression is taken in isolation, its reflected meaning or meanings are usually merely latent. It is the context that triggers these latent reflected meanings. In the example from *Les Flamboyants*, the reflected meanings of 'planté' and 'roulé' that are activated are appropriate to the situation. But there are others, such as 'planted' (as in gardening) or 'rolled' (as in butchery), that are irrelevant to this situation in this context. These are therefore very unlikely to occur to the listener/ reader. It is important to remember that being receptive to connotative meaning is not the same as looking up every possible use of a word in the dictionary and assuming that they are all relevant in the particular context in question.

It is easy to spoil a text by letting an inappropriate reflected meaning
15 creep in. There is an example in lines 15–16 of the TT in Practical 9.2: 'My grandmother had stripped her drawing-room of all its [. . .] knick-knacks'. The closeness of 'stripped' and 'knick-knacks' evokes 'strip naked' and 'knickers'. These are both reflected meanings, and together are most unfortunate. Note that neither would have been activated if the translator had used a different verb (e.g. 'cleared') or a different object (e.g. 'ornaments') – another illustration of the importance of context in realizing potential connotations. There may be another example of unsuitable reflected meaning in our own TT of *Les Flamboyants*: in this context of slime, secretion and filth, 'dumped' may well acquire a reflected meaning of 'defecated'. If there is a real danger of this unwanted reflected meaning intruding, a different TT would be needed, e.g. 'Le Mourmako had been left to steep and fester in the all-smothering mire.'

AFFECTIVE MEANING

Affective meaning is an *emotive effect which is worked on the reader or the person spoken to* by the choice of expression, and which forms part of its overall meaning. The expression does not merely denote its referent, but also hints at some attitude of the speaker or writer to the addressee.

Features of linguistic politeness, flattery, rudeness or insult are typical examples of expressions carrying affective meanings. Compare 'Taisez-vous, je vous en prie' with 'La ferme !' The expressions share the same core literal meaning of 'Stop talking', but the speaker's implied attitude to the listener has a different affective impact in each case: polite in the first, rude in the second.

Translators must obviously be able to recognize affective meanings in the ST. But they must also be careful not to introduce unwanted ones into the TT. For instance, in French, you might lend a book to a friend and say 'Tu me le rendras mardi'. A literal translation of this would sound rude in English: 'You'll give it me back on Tuesday', although the ST does not have that affective meaning at all. A better TT would avoid such brutal assertiveness: '(So) you'll give it me back on Tuesday, then?'

As we have seen, although these six types of connotative meaning are distinguishable from each other, it often happens that two or more occur together and nourish each other. In acquiring a translation method, it is useful to learn to distinguish exactly which sorts of connotative meaning are in play. Practical 10 involves detailed analysis of connotations, because it is designed to help in the acquisition of this ability. Once the ability has been acquired, however, it becomes relatively easy to respond to the sometimes complex connotations of a given piece of text without labelling every last component in them. All that remains then is to find a way of rendering them without too much translation loss!

PRACTICAL 10

10.1   Connotative meaning and translation

Assignment
Taking the expressions printed in bold type in the ST printed on pp. 156 and 158:

(i)   Categorize and discuss their connotative meanings.
(ii) Discuss the translation of them in the TT printed opposite, concentrating on how the connotations are rendered, and on any unwanted connotations that have been introduced. Where necessary, revise the TT to render the ST connotations more successfully into English, and explain why you think your TT is better.

Contextual information

The ST is from Act III of Ionesco's play *Rhinocéros* (1959). Among other things, the play satirically draws attention to conformism, racism and totalitarianism. It was inspired in part by Ionesco's horror at the rise of Nazism in Germany and Fascism in Romania, and his experience of the Nazi occupation of France. At this point in the play, all the characters but these three have turned into rhinoceroses, just as more and more people – even rigid conformists – were swept along by Fascism in the 1930s. Even Botard, the boss-hating man of the left, who had long remained sceptical about this so-called 'rhinoceritis', has suddenly succumbed to it. Dudard, too, will shortly join the blindly destructive herd. The TT was first published in 1960.

NB Remember that context plays an important part in triggering connotative meanings. Some will operate more or less regardless of context, but others remain latent until something in the context activates them. To take just two examples from the *Rhinocéros* ST, 'exploitants' is unlikely in this context to acquire a reflected meaning of 'farmers', and 'croissant' is surely not going to evoke patisserie.

Turn to p. 156

ST

BERENGER   Eh bien, réflexion faite, le coup de tête de Botard ne m'étonne pas. Sa **fermeté** n'était qu'apparente. Ce qui ne l'empêche pas, bien sûr, d'être ou d'avoir été un brave homme. Les braves hommes font les braves rhinocéros. Hélas ! C'est parce qu'ils sont de bonne foi, on peut les duper.

5   DAISY   Permettez-moi de mettre ce panier sur la table. (*Elle met le panier sur la table.*)

BERENGER   Mais c'était un brave homme qui avait des ressentiments...

DUDARD (*à Daisy, s'empressant de l'aider à déposer son panier*)   Excusez-moi, excusez-nous, on aurait dû vous débarrasser plus tôt.

10   BERENGER (*continuant*)   ...Il a été **déformé** par la haine de ses chefs, un complexe d'infériorité...

DUDARD (*à Bérenger*)   Votre raisonnement est faux, puisqu'il a suivi son chef justement, l'instrument même de ses exploitants, c'était son expression. Au contraire, chez lui, il me semble que c'est l'esprit communautaire

15   qui l'a **emporté** sur ses impulsions anarchiques.

BERENGER   Ce sont les rhinocéros qui sont anarchiques puisqu'ils sont en minorité.

DUDARD   Ils le sont encore, pour le moment.

DAISY   C'est une minorité déjà nombreuse qui va croissant. Mon cousin

20   est devenu rhinocéros, et sa femme. Sans compter les personnalités : le cardinal de Retz...

DUDARD   **Un prélat !**

DAISY   Mazarin.

DUDARD   Vous allez voir que ça va s'étendre dans d'autres pays.

25   BERENGER   Dire que le mal vient de chez nous !

DAISY   ...Et des aristocrates : le duc de Saint-Simon.

BERENGER (*bras au ciel*)   **Nos classiques !**

DAISY   Et d'autres encore. Beaucoup d'autres. Peut-être un quart des habitants de la ville.

30   BERENGER   Nous sommes encore les plus nombreux. Il faut en profiter. Il faut faire quelque chose avant d'être submergés.

DUDARD   **Ils sont très efficaces, très efficaces**.

DAISY   Pour le moment, on devrait déjeuner. J'ai apporté de quoi manger.

BERENGER   Vous êtes très gentille, mademoiselle Daisy.

35   DUDARD (*à part*)   Oui, très gentille.

BERENGER (*à Daisy*)   Je ne sais comment vous remercier.

DAISY (*à Dudard*)   Voulez-vous rester avec nous ?

DUDARD   Je ne voudrais pas être importun.

DAISY (*à Dudard*)   Que dites-vous là, monsieur Dudard ? Vous savez

40   bien que vous nous feriez plaisir.

DUDARD   Vous savez bien que je ne veux pas gêner...

BERENGER (*à Dudard*)   Mais bien sûr, Dudard, bien sûr. Votre présence est toujours un plaisir.

DUDARD   C'est que je suis un peu pressé. J'ai un rendez-vous.

TT

BERENGER   But now I come to think it over, Botard's behaviour doesn't surprise me. His firmness was only a pose. Which doesn't stop him from being a good man, of course. Good men make good rhinoceroses, unfortunately. It's because they're so good that they get taken in.

5   DAISY   Do you mind if I put this basket on the table? (*She does so.*)

BERENGER   But he was a good man with a lot of resentment . . .

DUDARD (*to Daisy, and hastening to help her with the basket*)   Excuse me, excuse us both, we should have given you a hand before.

BERENGER (*continues*)   . . . He was riddled with hatred for his superiors, 10   and he'd got an inferiority complex . . .

DUDARD (*to Bérenger*)   Your argument doesn't hold water, because the example he followed was the Chief's, the very instrument of the people who exploited him, as he used to say. No, it seems to me that with him it was a case of community spirit triumphing over his anarchic impulses.

15   BERENGER   It's the rhinoceroses which are anarchic, because they're in the minority.

DUDARD   They are, it's true – for the moment.

DAISY   They're a pretty big minority and getting bigger all the time. My cousin's a rhinoceros now, and his wife. Not to mention leading person-

20   alities like the Cardinal of Retz . . .

DUDARD   A prelate!

DAISY   Mazarin.

DUDARD   This is going to spread to other countries, you'll see.

BERENGER   And to think it all started with us!

25   DAISY   . . . and some of the aristocracy. The Duke of St Simon.

BERENGER (*with uplifted arms*)   All our great names!

DAISY   And others, too. Lots of others. Maybe a quarter of the whole town.

BERENGER   We're still in the majority. We must take advantage of that.

30   We must do something before we're inundated.

DUDARD   They're very potent, very.

DAISY   Well, for the moment, let's eat. I've brought some food.

BERENGER   You're very kind, Miss Daisy.

DUDARD (*aside*)   Very kind indeed.

35   BERENGER   I don't know how to thank you.

DAISY (*to Dudard*)   Would you care to stay with us?

DUDARD   I don't want to be a nuisance.

DAISY   Whatever do you mean, Mr Dudard? You know very well we'd love you to stay.

40   DUDARD   Well, you know, I'd hate to be in the way. . .

BERENGER   Of course, stay, Dudard. It's always a pleasure to talk to you.

DUDARD   As a matter of fact I'm in a bit of a hurry. I have an appointment.

45 BERENGER   Tout à l'heure, vous disiez que vous aviez tout votre temps.

DAISY (*sortant les provisions du panier*)   Vous savez, j'ai eu du mal à trouver de quoi manger. Les magasins sont **ravagés** : ils dévorent tout. Une quantité d'autres boutiques sont fermées : « **Pour cause de transformation** », est-il écrit sur les écriteaux.

50 BERENGER   **On devrait les parquer dans de vastes enclos, leur imposer des résidences surveillées**.

DUDARD   La mise en pratique de ce projet ne me semble pas possible. La société protectrice des animaux serait la première à s'y opposer.

DAISY   D'autre part, chacun a parmi les rhinocéros un parent proche, un 55 ami, ce qui complique encore les choses.

BERENGER   Tout le monde est dans le coup, alors !

DUDARD   **Tout le monde est solidaire**.

BERENGER   **Mais comment peut-on être rhinocéros ?** C'est impensable, impensable !

(E. Ionesco, *Rhinocéros*, © Editions GALLIMARD, 1988: 207–11)

45 BERENGER   Just now you said you'd got nothing to do.
DAISY (*unpacking her basket*)   You know, I had a lot of trouble finding food. The shops have been plundered; they just devour everything. A lot of shops are closed. It's written up outside: 'Closed on account of transformation'.

50 BERENGER   They should all be rounded up in a big enclosure, and kept under strict supervision.
DUDARD   That's easier said than done. The animals' protection league would be the first to object.
DAISY   And besides everyone has a close relative or a friend among
55 them, and that would make it even more difficult.
BERENGER   So everybody's mixed up in it!
DUDARD   Everybody's in the same boat!
BERENGER   But how can people be rhinoceroses? It doesn't bear thinking about!

(Ionesco 1962: 104–6)

10.2   Connotative meaning and translation

Assignment
(i)   You are translating the following text for a company that produces sea salt. Discuss the strategic decisions that you have to take before starting detailed translation of this ST, and outline and justify the strategy you adopt.
(ii)   Translate the text into English.
(iii)   Explain the main decisions of detail you took. Pay special attention to connotative meaning, but do not overlook other major decisions.
(iv)   Compare your translation with the published TT, which will be given you by your tutor.

Contextual information
The ST is printed, alongside an English TT, on a folded card tied round the neck of a pack of salt. On the front of the card it says: 'Fleur de sel. Récolte 1997. Méthode artisanale. « Cueillie à la main, non traitée. »' The ST and TT are printed in an italic sans serif font that looks like neat handwriting with an occasional flourish. Both are centred on the page. The ST is laid out as printed here.

Turn to p. 160

ST

> La *FLEUR DE SEL DE GUERANDE*,
> *fille naturelle du soleil et du vent,*
> *est une prestigieuse variante du sel marin breton.*
> *Son mode de cristallisation*
> *– exceptionnel en Europe –*
> *lui confère des qualités très précieuses.*

> *Alors que le sel commun se forme par saturation*
> *dans l'épaisseur des eaux de mer,*
> *la FLEUR DE SEL DE GUERANDE,*
> *elle, cristallise en flottant à la surface.*
> *Poussés par la brise, ses cristaux,*
> *en forme de petits esquifs,*
> *se rassemblent en nappe serrée :*
> *frémissante flotille, née d'un souffle*
> *et que le souffle suivant risque de noyer.*

> *Seule la paludière a le geste assez délicat et assez preste*
> *pour moissonner ce sel précaire*
> *avant qu'il ne coule irrémédiablement à pic :*
> *la FLEUR DE SEL DE GUERANDE est une denrée rare.*

> *Denrée savoureuse aussi : son arôme, très ténu,*
> *qui rappelle celui de la violette, sait avec bonheur, parfumer*
> *les pot-au-feu, courts-bouillons, bœuf gros-sel et l'ensemble*
> *de la cuisine gourmande.*

> *Rigoureusement sélectionnée,*
> *la FLEUR DE SEL DE GUERANDE*
> *est, en définitive, un sel de gala :*
> *ses cristaux blancs comme neige,*
> *aigus et scintillants comme le diamant,*
> *savent illuminer la table des plus grands chefs.*

(Salines de Guérande 1997)

Line numbers in left margin: 5, 10, 15, 20, 25

11

Language variety: Translation issues in register, sociolect and dialect

In this chapter, we look at characteristics in the way the message is formulated that reveal information about the speaker or writer. These stylistically conveyed meanings are connotations: they are not normally recorded in the dictionary, but are read between the lines, on the basis of widespread associations. For simplicity's sake, we shall call the information revealed 'speaker-related information', regardless of whether there is a written text or not; and we shall apply the terms 'speaker' and 'listener' to spoken and written texts alike.

There are two broad categories of speaker-related information that can be revealed through the way the message is formulated. The first comprises things that speakers intend to reveal, notably the effect they want their utterance to have on the listener. The second comprises things they do not necessarily intend to reveal, notably their social and regional affiliations. These things can occur together, of course, and they are sometimes hard to distinguish from one another. But, in analysing style, it is useful to keep them as clearly distinct as possible, because it helps the translator to pin down what features are textually important.

REGISTER

'Register' is a term used in so many different ways that it can be positively misleading. For our purposes, it is enough to distinguish two types of register.

Tonal register

The first is **tonal register**. Tonal register is the feature of linguistic expression that carries affective meaning. It is what is often simply called 'register' in dictionaries and textbooks on style. It is *the tone that the speaker takes* – vulgar, familiar, polite, formal, etc. The affective meaning of a feature of tonal register is conveyed by a more or less deliberate *choice* of one out of a range of expressions capable of conveying a given literal message – compare 'tu m'ennuies', 'tu m'embêtes', 'tu me fous les boules' and 'tu me fais chier'; or 'votre honneur ne me concerne pas', 'ça m'indiffère totalement, votre honneur' and 'je m'en branle de votre honneur'. The effect of tonal register on listeners is thus something for which speakers can be held responsible, in so far as they are *deliberately being* obscene, polite, etc.

It is important for the translator to assess where the ST expression comes on the SL politeness scale, and to render it with a corresponding TL degree of politeness. But it is not enough just to have a repertoire of expressions capable of injecting various affective meanings into a literal message. Equally important is the *situation* in which the expression is used. Different sorts of social transaction – preaching in church, defending a client in court, selling a car to a male customer, chatting in a bar, etc. – all imply different tonal registers. Another consideration is that the source culture and the target culture may have different expectations regarding the appropriate tonal register(s) for a given situation: awareness of such differences is as important as awareness of situation and having a repertoire of tonal registers.

Social register

A **social register** is a style from which the listener infers what social stereotype the speaker belongs to. A stereotype by definition excludes individual idiosyncrasies of people belonging to the stereotype; but, for better or for worse, we do tend to organize our interactions with other people on the basis of social stereotypes. These stereotypes range from broad value-judgemental labels such as 'coarse', 'genuine', 'chipper', etc. to increasingly specific stereotypical personality-types such as 'the pompous academic', 'the rugger-bugger', etc. In so far as each of these stereotypes has a characteristic style of language-use, this style is what we mean by social register. Social register therefore differs from tonal register in that the speaker-related information is not usually *intentionally* revealed by the speaker.

Whatever information the style conveys about the kind of person the speaker is, it will often be tentative. It is generally confirmed and refined by context and situation. Once these are taken into account, social register will carry information about such things as the speaker's educational background, social persona (i.e. a social role the speaker is used to fulfilling), occupation and professional standing, and so on. In other words, a social register is a style that is conventionally seen as appropriate to both a type of person and a type of situation. This is why a given genre requires a specific style, and often a specific jargon. Selecting the appropriate style and jargon is to a great extent a matter of fulfilling expectations with regard to social register: selecting the wrong social register risks undermining the speaker's social persona as a credible authority on the subject.

In translating an ST that has speaking characters in it, or whose author uses social register for self-projection, a major concern is constructing an appropriate TL register. In purely informative texts, this is relatively straightforward, the main problem being to find the conventional TL style for the genre. The more journalistic, political or literary the ST, however, the greater the importance of characterization, and therefore of social persona. When the translator is operating between Western European cultures, social stereotypes can sometimes be matched reasonably closely – guests at an aristocratic ball perhaps, or university students, or rugby fans. But even such parallels are far from exact: there are discrepancies between the stereotypes of British and French aristocrats, British and French university students, British and French rugby fans – and, for that matter, between Welsh and English rugby fans. And what about Jeeves and Wooster, or Giono's *paysans*? If there are social registers characteristic of these types, how does the translator convey them? Any strategy is going to involve loss, compromise and compensation. Whatever TL social register is finally decided on, it is most important to keep it consistent: if the *paysan* sounded like a cross between a gentleman farmer and a straw-chewing rustic, the effect could be ruined.

Social or tonal?

Social and tonal register are not always fully distinguishable. There are two reasons for this. First, it is sometimes not clear whether a style of expression reflects social stereotyping or the speaker's intentions towards the listener. Second, characteristics of particular social registers often include features of tonal register. Thus 'I am not prepared to tolerate further prevarication' may simply be typical of the way this person speaks (the social register of a rather formal authority-figure). Or it may be a tone put on to scare the listener into action (a formal and threatening tonal register). Or perhaps it only works as threatening because the speaker has authority in the first place, i.e. because of the speaker's social persona?

These ambiguities are found in the following extract from Georges Michel's play *L'Agression*. (*Contextual information*. The play shows the violent tensions between deprived urban youth and well-off middle-class adults. The youths are shown as being attacked by the shop-fronts with their complacent and ever louder and more garish displays of unaffordable consumer goods. Eventually the noise and lights become unbearable, and the kids react by smashing the shop windows in. The adults are often represented, as here, by a 'chorus' of anonymous voices. This extract comes early in the play. Nowadays, Jacquot would be wanting a Suzuki rather than a mobylette, and the boys would be into drugs as well as alcohol; but the attitudes and registers are as pertinent now as they were in 1968.)

AUTRE VOIX   Que dire de la dégradante et ignominieuse saleté de leurs cheveux.

[. . .]

UNE VOIX   Ils ont le regard dur et haineux...
AUTRE VOIX   La sournoiserie collée au visage...
5   AUTRE VOIX   Le sourire amer...
AUTRE VOIX   L'injure aux lèvres...
AUTRE VOIX   La parole aigre...
AUTRE VOIX   La fourberie au cœur...

[. . .]

AUTRE VOIX   On les voit flâner dans le quartier...
10   AUTRE VOIX   Avec des allures équivoques...
AUTRE VOIX   Demandant à l'alcool la consolation de leurs déboires...
AUTRE VOIX   L'oubli de leur turpitude et de leur souillure morale...

[. . .]

DANY   T'as raison, leur société, une vraie saloperie !... tous des enfoirés !
JEANNOT   Un peu, ouhai, c'est à dégueuler dessus...
15   (*Le chœur effrayé sort à reculons, quatre de chaque côté.*)
JACQUOT   Tu dis ça parce que t'as pas besoin de bosser... T'aurais pas ta frangine qui te glisse un fafiot par-ci par-là...
DANY   Et alors, pourquoi que tu veux que je les refuse ?... J'suis pas con comme toi à marner pour une mobylette...

(Michel 1968: 33–7)

The 'chorus' of voices has the social register of the typical self-important, censorious, middle-aged, middle-class conformist. But may it not be a deliberately adopted tone, by which the speakers try to impress on each other that they subscribe to this collective outrage at the excesses of the young? This tonal register would convey an affective meaning of 'I'm sure you agree it's a scandal and we need to unite against it'. But then again, perhaps the tone of outrage is an integral part of the social register of these people? Similarly, it may be that the sneering tone of the youngsters is part of their social register.

The importance of situation is a third complicating factor in assessing register. As Ken George points out:

formel v. informel

French is multiple, providing alternatives for a variety of social situations. [. . .] There are therefore several norms within French, depending basically on whether one is writing or speaking the language and whether the situation is formal or informal. Each variety and each register has its own conventions, which is why the term 'unconventional' is in the end unsatisfactory when applied exclusively to non-standard usage.

(George 1993: 166–7)

Most people do indeed vary their tonal register according to situation and genre, and most have several social registers. The essential thing for the translator is to be alert to the relation between register and situation, and to render that relation in the TT. As for distinguishing tonal and social register from each other, context usually makes this possible. Where it is impossible to disentangle them without lengthy analysis, it is acceptable in discussing translation simply to use 'register' as a cover-term.

SOCIOLECT

classe sociale

Whereas a social register belongs to a fairly narrowly stereotyped social persona, a sociolect is defined in terms of sociological notions of class. A **sociolect** is a language variety typical of one of the broad groupings that together constitute the 'class structure' of a society. Examples of major sociolects in the UK are those labelled as 'urban working class', 'white collar', 'public school', etc. These labels are vague. This is partly because British society does not have a rigid class structure, and partly because a 'class' label is often useless if not qualified by geographical reference. 'Public school' is relatively neutral to regional variation, but the further the speaker is from 'public school' on the scale, the more necessary it is to take class and regional factors together: compare 'urban working class', 'Leith urban working class', 'Leith youthful urban working class', etc. Mixed sociolectal/regional designations like these are often more helpful in recognizing language variants than purely sociological ones.

Sociolectal features can nevertheless convey important speaker-related information. If they are salient features of the ST, the translator cannot ignore them when deciding on a strategy. The first crucial factor to consider is what their function is in the ST. Thus, in translation of an eyewitness account of a crime for Interpol, sociolect (and register) would probably be subordinated to getting the facts clear. But if sociolect is not incidental, the translator may need to find a way of showing this in the TT. This is sometimes the case with journalistic texts, and often with literary texts. Even in such cases, however, a number of questions must be weighed in forming a strategy: What is the function of the ST sociolect(s), and how does it relate to the purpose of the ST? Would it not be safest to produce a TT in a bland 'educated middle-class' sociolect?

If the strategy is to incorporate some TL sociolectal features corresponding to those in the ST, the requirements are similar to those involved
in choosing social register. It has to be decided what sociolects are the
most appropriate, and there must be no inconsistencies in TT sociolect
(assuming there are none in the ST).

DIALECT

The fourth type of speaker-related information that can be inferred from
style concerns what part of the country speakers are from – where they
grew up, or where they live. This inference is based on **dialect**, a language
variety with features of accent, lexis, syntax and sentence-formation characteristic of a given region. Apart from being able to identify dialect
features in the first place, there are three things the translator has to think
about.

First, it has to be decided how important the dialect features in the ST
are to its overall effect. Similar considerations apply as to sociolect.
In purely informative texts, dialect is unlikely to be significant. But
in journalism, and especially in literary texts, the dialect(s) may have
important functions in realizing the purpose of the ST: one character may
habitually be incomprehensible to another; or dialect may carry vital
source-culture connotations; or it may give vital local colour to the ST,
as in Practical 5.1. In that practical, of course, the tight phonic/graphic
constraints of subtitling made it impossible to indicate dialectal features
even by compensation.

Second, if dialect does have such a function in the ST, an essential strategic decision is whether and why to use TL dialectal features. There are
very obvious dangers in using TL dialect. How do you decide which – if
any – TL dialects correspond to the ST ones? And will not a TL dialect
sound ridiculous on the lips of Alsatians or Marseillais? With luck, drop-
ping ST dialectal features will not incur really damaging translation loss. If
it does, but prudence warns against using dialect in the TT, the important
ST effects produced by dialect will probably have to be rendered through
compensation. The most useful technique is to make occasional exegetic
additions. The form these take will depend on the context. In an article on
a politician, the safest course is simply to insert a reference to e.g. 'his
much-loved/much-mocked Auvergne accent'. In other sorts of text, there
are sometimes more possibilities. Here, for discussion in class, is an example from Armand Lanoux's novel *Le commandant Watrin* (1956).
(*Contextual information. Capitaine* Bertuold and *sous-lieutenant* François
Soubeyrac are officers in the army. Their battalion consists of *Chtimis*
(northerners, from the Lille area). Bertuold commands a section of machine-

gunners, François a section of *voltigeurs* (light infantry). There is a sometimes violent rivalry between the two groups, though the officers get on
well. François, a talented storyteller and mimic, is recalling an episode when
his men relieved a section of Catalans garrisoning a frontier town.)

ST

Un de mes gars, aimable, Poivre, dit gentiment à un Catalan: « D'où
t'ch'est qu' t'es, ti ? – Hé, qu'est-ceu que tu me raconn'teu ? chante
l'autre. – Mi, j' to dis, d'où d' ch'est qu' tê ? – Oh ! putaing, je neu
comprin rien de rieng ! » Et ils se regardaient de travers, comme mes
voltigeurs et vos mitrailleurs, mon capitaine. Alors, j'interviens: « Il te
5 demande d'où tu es ? – Oh ! moi, putaing, je suis de Cerbère ! – Alors
tu dois connaître Vandarem, Carlos Vandarem ? – Bien sûr, que je le
connais, cet essepéditionnaire, mon lieutenin ! » Et mes Chtimis sont restés
figés devant ce miracle, leur lieutenant parlant avec des gitans olivâtres,
les entendant et se faisant entendre d'eux !
10
(Lanoux 1978: 53)

TT

One of them, a friendly lad, Poivre, but with an accent thick as beet, goes
up to a Catalan and asks him where he's from. The Catalan was just as
bad – had a real twang on him: 'What you bleedin' on about?' he says.
'I said "Where yer from," didn't I?' 'Can't understand a bleedin' word.'
And they were eyeing one another up, much the way your men and mine
5 do, Sir. So I step in and say, in my best twang: 'He's asking you where
you're from.' 'Oh, I'm from Cerbère!' 'Ah, you must know Vandarem
then – Carlos Vandarem?' 'Oh, the copyist – yes, course, I know him,
Sir!' And my northern lads just stood there wonderstruck, watching their
officer actually talking to these swarthy gypsies, and understanding them,
10 and them understanding him!

If, as here, ST dialectal features are closely associated with other features
of language variety, it is sometimes possible to use TL sociolect or register
to help compensate for the loss of connotations carried by the ST dialect(s).
A final possibility is wholesale cultural transplantation. This is rare. It is
generally only done with literary works, for commercial reasons. It often
requires such extreme adaptation that it can barely be described as translation, however brilliant the TL text may be.
   The third problem is one that applies to sociolect and register as well:
once a decision is taken to use TL dialect, it must be accurate, and it must
be consistent. Many literary TTs in particular are sabotaged by weaknesses in the translator's grasp of TL language variety. Among the many
skills a translator has to have is that of pastiche.

CODE-SWITCHING

Many people are adept at switching between language varieties, or even between languages. This is known as **code-switching**. People often do this for social camouflage or to avoid giving offence, matching their social persona to the particular situation they are in. Or they may do it for story-telling purposes, imitating the various characters in their story. Or it may be for persuasive purposes, sprinkling the text with expressions from different registers, sociolects or dialects. An excellent example of code-switching is François's virtuoso performance in the Lanoux extract, as he alternates between northern and south-western dialects and various registers and sociolects. Any text containing characters with recognizably different styles of expression is by definition marked by code-switching. In the extract from *L'Agression*, for example, the characters themselves do not code-switch, but the playwright does. Since code-switching is a definite strategic device, translators have to be prepared to convey in the TT the effects it has in the ST. In doing this, of course, they are subject to the requirements and caveats that we have outlined in discussing register, sociolect and dialect.

PRACTICAL 11

11.1 Language variety and translation

Assignment
   (i)   Imagine that you are translating for publication in the United Kingdom the text from which the following ST is taken. Concentrating on language variety, discuss the strategic decisions that you have to take before starting detailed translation of this ST, and outline and justify the strategy you adopt.
  (ii)   Concentrating on language variety, compare the ST and the published TT, printed underneath. Use this comparison to confirm or refine your own strategy.
 (iii)   Translate the ST into English.
 (iv)   Discuss any particularly significant decisions of detail you took in respect of language variety.

Contextual information
The text is from Marcel Pagnol's novel *Jean de Florette*. It is a letter from Attilio to Ugolin, both young Provençal *paysans*. Attilio has a Piedmontese father, who grows carnations for a living. He has promised Ugolin ten thousand carnation cuttings so that he can start up in business for himself. Ugolin has written to Attilio to ask how big a water supply he would need. This is Attilio's reply. Note that the narrative throughout the novel is in conventional French. Attilio's letter therefore stands out

in respect of language variety. Among the dialectal features in the text are some deriving from Piedmontese Italian: 'pourquoi' = 'parce que'; 'April' = 'avril'; the emphatic repetition of adjectives (here, 'sur sur sur' [*sic*]) is also an Italianate trait. The verb 'chasper' (l. 2) here means 'to feel up' (cf. Provençal 'chaspa', 'to feel/finger/grope').

ST

Collègue,

Je t'ai pas répondu de suite pourquoi ma sœur s'est marié avec Egidio, celui qui la chaspait tout le temps. Mintenant, s'est son droit. Pour les boutures, naturèlement que je t'en fais cadot. Mon père Monsieur Tornabua
5 est d'acort. Je lui ai pas dit que tu m'a demandé le prix. Cà lui aurait fait pêne. Elles seront prête pour le mois d'April. Prépare le champ, et surtout l'eau. Mon père Monsieur Tornabua dit que pour dix mille plante il te faut une réserve d'au moins quatre cents mètres cubes. Si tu les as pas sur sur sur, c'est pas la peine de comencer pour pas finir. Tu as bien
10 compris ? Quatre cent mètres. Et pas des mètres de longueur. C'est des cube, les mêmes qu'au certificat d'études : qu'à cause de ces mètres j'ai jamais pu le passer, et mintenant je m'en sers pour gagner des sous bien plus que l'essituteur ! C'est çà la vie ! Ecrit moi encore, mais fais un peu entention à ton ortografe ! On ni comprend rien, il faut toultan deviner !
15 Je dis pas sa pour te vexer. Moi aussi, samarive de pas bien connaître un mot comment ca s'écrie : alors, à la place, j'en met un autre !

　　Ton ami Attilio.

(Pagnol 1988: 59–60)

TT

Friend

I did not answer you immediately because my sister married Egidio, the one who chased her all the time. Now it's his right. As for the cuttings, naturally I'll make you a present of them. My father Monsieur Tornabua
5 agrees. I didn't tell him you asked me the price. That would hurt him. They will be ready for you in April. Prepare the field, and especially the water. My father M. Tornabua says that for ten thousand plants you should have a reservoir of at least four hundred cubic meters. If you haven't got that absolutely certainly certainly certainly it's not worth the trouble of starting
10 and not finishing. Do you understand properly? Four hundred meters. And not meters long. Cubes, the same as on the certificate of studies that I could never pass because of those meters, and now I use them to earn more sous than the teacher. That's life! Write to me again, but pay a little attention to your spelling! I didn't understand anything, I had to guess. I don't say this
15 to annoy you. Me too, it happens to me not to understand a word well when somebody writes it: so, in its place, I put another!

　　Your friend
　　Attilio

(Pagnol 1989: 39)

11.2   Language variety and translation

Assignment
(i)   You are translating for stage performance *L'Agression*, from which
       the extract on p. 164 is taken. Specifying where in the English-
       speaking world the TT is to be performed, and bearing the contextual
       information (pp. 163–4) in mind, discuss the strategic decisions that
       you have to take before starting detailed translation of this ST, and
       outline and justify the strategy you adopt.
(ii)   Translate the extract into English.
(iii) Discuss the main decisions of detail you took; pay special attention
       to language variety, but do not overlook other major decisions.

11.3   Language variety and translation

Assignment
(i)   You are translating for stage performance the play from which the
       following ST is taken. Specifying where in the English-speaking
       world the TT is to be performed, discuss the strategic decisions that
       you have to take before starting detailed translation of this ST, and
       outline and justify your own strategy.
(ii)   Translate the text into English.
(iii) Discuss the main decisions of detail you took; pay special attention
       to language variety, but do not overlook other major decisions.

Contextual information
The text is the ending of a satirical one-act play by Jean Tardieu, *La
Politesse inutile*. The action takes place in the teacher's house. Self-important and dogmatic, the teacher sententiously hectors a cringing pupil, who
leaves just as the mysterious 'visiteur' arrives. The visitor is scruffy,
relaxed and completely unimpressed by the teacher's flowery welcome.
Having said nothing, he suddenly tells the teacher his tie is crooked. The
teacher disconcertedly straightens his tie, and from this moment begins to
lose his poise. Trying to retrieve the situation with a further excessive
display of politeness, he offers the visitor a drink, saying that he will ask
his wife to get them something.

ST
LE VISITEUR (*soudain hilare*)   Vous avez une femme, vous ! Ah ! par
exemple ! (*Il rit avec cruauté*) Ah ! ah ! une femme ! ah ! non !... c'est
impayable !
LE PROFESSEUR (*très démonté, mais s'efforçant de rester aimable*)   Mais
5 bien sûr ! J'ai une femme ! la plus dévouée, la plus exquise, la plus...
LE VISITEUR (*sec*)   Ça suffit...

LE PROFESSEUR (*dans un sursaut de fierté*)   Mais à la fin, monsieur, quel jeu jouez-vous avec moi ? Que signifie votre attitude envers un homme de ma situation et de mon mérite ? (*Se montant un peu*) Savez-vous bien
10 que vous avez affaire à un professeur réputé, qui vit environné de l'estime de ses collègues, du respect de ses élèves, de l'affection des siens ? Je commence à trouver...

LE VISITEUR (*ironique et menaçant et comme s'il commençait à s'intéresser à la conversation*)   Ah ! vous commencez à trouver ?

15 LE PROFESSEUR   Parfaitement, je commence à trouver votre attitude singulièrement offensante à mon égard. A la fin, que me voulez-vous ?

LE VISITEUR (*se levant d'un bond et venant regarder le Professeur sous le nez*)   Tu veux le savoir ?

LE PROFESSEUR (*terrorisé et reculant vers la gauche*)   Oui, parfaitement,
20 je veux le...

LE VISITEUR (*de plus en plus menaçant*)   Tu veux le savoir, dis ? Eh bien, tiens ! (*Férocement, il lui donne trois ou quatre gifles violentes avec la paume et le dos de la main.*)

(J. Tardieu, *La Comédie de la comédie,*
© Editions GALLIMARD, 1990)

12

Scientific and technical translation

All texts can be categorized in terms of genre. There is no *a priori* reason for giving special attention to any one genre rather than any other. However, since most language students are not trained in science or technology, they are often in awe of 'technical' texts. Yet many professionals earn their living translating such texts. This is why we are devoting a whole chapter to the main translation issues they raise.

The 'technical' is not confined to science and technology. It is simply to avoid repeating 'scientific and technological' that we shall be using the term 'technical texts' to denote texts written in the context of scientific or technological disciplines. In fact, of course, *any* specialist field has its own technical terms and its own genre-marking characteristics: a look at a hobbies magazine, or a review of the rock scene, or the sport or business pages in the paper, quickly confirms this. Texts in these and any other specialized field are properly speaking 'technical' texts. Nevertheless, the fact that scientific and technological texts are so very unfamiliar for many language students makes them clear illustrations of two important points in the translation of all specialist texts. First, the translator must be just as familiar with technical terms and genre features in the TL as in the SL. Second, the problems met in translating specialist texts are mostly no different from those met in translating in any other genre, specialized or not. A textual variable is a textual variable, a hyponym is a hyponym, whatever the genre and whatever the subject matter; and the relative merits of literal and free translation need to be considered in translating any text.

Taking 'technical' in the narrow definition we have given it, we can say that most technical texts are relatively inaccessible to the non-specialist reader. There are three main reasons for this inaccessibility. One is lexical, the others are conceptual. In illustrating them, we shall refer to the following text:

CONSTRUCTION ET CARACTERISATION D'UN ELECTROLY-
SEUR POUR LA REDUCTION ELECTROCHIMIQUE DE LA
VAPEUR D'EAU A 850°C. RAPPORT FINAL

Une nouvelle cellule plane d'électrolyse de la vapeur d'eau utilisant un
disque d'électrolyte solide de zircone yttriée de 50cm² de surface utile
a été mise à l'épreuve à 850°C. Les problèmes d'étanchéité ont été
résolus, mais l'épaisseur du disque reste le paramètre critique de la technologie de cet assemblage. Vers 300 microns une fissuration apparaît,
soit au moment de l'usinage soit, dans la cellule, au cours de la montée
en température.
   L'effet de dopage de l'interface cathodique par oxyde de cérium a
été étudié sur des cellules de petite dimension. Sous l'effet du changement de l'état, d'oxydation du cérium, la réactivité de la cathode se
trouve augmentée quand la concentration en eau du mélange gazeux
décroît. On a calculé que cet effet peut élever le rendement des cellules
tubulaires connectées en série de 50%. Cette amélioration électrochimique, donne un regain d'intérêt au dispositif tubulaire, dont la technologie
d'assemblage est par ailleurs bien maîtrisée.

                                                    (Viguie 1983)

There are three sorts of lexical problem arising from the specialized use
of technical terms. First, there is the obvious problem of terms not used
in everyday, ordinary language, and which are therefore totally unfamiliar
to the lay translator. The text given above contains a simple example of
this problem. A term such as 'zircone yttriée' is instantly recognizable as
belonging only to specialized scientific contexts. Without specialist knowledge, the translator can neither guess the exact meaning nor make an
informed guess at the correct TL term.
   The second problem is that of terms whose everyday uses are familiar to
the translator, but which look as if they are being used in some specialized
way in the ST. An example in this text is 'dopage', which regularly denotes
the doping of racehorses, or drug abuse by athletes, etc. These meanings do
not look as if they apply, but the translator cannot be sure that 'dopage'
here does not have some related pejorative meaning, e.g. unacceptably
distorting performance by introducing foreign bodies. Only a specialist
will be able to confirm that the correct term is 'doping' – i.e. adding an
impurity to a semiconductor to produce its desired characteristics.
   Third, a term may have an everyday sense that is not obviously wrong
in the context. This is the most dangerous sort of case, because the translator can easily fail to recognize the term as a technical one, and mistakenly
render it in its everyday sense. There are good examples in the electrolysis text. First, 'étanchéité' looks as if it is used in its everyday sense of
'watertightness'. This seems to fit the context, and a translator might well
opt for it without even suspecting that there is a problem here. The problem

is that the apparatus needs to be impermeable not to liquids, but to gases. So the appropriate rendering of 'étanchéité' in this context is not 'water-tightness', but 'gas tightness'.

Similarly, 'cellule plane' seems to be a perfectly ordinary collocation of everyday words. The non-specialist might well translate this expression simply as 'flat cell', without recognizing it as a technical term with an English synonym, 'planar cell'.

As these examples show, access to up-to-date specialist dictionaries and databases is essential for technical translators. Of course, even the most recent materials will sometimes be slightly out of date, because scientific and technological fields are constantly developing. In any case, even the best reference material does not always give a single, unambiguous synonym for a particular technical term. This means that the normal caveats concerning use of dictionaries also apply to technical translation. That is, translators can only select the appropriate TL term if they have a firm grasp of both the textual context and the wider technical context. The problem is not lessened by the fact that some of the context may remain obscure until the correct sense of the ST terms has been defined! This brings us to the two conceptual reasons why technical texts may be difficult to translate.

The first type of conceptual problem arises from ignorance of underlying knowledge taken for granted by experts, but not understood by non-specialists and not explicit in the ST. This, too, can be illustrated from the electrolysis text. Take the following sentence:

On a calculé que cet effet peut élever le rendement des cellules tubulaires connectées en série de 50%.

The construction of the sentence is ambiguous, because of the position of '50%'. Purely syntactically, '50%' may modify either 'série' ('a 50% series') or 'élever' ('increase by 50%'). If '50%' had been placed immediately after 'élever', of course, there would have been no ambiguity. Yet the possibility that the sentence is ambiguous would presumably never even occur to a specialist who knows that there is no such thing as 'connecting cells in a 50% series'. However, this 'obvious' piece of background knowledge is not explained in the immediate context, and may not be obvious at all to the non-specialist – 'a 50% series' sounds no more outlandish to the lay person than many genuine technical terms. Without such background knowledge, the translator may suspect that 'tubular cells connected in a 50% series' is wrong, but cannot be certain that 'increase the yield of tubular cells by 50%' is right.

The conceptual unfamiliarity of technical texts makes it easy for an inexperienced translator to misconstrue the syntax. A single mistake like this can make the TT nonsensical. There is a simple example in the electrolysis text:

un disque d'électrolyte solide de zircone yttriée de 50cm^2 de surface utile

This translates correctly as 'a solid electrolyte disc of yttriated zirconia with a working surface of 50cm²'. But it is easy to misconstrue the syntax in a number of ways, e.g. as 'a solid electrolyte disc of zirconia yttriated with 50cm² of working surface', or 'an electrolyte disc solid with yttriated zirconia. . .'. And how is the non-specialist to be sure that these are not right?

The second type of conceptual problem concerns what might be called the 'logic' of a discipline – methods of argumentation, the development of relations between concepts. There is a minor example in the electrolysis text. Without a grasp of the principles of electrolysis and the ideas behind the development of the new type of cell, the translator cannot be sure whether 'dispositif tubulaire' refers to the same thing as 'cellule tubulaire' or to a different piece of equipment. This type of problem is the most intractable of all in technical translation. Non-specialists are always likely to reach a conceptual impasse from which no amount of attention to syntax or vocabulary can rescue them. In that case they have only two options: learn the concepts of the field in which they wish to translate, or work in close consultation with experts. In practice, trainee technical translators generally do both, quickly becoming experts themselves with the help of specialist supervisors. However, not even expert translators can expect to keep abreast of all the latest research while at the same time doing translation, and they will sooner or later come up against problems that can only be solved by consulting other experts, databases or, if possible, the author of the ST.

These remarks about the need for consultation are not to be taken lightly. They raise the important question of the responsibility – and perhaps the legal liability – of the translator. There is a difference here between technical translation and, say, literary translation. It is not that literary translators are not held responsible for their work, but the implications of mistranslation are generally less serious for them than for technical translators, where one mistake could cause financial damage or loss of life. This is another respect in which technical translation is exemplary, bringing out extremely clearly a golden rule which is in fact essential to all translation: never be too proud or embarrassed to ask for help or advice.

Even after every precaution has been taken in translating, it is often necessary for the translator to attach a legal disclaimer to the TT. Here is an example:

> While every due care has been taken in the preparation of the work accompanying this, neither the ***** Ltd, nor its staff, consultants or translators can accept legal liability for any damage or loss arising from error therein, howsoever caused.

The spectre of legal liability is a reminder that even the minutest error of detail on any level of textual variables is typically magnified in a technical text. It is all too easy in translation to confuse similar words, as in this example from a tourist leaflet on Carcassonne:

ST	TT
Au XIIIe siècle, le pouvoir royal dote la ville d'une seconde ligne de remparts.	In the thirteenth century royal power gilded the town with a second line of ramparts.

And we have lost count of the number of times 'de vieux samovars de cuivre' has been translated in class as 'old leather samovars'. Luckily, when that happens, everyone has a laugh and the student promises to be more careful in future. But it is much more dangerous to confuse closely similar technical names. Consider how similar are some of the prefixes and suffixes that can be attached to the root 'sulph', and how many possible permutations of them there are:

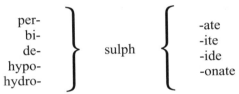

The slightest error in affixation here will be a major factual error, whereas, in non-technical language, affixation may sometimes be a matter of style. For example, in French, there is a distinction between 'continu' and 'continuel', if they are precisely used. Something that is 'continu' lasts without interruption, in space or time; something that is 'continuel' may last without interruption, but may also occur as a succession of repetitions, with possible intervals, in time. 'Continuous' and 'continual' correspond closely to 'continu' and 'continuel' respectively. But in non-technical texts the translator often does not need to make a distinction in literal meaning between the two. Similarly, there is generally little difference in practice between '*dis*believing' and '*un*believing', or between '*in*excusable' and '*un*excusable'. In literary texts, the choice between affixes can often depend on context, euphony or personal taste. But with technical terms in specialist texts of any kind (not just scientific and technical texts), the temptation to be guided by such considerations must be resisted absolutely. Thus, in the electrolysis text, students have pointed out more than once that 'tubular cells' sounds comically like 'tubular bells', but that is just too bad – 'tubular cells' is the correct term, and the translator should on no account replace it with 'tube cells', 'tubiform cells', 'tube-shaped cells', or whatever.

Even professionals sometimes let stylistic considerations interfere with the strict logic of the message. We can show this from the translation of an example quoted in Chapter 2. (*Contextual information*. This is the conclusion of a text on the transport of nuclear fuels. It concerns the level of radiation to which people in the vicinity of the transport are exposed; these are slightly different depending on whether the fuel is U/MOX or UO_2 – whence 'différentiel'.)

> Les équivalents de dose effectifs collectifs différentiels annuels reçus par les riverains et par les passagers d'autres véhicules sont du même ordre de grandeur.

Here is the published TT:

> The effective, collective, annual differential dose equivalents received by people living alongside and passengers in vehicles are of the same order of magnitude.

The order of the adjectives and the insertion of commas undermine the ST message. In the ST, the absence of commas has a rigorous semantic function, showing that what is referred to is a very precise subset of 'équivalent de dose'. This subset consists of five specific elements. The basic element is 'équivalent de dose' ('dose equivalent'). This is then narrowed down to a particular subcategory of dose equivalent:

équivalent de dose *effectif*   *effective* dose equivalent   *— placement des adjectifs*
(vs e.g. 'potentiel')

This subcategory is then itself narrowed down to another one, a particular *sort* of effective dose equivalent:

équivalent de dose effectif *collectif*   *collective* effective dose equivalent
(vs e.g. 'individuel')

And *this* subcategory is narrowed down still more precisely:

équivalent de dose effectif collectif   *differential* collective effective
différentiel (vs e.g. 'standard')   dose equivalent

Finally, this narrow sub-sub-subcategory is refined into an even narrower one:

équivalent de dose effectif collectif   *annual* differential collective
différentiel *annuel* (vs e.g.   effective dose equivalent.
'mensuel')

The point about this final, highly specific subset of 'équivalent de dose' in the ST is that it is an *indivisible unit*. The adjectives are not tacked onto the noun at random or as optional extras, but combine with it to form an integral whole. In other words, the ST adjectives *define* the dose equivalent, they do not *describe* it. If they described it, there would be commas between them, perhaps with an 'et' instead of a comma before 'annuels'. This describing function is in principle endless – you can go on accumulating qualities as and when you see them, as in:

> Here's a dose equivalent. Oh, and look – it's effective. And gosh, it's collective as well. And wouldn't you say it's a bit differential, too? And definitely annual, with it. Turn it over, let's see what it's like on the other side – hey, it's green and hairy . . . etc.

The defining function, by contrast, is tantamount to creating a compound noun: 'équivalent-de-dose-effectif-collectif-différentiel-annuel'. This compound expression must be read and understood as an indivisible unit, and it has to be translated as such.

The published TT is thus defective on two counts. First, by interfering with the order of the adjectives, it implies a different subcategory of dose equivalent. Second, this new subcategory is at best never more than implicit, because the commas in any case give 'effective' and 'collective' a describing function, not a defining one. It may well be, of course, that in view of the context a specialist reader would see through the fog and interpret this sentence correctly. But the translator cannot afford to take the risk of playing fast and loose with the ST. The best rendering may not sound beautiful, but at least it is accurate and clear:

> The annual differential collective effective dose equivalents received by other road-users and by people living along the route are of similar orders of magnitude.

Another temptation students often succumb to is that of 'improving on' the ST. This is risky in any genre, but disastrous in technical translation. We saw a good example on p. 24, in respect of this same sentence on nuclear physics. For purely phonic and prosodic reasons, 'different' and 'efficacious' were preferred to 'differential' and 'effective', and the word order changed. This made nonsense of the text:

> The different annual collective efficacious equivalent doses received by people living along the route and passengers in other vehicles are of the same order of magnitude.

Some parts of technical texts may be formulated in mathematical symbols. These need minimal effort in translation, although they cannot always be literally transcribed. Careful attention must be paid to any differences between SL and TL convention, as in the following:

French	*English*
$0{,}35 \cdot 10^{-4} \, bar^{-1}$	$0.35 \times 10^{-4} \, bar^{-1}$

[handwritten:] les maths

The technical translator's paramount concerns, then, are accuracy and conformity with the requirements of genre. In so far as the requirements of genre imply style, register is also important: the wrong tonal or social register may alienate the reader and undermine confidence in the TT or even in the author of the ST.

The relation between accuracy and style is not always straightforward, however. If an ST is badly written or ungrammatical, should this be reflected in the TT? The question applies to all translation, of course. In our view, translators are not in principle responsible for 'improving' defective STs. However, this is sometimes necessary with purely informative texts, because the crucial thing is factual accuracy. If there is any potentially misleading or dangerous ambiguity or obscurity in the ST, there is every reason to keep it out of the TT – if necessary after consultation with the author or an expert. The electrolysis text contains two instances of bad punctuation. The first is unforgivable:

Sous l'effet du changement de l'état, d'oxydation du cérium, la réactivité de la cathode se trouve augmentée

Perhaps the needless comma after 'état' will not destroy the meaning for an SL specialist reader. It certainly does flummox student translators: they think there is a conceptual problem (Is there a phenomenon in electrolysis called 'changement de l'état'?), and (not surprisingly) they cannot work out the grammar of 'd'oxydation du cérium'. There should surely be no question of trying to replicate the effect of this illiterate comma in the TT. The other example is less serious: *[handwritten: entre le sujet et le verbe]*

Cette amélioration électrochimique, donne un regain d'intérêt

The comma here reflects a prosodic emphasis (a stress on '-ique' and a slight pause). It is ungrammatical, but it does not seem to prevent the sentence being understood. Again, however, it would be safer not to have a corresponding TT comma.

The position of '50%' at the end of its sentence is another poor piece of writing. This would be unorthodox and inelegant in most texts. In this one, as we have seen, it can certainly pose problems of comprehension to the inexperienced translator. Fortunately, once the ST sentence has been worked out, translating it is relatively straightforward: English readily accommodates short adverbial phrases at the end of the sentence; and there is less danger of ambiguity than in the ST, because 'de' here translates as the hyponym 'by'. But the translator may well feel that keeping the ST order might make the sentence difficult to understand at a first reading; if so, the obvious place for 'by 50%' is immediately after the verb 'increase'.

Before embarking on the Practical, it will be useful to note some of the characteristics of technical texts in English. First, the language is usually informative, and often includes expressions denoting purpose or role, and explanations of method or process. Second, in accounts of experiments or research programmes, the passive is used extensively, which keeps the style impersonal. This is also true of French technical texts, as in the electrolysis text (ll. 3 and 8–9). Sometimes, the impersonal 'on' is used as well as the passive (l. 12); both forms are generally rendered with the passive in English.

Another typical feature of technical texts is the frequent use of compound nouns (e.g. 'website design', 'fine-coal dewatering centrifuge', 'stability problems') and indeed of nominalization in general. By **nominalization** we mean the use of a noun which, in the same language or in a TT, could be replaced by an expression not containing a noun. Nominalization as such is discussed in Chapter 16; we shall just note here its prevalence in technical texts. The electrolysis text contains good French examples of nominalization and some of its effects. Here, for discussion, are ll. 5–7 and an alternative formulation without nominalization:

Vers 300 microns une fissuration apparaît, soit au moment de l'usinage soit, dans la cellule, au cours de la montée en température.	Vers 300 microns le disque se fissure, soit quand on l'usine, soit, dans la cellule, pendant que monte la température.

It must be remembered, however, that even non-technical French makes much more use of nominalization than non-technical English does. So, in translating technical texts, it should not be assumed that all ST nominal structures must necessarily be rendered with TL nominal structures. The sentence we have just looked at contains an example; compare two possible renderings of 'au cours de la montée en température': 'during the rise in temperature' vs 'as the temperature rises'.

The examples we have been looking at illustrate the features of scientific and technological language that Pinchuk neatly categorizes as follows:

1. [Technical language] is specialized and tends to become more and more specialized in contrast to the versatility of ordinary language. [Everyday] language tends towards liveliness and multiplicity of meaning, but the controlled language of science is manipulated in the direction of insipidity and colourlessness.
2. It seeks the most economic use of linguistic means to achieve standardization of terms and usage.
3. It seeks to avoid ordinary language associations and endeavours to define terms accurately.

(Pinchuk 1977: 165)

As Pinchuk points out (246–51), before embarking on a translation it is important to ascertain whether the work has already been translated. He provides a list of organizations which have registers of available translations, including Aslib (The Association of Special Libraries and Information Bureaux). And of course technical translation, like translation in any genre, requires familiarity with SL and TL material of a similar type, to serve as a source of information and as a stylistic model. The translator may well need some time to find the information sought (e.g. concepts or lexis). Useful sources of information include monographs, abstracting and indexing journals, periodicals, yearbooks, textbooks, encyclopedias, standards and trade literature, theses and dissertations. Increasingly, the Internet is being used for up-to-date information. Some organizations keep databases containing centrally agreed translations of technical expressions; an example is Eurodicautom, the European Commission's multilingual termbank. These databases are continually added to, and translators are expected to conform to the agreed renderings, in the interests of organization-wide consistency and clarity.

We have quoted a number of times from the text on p. 173. In preparation for Practical 12, the problems it poses should be analysed, and a translation attempted. The exercises in Practical 12 will show that, apart from the lexical and conceptual problems outlined above, technical translation is not essentially different from most other sorts of translation: as long as specialist help can be called on, there is no reason why anyone should not confidently tackle technical translation in any field. Trainee translators, of course, with the help of their seniors, very rapidly become fully competent in their specialist areas.

PRACTICAL 12

12.1   Scientific and technical translation

Assignment
After class discussion of problems encountered in translating the electrolysis text, compare your TT with the published one, which will be given to you by your tutor. (We give no contextual information for this text, apart from the points made in the chapter. This is so that you can distinguish clearly between the problems requiring specialist knowledge and the usual characteristic differences between French and English.)

12.2   Scientific and technical translation

Assignment
(i)   You are translating the following ST for publication in a monthly journal of abstracts of recent research. Discuss the strategic decisions

that you have to take before starting detailed translation of this ST, and outline the strategy you adopt.

(ii)   Translate the text into English.
(iii) Explain the main decisions of detail you took.
(iv)   Discuss the published TT (ECSC-CERCHAR 1987: 21), which will be given to you by your tutor.

Contextual information

The text is part of an abstract of a study on safety in mines. In line 23, translate 'tubbings' as 'segmental linings'. The reference is to the technique of lining a tunnel with metal or concrete as it is dug. The lining is prefabricated, and is installed in segments ('tubbings').

ST

PRESENTATION DU PROBLEME A ETUDIER

Les moyens de lutte contre les feux ont considérablement évolué au cours de ces dernières années, en particulier grâce à l'utilisation de l'azote.

Cela a permis une intervention plus rapide, mais aussi plus progressive,
5   la fermeture de l'enceinte dans laquelle se développe un feu pouvant être limitée à des barrages légers qui seront ensuite déposés en cas de retour dans le chantier traité ou renforcés dans le cas contraire.

La réussite de la méthode est d'autant plus probable que sa mise en œuvre est plus rapide.
10 D'autre part, l'édification de tout barrage à proximité d'une zone en échauffement ou en feu présente certains risques qu'il est nécessaire de réduire au minimum.

PLAN DE TRAVAIL

Une voie de recherche consiste en l'utilisation de matériaux plus légers
15 ou plus facilement transportables afin d'en accélérer l'acheminement au lieu du barrage. A cet égard, l'utilisation de mousses incombustibles est susceptible d'apporter une amélioration considérable.

Une autre voie vise à réaliser le barrage, ou au moins la plus grosse partie du barrage, à distance. Il pourra s'agir d'essais de nouvelles struc-
20 tures gonflables, mais surtout d'un mode approprié de mise en œuvre de mousses à prise rapide.

Un troisième domaine sera exploré : la réalisation de barrages rapides et adaptés pour la fermeture des tubbings de dressants.

(ECSC-CERCHAR 1987: 21)

grammatical transposition

13

Legal and financial translation

For the lay translator, the many genres of legal and business text can be just as disconcerting as technical texts, and for exactly the same lexical and conceptual reasons. There is an added complication, however. Technical texts may be unfamiliar to the lay person, but at least they are talking about the same set of phenomena, whatever the language – *CrMo steel* is *CrMo-Stahl* is *acier au CrMo*, etc. But there are real differences between, say, the French and English legal, financial and tax systems (not to mention the difference between Scottish and English law). So translators have not only to master SL and TL terminology, but also to familiarize themselves with the different systems and have a clear idea of the closest equivalences between them. Still, foreign trade does take place, British people do buy houses abroad, Europol does function, and so on. So translation between the systems is possible. The translator has two broad functions in enabling these things to happen. The first is to translate texts that have the force of law (e.g. legislation, constitutions, contracts) or are required by law (e.g. financial statements). The second is to translate legal or financial texts not as legally binding documents, but for other purposes, such as giving or requesting information.

We shall look first at translating texts that have the force of law. The vital things here are scrupulous accuracy and, usually, no matter how complex the ST may be, to produce a TT that respects the ST layout. Some French and English genres have similar layouts in any case, although the style is often more heavily nominalized in French and may need local grammatical transposition. But there is no question of large-scale textual reorganization in such texts. And, where an organization is multinational, like the European Union, it is especially important to keep the same format for the text in each language. We saw an example of this on pp. 104–5, in the context of grammatical and sentential issues.

Contracts and legally binding agreements must be translated with similar considerations in mind to legislative or constitutional texts. Here, as
samples, are excerpts from typical French and English publishers' contracts:

French text
ENTRE LES SOUSSIGNES :
- Monsieur [*author's name*], demeurant [*author's address*], agissant en
tant qu'auteur, ci-dessous dénommé 'AUTEUR', d'une part,
- et la Société à responsabilité limitée [*name of publisher*], dont le siège
5 est à [*address of publisher*], ci-dessous dénommée 'L'Editeur', d'autre
part,
IL A ETE CONVENU CE QUI SUIT :
- Monsieur [*author's name*] cède à la Société à responsabilité limitée
[*name of publisher*] qui accepte pour elle et ses ayants droit, dans les
10 termes des dispositions ci-après énoncées, le droit exclusif d'exploiter sa
propriété littéraire sur l'ouvrage [*title of book*].
    Dans le cadre du présent traité, l'Auteur cède à 'L'Editeur' le droit
exclusif d'imprimer, publier, reproduire et vendre ledit ouvrage sous forme
d'éditions de tous formats, ordinaires, illustrées, de luxe ou populaires, à
15 tirage limité ou non.
    De son côté, 'L'Editeur' s'engage à assurer à ses frais la publication
en librairie de cet ouvrage et il s'emploiera à lui procurer, par une diffu-
sion dans le public et auprès des tiers susceptibles d'être intéressés, les
conditions favorables à son exploitation sous toutes les formes. En consid-
20 ération de cet engagement pris par 'L'Editeur', et une telle publication
étant susceptible d'apporter à l'ouvrage une exploitation plus étendue,
l'Auteur cède en outre à 'L'Editeur' qui aura seul le pouvoir de les gérer
et d'en disposer, tous les droits patrimoniaux d'adaptation, de reproduc-
tion et représentation de l'ouvrage.
    [. . .]
25 1. - L'Auteur remettra le texte dactylographié de son texte, ainsi que
l'ensemble des documents photographiques à reproduire, à 'L'Editeur'
dans les meilleurs délais.
    Le manuscrit doit être définitif et complet (avec les documents d'illus-
trations), en double exemplaire, dactylographié à double interligne au recto
30 seulement, et soigneusement revu et mis au point pour l'impression.
'L'Editeur' ne pourra donc supporter les conséquences de modifications,
remaniements ou mise au point ultérieurs du texte, ni quant aux frais ni
quant aux délais.
    Les épreuves communiquées à l'Auteur devront être retournées avec le
35 bon à tirer dans les dix jours suivant leur réception par l'Auteur. A défaut,
'L'Editeur' pourra procéder au tirage sans attendre davantage.

English text
AN AGREEMENT
dated [*date*] between
(1) [*author's name*] of [*author's address*] (the 'Author', which expression
shall, where the context admits, include the Author's executors, adminis-
5   trators and assigns or successors in title as the case may be)
and
(2) [*name of publisher*] of [*address of publisher*] (the 'Publishers', which
expression shall, where the context admits, include any publishing imprint
subsidiary to or associated with the Publishers and the Publishers' admin-
10 istrators and assigns or successors in business as the case may be).

Recital/Background
The Author is writing, compiling or editing an original work at present
entitled [*title of book*] consisting of the materials indicated in Schedule
A, attached (hereinafter called 'the Work').

15 **Delivery of the Work**
1. (a) The Author undertakes to deliver the Work as specified in Schedule
A (attached) ready for the printer in content and form acceptable to the
Publishers and conforming to the Publishers' house style by [*date*] unless
otherwise mutually agreed in writing.
20   (b) Time is of the essence for delivery of the work. Should the Author
fail or neglect to deliver the completed Work by the prescribed date the
Publishers may, if they think fit, decline to publish the Work, and shall
be entitled upon giving notice to this effect to terminate this Agreement
forthwith. [. . .]

25 **Publishers' Obligations**
3. Provided that the Author has complied with all his/her undertakings
under the terms of this Agreement the Publishers shall, unless prevented
by war, strikes, lock-outs or other circumstances beyond the Publishers'
control, unless otherwise agreed with the Author, at their own risk and
30 expense produce and publish the Work. The Publishers shall have the
entire control of the publication, and the paper, printing, binding,
jacket and embellishments, the manner and extent of advertisement, the
number and distribution of free copies for the Press or otherwise, and the
price and terms of sale of the first or any subsequent edition shall be in
35 their sole direction. The Publishers shall not be responsible for any
accidental loss or damage to the Work, by fire or otherwise, while it is
in their custody or in the course of production. [. . .]

Grant of Rights

5. In consideration of the payments hereinafter mentioned the Author
40   grants to the Publishers the sole and exclusive right and licence to produce
and publish, and to license others to produce and publish, the Work or
any adaptation, abridgement or translation of the Work, or any part of the
Work, in all forms and media whether now in existence or invented after
the date of this Agreement in all languages throughout the world for the
45   full term of copyright, including all renewals and extensions thereof and
including all vested and contingent and future rights of copyright whether
now or hereafter known and also the right to renew and extend such copyright and other rights. [. . .]

Proofs, Index, Copyright Fees and State of the Manuscript

50   7. (a) The Author undertakes to read and correct the proofs of the Work
and to return the proofs to the Publishers promptly. In the event of the
Author failing to return the proofs to the Publishers within the time specified by the Publishers, the Publishers may consider the proofs as passed
for press.

These two texts are very differently organized from each other. In part
this reflects differences between French and British practice, and in part
it shows that different publishers prioritize different things. As we have
seen, in many genres, TL conventions imply that the TT should be arranged
differently from the ST, to conform with TL genre requirements. But a
contract normally only has legal force under source-culture law, and is
translated essentially for information. There is thus no point in embarking
on a rearrangement, especially given the differences between different
publishers' priorities. The main thing, then, translating a contract or agreement, is to respect the arrangement and detail of the ST, making sure that
the content is clear.

Bearing these comments in mind, compare the two texts carefully, and
then translate the last 12 lines of the French text into English.

A particularity of contracts in English, as of constitutional texts, is the
use of third-person 'shall' to signify a binding obligation or prescription.
If 'will' is used in a contract, it signifies that the event is a matter of fact
rather than of obligation.

A less traditionally formal genre is what might be called the 'summary
of terms and conditions', such as might be sent with a credit card or a
club card. Certainly in English-speaking countries, these tend to use 'we'
and 'you' rather than third-person forms, and to use everyday verb tenses
rather than 'shall'. But if one signs a declaration that one has read the
terms and conditions and agrees to abide by them, these texts are just as

binding as more formally drafted ones. In France, even when they are purely informative and not binding, they are often less personal, and it would be prudent not to produce TTs as informal as the conventional English ones: too personal a text might be perceived as undermining the dignity of the company, or as trivializing the arrangement proposed. On the other hand, you may not want to make the company sound pompous to a target public; in that case, it is normally acceptable to avoid where possible the legal 'shall', even where the ST is in the third person. There was an example of this kind of text in Practical 5.4. If you did not do that assignment, it would be useful to look at it for Practical 13.

To come now to translating legal texts that do purely and simply give or request information. Here, while accuracy is essential, there is sometimes more scope for flexibility in respect of layout and style in the TT. To take a hypothetical case, imagine that a *juge des enfants* writes to the competent foreign authorities to make certain enquiries in connection with the guardianship or custody of a child. It is an official request, made with reference to certain French laws, listed in the letter. As the laws do not apply as such outside France, the *juge* encloses photocopies of the relevant parts of the *Code civil* and the *Code de procédure civile* to show the basis on which he has made the request. These obviously need to be translated, and the translator must use appropriate legal terms where necessary, but there is no need to adopt the formal language of UK parliamentary acts in translating what is in any case a digest of a number of *lois* and *décrets*. Here are two of these extracts, for class discussion and translation. The first is from the section of the *Code civil* dealing with *assistance éducative*; the second is from the section in the *Code de procédure civile* on *commissions rogatoires*.

ST 1 (i)

Art. 375 Si la santé, la sécurité ou la moralité d'un mineur non émancipé sont en danger, ou si les conditions de son éducation sont gravement compromises, des mesures d'assistance éducative peuvent être ordonnées par justice à la requête des père et mère conjointement, ou de l'un d'eux,
5 *(L. n° 87 – 570 du 22 juill. 1987)* « de la personne ou du service à qui l'enfant a été confié » ou du tuteur, du mineur lui-même ou du ministre public. Le juge peut se saisir d'office à titre exceptionnel.

Elles peuvent être ordonnées en même temps pour plusieurs enfants relevant de la même autorité parentale.
10 *(L. n° 86 – 17 du 6 janv. 1986, art. 51)* « La décision fixe la durée de la mesure sans que celle-ci puisse, lorsqu'il s'agit d'une mesure éducative exercée par un service ou une institution, excéder deux ans. La mesure peut être renouvelée par décision motivée. »

ST 1 (ii)

COMMISSIONS ROGATOIRES A DESTINATION D'UN ETAT ETRANGER

Art. 733 Le juge peut, à la demande des parties, ou d'office, faire procéder dans un Etat étranger aux mesures d'instruction ainsi qu'aux autres actes judiciaires qu'il estime nécessaires en donnant commission rogatoire soit
5 à toute autorité judiciaire compétente de cet Etat, soit aux autorités diplomatiques ou consulaires françaises.

Art. 734 Le secrétaire de la juridiction commettante adresse au ministère public une expédition de la décision donnant commission rogatoire accompagnée d'une traduction établie à la diligence des parties.

Art. 735 Le ministère public fait aussitôt parvenir la commission roga-
10 toire au ministre de la justice aux fins de transmission, à moins qu'en vertu d'un traité la transmission puisse être faite directement à l'autorité étrangère.

A common form of legal translation for information purposes concerns court cases conducted, under French law, between, say, a French citizen and a British company. Here, for the British lawyers, the translator's job is typically to translate the background information and the texts of any judgements and appeals. So it is not unusual (though of course deeply alarming) to be confronted with a sentence like this:

Pour rejeter le moyen de la société [*name of company*] suivant lequel la chambre de la cour d'appel ne pouvait connaître de l'appel du jugement sur le fond dès lors que, par l'intermédiaire d'un magistrat ayant siégé dans les deux formations, elle avait précédemment connu de l'appel d'une ordonnance de référé attribuant une provision à M. [*name of*
5 *party*] et porté à cette occasion des appréciations sur des points qui étaient de nouveau en litige au fond, la cour d'appel a énoncé que, bien qu'elle ait déjà statué sur des points de droit à nouveau soumis à son examen, elle n'avait pas à se dessaisir dès lors que les deux instances n'étaient pas de même nature s'agissant, d'une part, d'un appel contre
10 une ordonnance de référé qui n'a pas au principal l'autorité de la chose jugée, d'autre part, d'une instance au fond, de sorte qu'en se prononçant sur l'appel du référé la Cour ne pouvait être considérée comme s'étant déjà prononcée sur le litige au fond et que la distinction des deux actions concernées ne permettait pas à la société [*name of company*] d'exciper
15 utilement de l'article 6,1° de la Convention européenne de sauvegarde des droits de l'homme et des libertés fondamentales pour solliciter le dessaisissement de la troisième chambre de la Cour.

Clearly, the translator has to know what the technical terms mean ('moyen', 'connaître de', the uses of 'fond', etc.), but an even bigger problem is working out the structure of the sentence. Luckily, once this has been done, it is legitimate to recast the sentence or split it up, so that the message is instantly clear. Certainly, as with the excerpts from the *Codes*, the TL barrister or advocate requires an accurate TT. But as the TT is for information only, there is every reason to produce a user-friendly combination of accuracy with clarity: the outcome of the case may depend on it.

This is one reason why, with texts of this type or with contracts, it is standard practice for the translator to add a disclaimer declining responsibility for the legal consequences of the TT, or for any obscurity arising from differences between the two legal systems. In fact, the safest thing is to do this with *any* legal translation. It is the reponsibility of the end-user of the translation to find out the precise implications of source-culture bodies, courts and legal terms, and to act accordingly. Thus a typical disclaimer might read:

> This translation is not intended, and may not be interpreted, to consti-tute legal advice; only a lawyer admitted to practise in the jurisdiction in question can give advice about the meaning of this law. Nor can there be any assurance that a regulatory agency or court of law has not construed, or will not construe, the original statute/regulation in a way inconsistent with this translation.

Another commonly translated genre is the annual report and financial statements to shareholders. These may be in abbreviated or full form. A typical statement will be preceded by a substantial overview of the year, called a *rapport d'activité* (business review). The report proper will then typically comprise a *rapport de gestion* (management report), the *bilan* (balance sheet), the *compte de résultat* (statement of income), and perhaps a *tableau de flux de trésorerie* (cashflow statement) and a *tableau de financement* (statement of changes in financial position; the type of infor-mation given under this heading in one company's report may well appear piecemeal under different headings in another's). Whatever other head-ings are used in a particular company's accounts, they will always be followed by an *annexe* (notes to the financial statements), saying what accounting policies have been used and giving further disclosure relating to items in the statements. Finally, companies are required by law to have the accounts audited by an independent auditor (or two, in the case of publicly quoted companies); the document must include an 'auditor's report', stating that in the auditor's opinion the accounts present a true and fair view of the company's financial results.

The language of finance and accountancy is as esoteric in French as in English: as with scientific and technological texts, translators have to famil-iarize themselves with SL and TL terminology, partly with help from a mentor, partly by looking at representative TL texts. Once the terminology, conventions and different national systems have been mastered, there are three other factors which may come into play.

First, given the differences in accounting practice between France and English-speaking countries, the translator must decide how to lay out the TT. In fact, there is little choice: there are official internationally agreed translations of accounting captions, and these are normally used. It is usual to copy the ST arrangement in the TT. It is emphatically not the translator's job to supply more, or less, information than is given in the ST.

One things translators do typically come up against is the request to use exactly the same headings and terminology as in the client company's previous annual reports. Even where the translator points out that a given TL rendering is inappropriate, the company will not agree to a change, for fear of being flooded with phone calls from analysts wondering what they are trying to hide.

Second, if the accounts are produced in conformity with different legal requirements from target-culture ones, a gist and/or exegetic translation may be in order. This is something to check with the company. We saw an extreme example on p. 10, but it really is not uncommon to see TTs like the following:

ST	*TT*
Les comptes consolidés de ***** SA sont établis conformément à la loi du 3 janvier 1985 et son décret d'application, étant précisé à cet 5 égard que l'option retenue de présentation des postes du bilan est celle du classement long terme et court terme conformément aux principes comptables généralement 10 admis au plan international.	The consolidated financial statements of ***** SA have been prepared in accordance with French generally accepted accounting principles and with the international accounting principles recommended by the International Accounting Standards Committee (IASC).

In this case, both ST and TT have clearly been drafted on a need-to-know basis. Strictly speaking, the TT does not correspond to the ST. 'In accordance' only applies to order by maturity (i.e. 'classement long terme et court terme'); and the IASC system is only one option among international accounting principles (there is also e.g. the United States Generally Accepted Accounting Principles). What probably lies behind this TT is that the translators identified the headings in the accounts as IAS headings, asked the client to confirm that this was the case, and indicated as much in their text.

It is, however, also common to see a faithful TT, however esoteric the French legal details may seem to TL readers, as here:

ST	TT
Les comptes consolidés de ***** sont établis suivant les règles comptables généralement admises au plan international, préconisées 5 par l'International Accounting Standards Committee (IASC).	*****'s consolidated financial statements are drawn up according to internationally accepted accounting principles, as recommended by the International Accounting Standards Committee (IASC).
Ils sont également en accord avec la loi du 3 janvier 1985 et son décret d'application du 17 10 février 1986.	These statements also conform to the law of January 3, 1985, enacted by decree dated February 17, 1986.

As these two examples suggest, there is often more freedom for sentential reorganization in this kind of text than in a text having the force of law, although there are existing IASC translations of such texts. Using this freedom, have a go at translating this sentence from some Notes to financial statements ('MdF' = 'Milliards de Francs'):

ST 2

La mise en œuvre rigoureuse des actions décidées et renforcées tout au long de l'année, afin d'adapter le potentiel de l'entreprise au contexte économique, à savoir :

- réduction drastique des frais de fonctionnement,
5 - réduction des cadences et adaptation, en conséquence, du potentiel,
- freinage de l'investissement (1,7 MdF contre 2,8 MdF l'année précédente),
- réduction des dépenses de recherche et de développement autofinancées, 4,3 MdF contre 5,2 MdF, tout en améliorant leur productivité et leur 10 efficacité,

ont permis de ramener la perte d'exploitation de 1,22 MdF à 0,26 MdF et de diminuer le besoin de fonds de roulement de 4,36 MdF.

(Aerospatiale 1994a: 42)

Finally, in terms of genre, big companies typically produce a hybrid text, combining the statutory financial statements with a lavishly illustrated narrative report of the firm's activities which amounts to an advertising pitch. A further element here is that the glossy description inevitably contains a lot of technical material, depending on what the company manufactures. So the translator may well need to be familiar not just with the language of accountancy, but with e.g. the latest in computer software or ski technology or aeronautical engineering. Some translation firms will give the financial statements to one translator and the glossy material to another – but even then, the person doing the advertising material will not be able to escape the language of finance entirely. There is an example of this in Practical 2.1. If you did this assignment, we recommend looking at it again as an illustration of some of the points made in the present chapter. If you did not, it is worth doing as part of Practical 13.

Here is a more purely financial ST than the one in Practical 2.1, for comment on salient features and draft translation. Make notes on the elements that raise translation problems, and how they can best be tackled. If necessary, consult friends studying economics, management and accountancy. The text is from the *rapport d'activité* of an electrical engineering firm with many subsidiaries in France and abroad.

ST 3

Au 31 décembre 1996, le chiffre d'affaires consolidé s'est élevé à 43,8 milliards de francs, soit + 4,6% par rapport à l'exercice précédent. A périmètre et taux de change comparables, cette progression aurait atteint + 4,7%. L'incidence de la traduction en francs français des chiffres d'af-
5 faires libellés en devises s'est élevée à + 545 millions de francs.

Le chiffre d'affaires réalisé en France s'est légèrement redressé au cours du dernier trimestre limitant ainsi la baisse du chiffre d'affaires à 3%, dans un contexte de faiblesse de l'investissement industriel et de la construction non-résidentielle.
10 En Europe la croissance de l'activité des filiales s'est maintenue à un niveau satisfaisant : + 7,3% à périmètre et taux de change constants, toujours entraînée par l'activité des sociétés de Grande-Bretagne, d'Espagne et d'Italie.

En Amérique du Nord, la croissance s'est élevée à 6,4% à périmètre et
15 taux de change comparables en raison, d'une part, de la croissance continue du marché résidentiel aux USA et, d'autre part, de la sensible progression de l'activité des filiales canadienne et mexicaine.

(Schneider 1997a: 38)

To sum up, in translating French legal and financial texts the accent will be on accuracy, clarity and avoidance of ambiguity. In TTs that do not have the force of law, some referring expressions (e.g. 'le Code civil', 'l'article 103 de la loi du 24 juillet 1966') may need a touch of exegesis and/or gist to show that they refer to the SL culture and not the TT culture: 'the French Civil Code', 'French corporate legislation'. If the TT does have the force of law (e.g. a contract), there is no such latitude: there will still need to be reference to the French Civil Code, but details of specific laws and articles must also be spelt out as in the ST. With some texts, it may be necessary to include footnotes or translator's notes. But it is essential to remember that it is *never* the translator's job to add anything that amounts to comment on, or interpretation of, substantive points of law (see Hickey 1998: 224–6). The prerequisite is to know what the purpose of the TT is. Is it being used in a legal action? Is it the subject of controversy or dispute? No text of any kind is produced in a vacuum, and the more that is known about the subject matter of the ST, the more fit for its purpose the TT will be.

As with any area, the debutant translator should build up for reference purposes a portfolio of 'parallel texts' in both languages, such as contracts and tenders, balance sheets, certificates and official documents. This makes it possible to get a feel for different types of document and register, to understand how they work, what they are for and the specialist language used. The conventions used in both languages will gradually become apparent, and can be automatically applied in translation. The Internet is an increasingly useful source of such information, e.g. www.findlaw.com, www.freshfields.com, and the LIFT network of the Institute of Translation and Interpreting (see www.iti.org.uk for details). And for this and many other areas of professional translating activity, there is an excellent information and advice service called 'The Bottom Line', by Fire Ant & Worker Bee, at www.accurapid.com/journal.

PRACTICAL 13

13.1 Legal translation

Assignment
After class discussion of problems encountered in translating the excerpt from the publishing contract (p. 184), compare your TT with a specimen given you by your tutor.

13.2 Legal translation

Assignment
After class discussion of problems encountered in translating STs 1 (i) and (ii) on pp. 187–8, compare your TT with a specimen one given you by your tutor.

13.3 Legal translation

Assignment
(i) You are translating a contract, from which the following ST is taken. The contract is for the sale of property, under French law, by a French person to a Briton. The French and English texts will be printed alongside one another throughout the contract; articles and paragraphs should therefore be numbered identically in ST and TT. Discuss the strategic decisions that you have to take before starting

detailed translation of this ST, and outline and justify the strategy you adopt.

(ii)   Translate the text into English.

(iii) Explain the main decisions of detail you took.

Contextual information

The contract is headed 'Contrat de vente immobilière sous conditions suspensives'. It consists of four pages of general conditions and four of special and specific conditions. The general conditions comprise thirteen articles relating to designation of the parties, description of the property, terms, etc. The special and specific conditions consist of a set of forms to be filled in with details of the actual parties concerned, the property, methods of financing the purchase, etc. The ST consists of two extracts from Article 8 of the 'Conditions générales', which covers protection of the borrower if the purchase is financed by a loan. The 'rédacteur' is the lawyer who is drawing up the contract.

ST

Dans le cas où la présente vente serait conclue à l'aide d'emprunt, l'ac- quéreur remplira les informations demandées au 8.b des conditions particulières, et la présente vente sera alors soumise à la condition suspen- sive de l'obtention du ou des prêts qui seront sollicités par l'acquéreur
5   (et, le cas échéant, par le rédacteur dûment mandaté à cet effet) et dont les caractéristiques seront définies au 8.b des conditions particulières.

Cette condition est stipulée au seul profit de l'acquéreur.
Elle est définie de la façon suivante :

1) Durée et réalisation de la condition suspensive :

10   La durée et la validité de la présente condition suspensive est fixée au 8.b § G des conditions particulières, étant entendu qu'elle ne peut être inférieure à un mois conformément à l'article 17 de la loi n° 79–596 du 13 juillet 1979.

La présente condition suspensive sera considérée comme réalisée dès
15   que l'acquéreur aura obtenu, dans le délai fixé, un ou plusieurs prêts couvrant le montant global de la somme à financer par emprunt et répondant aux caractéristiques définies au 8.b des conditions parti- culières. [. . .]

4) Non réalisation de la condition suspensive :

20   Si la condition suspensive n'est pas réalisée dans le délai prévu au 8.b § G des conditions particulières, sans que ce défaut incombe à l'ac- quéreur, et sauf renonciation par ce dernier à ladite condition dans la forme prévue ci-après au paragraphe 5), chacune des parties retrou- vera sa pleine et entière liberté, sans indemnité de part et d'autre.
25   Dans ce cas, tout versement effectué par l'acquéreur lui sera immédi- atement et intégralement restitué.

En revanche, si la non-obtention des prêts a pour cause la faute, la négligence ou tout abus de droit de l'acquéreur comme en cas de comportements ou de réticences de nature à faire échec à l'instruction des dossiers ou à la conclusion des contrats de prêts, le vendeur pourra demander au tribunal de déclarer la condition suspensive de prêt réalisée, en application de l'article 1178 du Code Civil avec attribution de dommages-intérêts pour le préjudice subi du fait de l'immobilisation abusive des biens à vendre.

13.4 Financial translation

Assignment
After class discussion of problems encountered in translating ST 2 on p. 191, compare your TT with the published one, which will be given you by your tutor.

13.5 Financial translation

After class discussion of problems encountered in translating ST 3 on p. 191, compare your TT with the published one, which will be given to you by your tutor.

14

Translating consumer-oriented texts

All texts, including translations, are produced for a purpose. The purpose is always a major factor in deciding a strategy. Translating consumer-oriented texts makes the importance of purpose especially clear. This, together with the fact that many translators earn their living with these sorts of text, is why we are giving them a chapter to themselves.

By 'consumer-oriented texts', we mean texts which try to persuade the public to buy something, or tell purchasers how to use what they have bought, or advise on commodities that might be bought or on courses of action that might be taken. The range thus includes advertisements, tourist brochures, user manuals, consumer magazines, recipe books, CD booklets, public notices, information leaflets, etc. – even propaganda can be classified under this heading. Consumer-oriented texts may therefore fall into the category either of persuasive or of empirical genres, or both. Often, they have literary, religious or philosophical genre-features as well. Sometimes, they are so specialized that they are given to technical translators; even then, the translator has to keep consumerist criteria in mind (compare e.g. 'If the battery goes flat' and 'In the unlikely event of your battery going flat').

The most extreme instance of consumer-oriented translation is translating advertisements. This is often as much a question of writing original copy as of translation. In fact, big firms are likely to ask an agency to produce a tailor-made advertisement for the target culture. But it is not rare for translators to be asked to translate advertisements, and intra-trade publicity is commonly translated. Many multinationals, keen to ensure a distinctive brand image world-wide, either have all their translating done in-house, in close cooperation with other departments (e.g. marketing), or commission all their translations from one agency, with which they work closely in ensuring presentational norms of all kinds (see Guidère 2000: 14–15). This cooperation is in fact often two-way: in order to avoid potential difficulties posed by the varying requirements of different target cultures, and thus to ensure quicker and more efficient translation, the agency draws up its own style sheet and presentational recommendations, and urges companies to produce STs that conform with these. For our needs in this course, translating advertising material is certainly a good way of focusing attention on the dimension of purpose in textual genre. If you did not do Practicals 3.1, 3.2, 6.1 or 10.2, we recommend that you at least look at them for this chapter.

Translating advertising material also obliges the translator to consider carefully the central question of cultural differences between SL public and TL public: nowhere more clearly may inter-cultural differences make literal translation unwelcome, even where it is possible. Different cultures value different things, and have different taboos. There is also evidence that different cultures stereotype consumers differently. These sorts of differences are just as important in consumer handbooks as in advertisements. In fact, many handbooks have an important publicity function as well, flattering purchasers and trying to cement their loyalty to the brand ('Congratulations! Now that you are the proud owner of . . .', etc.). Apart from such cultural factors as religion, race, diet, attitudes to sex, etc., it is also vital to choose the right language variety both in STs and in TTs. For instance, while the language of consumerism is more relaxed today in the West than it was even ten years ago, comparing different continental European versions of a typical computer handbook suggests that some cultures are still more resistant than others to chirpy informality in such texts.

It is impossible to generalize on the basis of one or two examples, but, as indicators of possible differences in cultural expectation that might influence translation choice, here are two pairs of texts for analysis and comparison (and not necessarily imitation!). The first is from computer literature, the English and French versions of the Windows 95 user manual:

ST	TT
If you asked a rocket scientist to explain what Windows is, he'd probably tell you that it's a computer operating system with a graphical user interface and a rich set of applications. Whatever that means. That definition certainly doesn't give you a clue as to why you'd want to use Windows, does it? So let's try the same question again, this time in plain English.	Si vous demandiez à un ingénieur en aéronautique de vous dire ce qu'est Windows, il vous répondrait certainement qu'il s'agit d'un système d'exploitation pour ordinateur qui dispose d'une interface utilisateur graphique et d'un grand nombre d'applications. C'est bien beau mais cette définition n'éclaire sans doute pas votre lanterne. Reformulons donc notre question afin d'obtenir une réponse plus directe.

The second pair of texts is from the English and French introductions to a recipe book supplied with the Braun Multipractic Plus food processor. Comparing the two may be particularly revealing, because neither is a translation of the other. They have been derived from a German original. Each is thus a clue to the cultural presuppositions that will have guided the respective translator/writers. The presuppositions comprise two things: a stereotype of consumer attitudes, behaviour and lifestyle; and recognition of the stylistic features typical of the genre. When it comes to actually translating such texts, these presuppositions are foremost amongst the target-culture expectations which the translator is required to prioritize. Compare the two in class, making detailed notes on how they resemble and differ from one another. In the practical, you will be given the rest of the French text and asked to produce an appropriate English TT.

French text

INTRODUCTION

Ce livre de cuisine ne prétend pas vous apprendre à cuisiner. Au contraire, nous supposons que vous le
5   savez déjà. Non, ce livre de cuisine voudrait vous ouvrir d'autres horizons en vous présentant des exemples de recettes de tout genre réalisables plus facilement, plus
10 rapidement et mieux encore à l'aide du Multipractic Plus.

  Le principe du Multipractic Plus est très simple : il fait tout ce qu'il fait en une fois en ne
15 nécessitant, dans la majorité des cas, qu'un seul accessoire, le bloc-couteau. Il en résulte trois avantages.

  D'abord, il ne vous sera plus
20 nécessaire, avant de commencer votre cuisine, de monter et démonter les pièces de l'appareil avec plus ou moins de difficulté. Ainsi, vous aurez moins de
25 vaisselle à laver et à ranger. Deux grands avantages que n'ont pas la majorité des appareils de cuisine ménagers : ils ne sont que peu ou pas utilisés, non pas en raison

English text

COOKING THE MODERN WAY

The object of this book isn't to teach you how to cook – we assume you're past the beginner stage! But now you have your Multipractic Plus to help you, there are so many recipes (not just complicated ones) that you can make faster, easier – and better.

  Basically, the Multipractic Plus is a very simple unit that does everything in just one working bowl. And for most purposes, you'll only need to use one attachment (the blade). This has three important advantages.

  First, you don't have to go through all the fuss and bother of sorting out which attachments you're going to need for a given recipe, and getting them all assembled and ready to use. Second, there's hardly anything to wash up and put away afterwards – the major timesaver. Too many kitchen appliances sit around in the cupboard and are hardly ever used, simply because they're more trouble to set up and clean than

30 d'un fonctionnement déficient, mais parce que leur assemblage, démontage et entretien prennent trop de temps.

(Braun 1981: 7)

they're worth. But your Braun Multipractic Plus has been specially designed to be quick to use and quick to clean.

(Braun 1981: 7)

The point is that, as ever, part of the translator's preparation must be to study examples of appropriate TL texts, so as to become familiar with the requirements and assumptions of the genre that is intended for the TT. It is just as important, of course, to be aware of stylistic features and cultural assumptions that are *not* characteristic of the intended TL genre. Even intralingually, if the style of the *Brownie Cookbook* were used in Delia Smith, her readers would be insulted, and would not not take her seriously. Conversely, Delia's style might be too adult for the Brownie. Either option would be commercial suicide. The trendy twenty-something niche requires something else again. In translation, putting notes for a Schubert CD booklet into *New Musical Express* style would be an act of commercial sabotage – as would translating M.C. Solaar notes into the English of Schubert criticism.

All these sorts of consideration will apply in Practical 14. It is, however, also important to remember that many changes in structure, vocabulary and register result more from standard differences between languages than from genre-specific cross-cultural differences. You will have seen this in comparing the Windows texts. Thus for instance 'a computer operating system' is rendered as 'un système *d'*exploitation *pour* ordinateur'; and 'with a graphical user interface' is rendered as '*qui dispose d'*une interface utilisateur graphique'. The greater length of the French expressions has nothing to do with tonal or other stylistic requirements of the genre; they are simply standard grammatical constraints which apply in the translation of any kind of text (alternatives to 'dispose de' here would be 'disposant de' or 'ayant'). Similarly, compare the following extracts from the bilingual leaflet accompanying a tube of French-made whitening toothpaste:

ST

De nombreux facteurs extérieurs provoquent l'apparition sur l'émail des dents, de taches plus ou moins étendues et plus ou moins colorées :

5 - L'usage du tabac entraîne une coloration qui varie du jaune au noir et dont l'intensité augmente avec la consommation.

- L'alimentation, certaines bois-
10 sons, favorisent également l'apparition de taches brunes tenaces qui s'incrustent dans l'émail.

TT

Many external factors can cause areas of coloured staining on the surface of teeth enamel:

- The use of tobacco causes a yellow to black coloration which becomes deeper when food is consumed.

- Food and some drinks also encourage the appearance of stubborn brown stains which build up on the enamel.

- La présence de tartre accentue le
phénomène car sa surface rugueuse
15 facilite la formation de dépôts.

- The presence of tartar intensifies
this phenomenon as its rough
surface encourages deposits to
form.

Whatever the genre, if the ST were translated literally into English, the
nominalization would sound over-formal or pompous. The TT avoids this
pitfall and, apart from 'teeth enamel', is accurate and idiomatic.

Finally, the same point can be made 'negatively', by comparing an ST
with a TT that, for whatever reason, has not taken grammatical and
idiomatic differences between SL and TL sufficiently into account. The
TT repays analysis and discussion in class. The texts are taken from a
leaflet supplied with a tube of 'Pâte Magique':

ST

POUR FAIRE UN BALLOON
1° Après vous être humecté les
doigts, prélevez un peu de Pâte
Magique, la valeur d'une cerise.
5 Enfoncez le chalumeau jusqu'au
centre et par légères pressions sur
la pâte faites-la bien adhérer au
chalumeau.
  2° Souffler doucement pour
10 commencer (jamais fort). Quand
le ballon aura dépassé la taille
d'une orange vous pouvez souffler
plus fortement. Cessez le gonfle-
ment alors que le ballon est
15 encore souple au toucher (ne pas
pousser jusqu'à parois rigides).
  3° Pour fermer le ballon, pincez-
le au-dessous du chalumeau, entre
pouce et index, pour rapprocher et
20 coller ses parois. Le chalumeau
étant ainsi isolé du ballon, retirez-
le doucement de l'autre main. Si,
par hasard, un trou se produit,
pincez le ballon à l'endroit du
25 trou, soit entre les doigts, soit
entre les lèvres.

TT

MAKING A BALLOON
1° With wet fingers, take a little
bit of Magical Paste, like a
cherry. Drive in the straw pipe to
the middle, then with light pres-
sures the paste must well adhere
to the straw pipe.
  2° Blow lightly for beginning,
never strongly. When the balloon
will be bigger than an orange, you
can blow stronger.
  Stop of blowing when the
balloon is still supple.
  3° For shutting the balloon,
pinch it under the straw pipe
between the thumb and the
forefinger, bring and stick its sides
together.
  The straw pipe being so cut off
from the balloon, pull it back
slightly with the other hand. If, by
chance, there is a hole, pinch the
balloon on the place of the hole,
either, with fingers or with lips.

PRACTICAL 14

14.1 Consumer-oriented translation

Assignment

(i) You have been commissioned to translate the recipe book supplied with a food processor. The ST is actually a continuation of the French Braun text of which we gave the first three paragraphs on pp. 198–9. Your TT should follow on clearly from the third paragraph of the English version of the text. This exercise is thus not a common 'real-world' one, because the ST is itself a translation of a German ST. However, for present purposes, you should imagine that it relates to a French product, and treat the English text on pp. 198–9 as evidence of the company's perception of how it needs to market its products in the United Kingdom; in commissioning the translation, the company will have given you guidelines on this matter. (This *is* akin to a real-world situation – see the comments on multinationals on p. 196.) Discuss the strategic decisons that you have to take before starting detailed translation of this ST, and outline and justify the strategy you adopt.

(ii) Translate the text into English. (If you know anyone with a Braun, resist the temptation to look at the recipe book: the published English version will be discussed in class.)

(iii) Explain the main decisions of detail you took.

(iv) Compare your translation with the published English version, which will be given to you by your tutor. In discussing these, it may be interesting to reflect on how far the published texts, which first appeared twenty years ago, accurately reflect contemporary cultural expectations.

Contextual information

The titles and the opening three paragraphs of both texts, printed on pp. 198–9, are useful contextual information. In line 3, translate 'le couteau' as 'the blade'.

ST

Ce n'est certainement pas le cas avec le Multipractic Plus qui présente encore un troisième avantage et non des moindres. La majorité des recettes se prépare dans le bol unique, à l'aide du seul couteau du Multipractic Plus. Par conséquent, il est possible d'effectuer plusieurs opérations succes-
5 sives sans avoir à vider ou nettoyer le bol à chaque reprise.
Pour profiter de cet avantage, il est indispensable de réfléchir d'abord à l'ordre de succession des opérations. Il convient ensuite de bien connaître comment le Multipractic Plus transforme les ingrédients selon qu'ils sont séparés ou mélangés.

Douze chapitres de ce livre y sont consacrés pour vous en parler et
vous le démontrer. Chaque chapitre traite une fonction essentielle du
Multipractic Plus, depuis le hachage des fines herbes jusqu'à la préparation d'une pâte à brioche. Toutes les opérations nécessaires sont expliquées
et illustrées, les résultats obtenus décrits et les tours de main révélés.
Chacun de ces chapitres est suivi de recettes illustrant une fonction de
base de l'appareil. Ainsi on trouvera de nombreuses recettes utilisant des
fines herbes hachées, ou une pâte à brioche, etc.
Afin de vous permettre de vous y retrouver plus facilement, nous avons
classé les recettes de façon habituelle en « entrées », « potages », « viandes »,
etc.
(Braun 1981: 7)

14.2   Consumer-oriented translation

Assignment
(i)   You have been commissioned to translate a catalogue presenting
        the full Spring/Summer range of a lingerie manufacturer. This extract
        comprises the introductory blurb and the presentation of 'Eclair',
        one of the ranges in the collection. Discuss the strategic decisions
        that you have to take before starting detailed translation of this ST,
        and outline and justify the strategy you adopt.
(ii)   Translate the text into English.
(iii) Explain the main decisions of detail you took.
(iv)   Compare your translation with the published TT, which will be given
        to you by your tutor.

Contextual information
The ST was published in early 2000, and refers to the Spring/Summer
collection from the corsetier Huit. 'Magic Huit', '2008 Sans Coutures'
and 'Actuels' are three of the ranges in the collection. Consulting cata-
logues at the local lingerie shop would be useful preparation for the
translation.

ST
Avec sa collection Printemps-Eté 2000, Huit diffuse un nouvel air empreint
de FRAICHEUR, de PURETE et de LEGERETE, pour envelopper la femme
dans une bulle de quiétude et de sérénité absolue.
Les COULEURS s'enhardissent d'un halo de luminosité à travers une
gamme osée de rose poudré, fuchsia, parme, vert anis, camel et gris.
Les MATIERES s'assagissent en puisant dans les ressources naturelles
du coton, la douceur des microfibres, la souplesse des dentelles et la trans-
parence des tulles irisés. [. . .]

Quand l'expérience fait la différence...

10 Une fois encore, le corsetier visionnaire nous éblouit par son savoir-faire et son sens de la créativité. Il joue avec les formes et les détails pour proposer une très large palette de modèles parfaitement adaptables à la morphologie de chaque femme :

- *des formes uniques et des concepts innovants* : l'incontournable Magic
15 Huit, l'avant-gardiste 2008 Sans Coutures, Les Actuels à l'allure intemporelle...

- *des fibres « intelligentes »* : l'ultra douceur de la Méryl® Microfibre, la tonicité de la Microfibre Sensitive Light Soft, la brillance du voile Sparkling, le confort inégalable du Jacquard Tubulaire et l'élasticité des
20 dentelles ouvragées, placées et parfois moulées – comme la moderne dentelle Fascination d'H_2O...

- *des finitions parfaites* : strass SWAROVSKI, doubles bretelles, délicats anneaux dorés à l'or fin...

Coup de foudre pour l'élégance...

25 Délicieux mariage de pureté et de sophistication, ECLAIR annonce de fabuleuses perturbations...

En gris perle et rose saumon, cette ligne éblouissante, tout en microfibre, offre une panoplie de modèles élégamment rehaussés d'étincelants strass SWAROVSKI : balconnet aux bonnets ourlés « pétales de tulipe », soutien-
30 gorge triangle padding, gainette, shorty et caraco...

Plus électrisante, la femme en l'an 2000 sera !

(Huit 2000)

14.3 Consumer-oriented translation

Assignment
(i)   You are translating a series of patient information leaflets for a French pharmaceutical company. The leaflets will have French on one side and the English on the other. The one from which this ST is taken is for inclusion in packs of antibiotics. Discuss the strategic decisions that you have to take before starting detailed translation of this ST, and outline and justify the strategy you adopt.
(ii) Translate the text into English.
(iii) Explain the main decisions of detail that you took.
(iv) Compare your translation with the published TT, which will be given to you by your tutor.

Contextual information
This is the first half of the text, giving information on the medicament contained in the pack. The second half is more discursive, and contains

general information on antibiotics and how to take them. The best preparation for translating this text is to look at a few leaflets supplied with similar target-culture products. It may also help to consult the local pharmacist. (It cannot always be assumed, of course, that the translator will be given a completely free hand in deciding style and layout by the firm commissioning the translation.) NB The spellings 'roxythromycine' and 'roxithromycine' are both *sic*.

ST

RUliD® 150mg roxythromycine

COMPRIMES/ADULTE

composition
Roxithromycine .... cent cinquante milligrammes
5 Excipient q.s.p. .... 1 comprimé enrobé
présentation
Boîte de 10 comprimés enrobés sous plaquette thermoformée.
indications
- Infections dues aux germes sensibles au **Rulid**, notamment dans les
10 manifestations O.R.L., bronchopulmonaires, génitales (à l'exception des infections gonococciques), cutanées.
contre-indications
- Allergie à la roxithromycine
- Association à l'ergotamine et à la dihydroergatomine.
15 **précautions d'emploi**
Prévenir le médecin traitant en cas de :
- insuffisance hépatique,
- prise associée à d'autres médicaments,
- allaitement,
20 - grossesse.
autres effets possibles du médicament
- Manifestations digestives :
    - nausées
    - vomissements
25   - douleurs d'estomac
    - diarrhées ;
- Manifestations allergiques.
- Vertiges.
effets sur la capacité de conduire des véhicules ou d'utiliser des
30 **machines**
Les risques de sensations vertigineuses peuvent rendre dangereuse la conduite automobile ou l'utilisation de certaines machines.
posologie et mode d'administration
Adulte : absorber 1 comprimé matin et soir, de préférence avant les repas.

15

Revising and editing TTs

Throughout the course, we have considered translation sometimes as a process, and sometimes as a product. The assessment of existing TTs has been an important feature in practicals. This chapter looks exclusively at the final stage of translation as a process, where the proposed TT is actually examined as a product.

Any form of post-translation process is an operation carried out in writing on a pre-existent text. Revision is concerned with ensuring accuracy by eliminating errors and inconsistencies. Errors of accuracy can be relatively minor, such as spelling mistakes or punctuation, but they can also include ungrammatical or misleading constructions. And it is not only the language of the TT which may be wrong or unsuitable: the concepts themselves may have been distorted in transmission. The TT is the sum not only of a translator's ability in the two linguistic systems concerned, but also of knowledge of the subject matter in question. So, for example, a translator may be equipped linguistically to tackle a text on computer software, but not have the expertise necessary to make the right terminological and practical decisions, thereby undermining the TT's authoritativeness.

In this chapter we shall refer to **revision** where the task concerns checking a TT against the ST for accuracy, and to **editing** where the TT requires 'polishing' after the revision process. The two overlap to some extent, especially where TT peculiarities are not so much errors as features of style.

As a preliminary exercise, it will be useful to assess the quality of the following TT and point out where the faults lie. It is from the abstract of a report on research into ultrasonic detection of clusters of impurities in sheet steel.

ST

L'étude dont il est rendu compte ici portait sur les possibilités de détection des amas inclusionnaires dans les tôles minces.

5 Le premier problème que nous ayons eu à résoudre est celui de l'approvisionnement en échantillons contenant des défauts significatifs. Plusieurs techniques
10 pouvant conduire à la création artificielle de tels échantillons furent essayées mais nous conduisirent à des échecs. Ce problème n'a été résolu que
15 lorsque l'usine d'Isbergues d'USINOR Châtillon a été équipée de moyens de contrôle industriel et a pu nous fournir des échantillons contenant des défauts
20 naturels. [. . .]

Nos échantillons étant principalement en aciers inoxydables, nous avons été conduits à mettre au point un logiciel permettant de
25 calculer les diagrammes de vitesses de phase et de vitesses de groupe pour ces aciers. [. . .]

En émission piézo-électrique nous avons étudié plus parti-
30 culièrement la réponse relative des défauts naturels en fonction du mode d'onde de Lamb et de la fréquence de l'émission ultrasonore utilisée. Pour un même
35 défaut, cette réponse varie de façon importante d'un mode à l'autre mais aussi, pour un même mode, avec la fréquence.

(Albert 1987: 510)

TT

The study here discussed was concerning the possibilities of detection of inclusion clusters in thin sheets.

The first problem which was solved is the one of making available samples involving significant defects. A few techniques were used in order to artificially make such samples but they all revealed being unsuccessful. This problem was solved when the USINOR Plant Chatillon at Isbergues was equipped with industrial control installation and was able to deliver samples with natural defects. [. . .]

Our samples were mainly stainless steels so that we were led to engineer a software allowing to calculate the phase and group velocity diagrams for these steels. [. . .]

With the piezoelectric emission we have particularly studied the response corresponding to natural defects in function of the Lambwaves mode and in function of the frequency of the used ultrasonic emission. For a same defect this response noticeably varies from a mode to another but for a same mode with the frequency.

(Albert 1987: 510)

One obvious quirk of the ST is the use of 'nous'. In French technical texts, 'on' or the passive is normal, but 'nous' is sometimes used where the text is reporting on (and perhaps promoting) the work of a company.

The TT is typical of an increasing number of science and engineering texts by Continental writers, in that it does not seem to have been translated by a native English speaker. The translator (most probably the author) has a good grasp of the TL technical terms – 'inclusion clusters', 'phase and group velocity diagrams', etc. – although 'Lambwaves' is better written as two words (cf. 'Lamb shift'). What does sometimes need revision is TL grammar and idiom.

In the first sentence, the archaic 'The study here discussed' sounds like something from a law court. More seriously, 'was concerning' is a classic mistake in translating the French imperfect. Errors in verb tense are common in English TTs produced by native French-speakers. The perfect, or *passé composé*, is as fertile in difficulties as the imperfect. In the above TT, there is actually only one example of this particular fault: in l. 25, 'we studied' is preferable to 'we have studied'. But obtrusive present perfects like this often mar English translations of scientific reports, as in the following text on blast-furnaces:

In order to detect and control the position and the shape of the softening-melting zone, several complementary methods have been used. [. . .] A special device allowed the measurement [. . .] from which the cohesive zone shape has been deduced. [. . .] the position of the cohesive zone foot has been derived. [. . .] The response of the softening-melting zone [. . .] has been studied [. . .], etc.

(ECSC-CRM (Belgique) 1987a: 502)

Even for a native English-speaking translator, the choice between English preterite and present perfect is not always obvious, of course. The deciding factor is usually context. Sometimes, the present perfect *is* the appropriate tense, as in this report, written in English by British engineers:

The majority of coalfaces in the United Kingdom are constrained by geology . [. . .] Monitoring and control systems are making a contribution to improving the efficiency of the longwall system . [. . .] Lost time due to machine breakdowns has been reduced, [. . .] and [. . .] it has been possible to expose the problem areas . [. . .] Face conditions and extraction have been improved . [. . .] These monitoring and control systems have been tested and evaluated [. . .] , etc.

(Barham and Cutts 1987: 481–2)

This text refers to the *still ongoing effects* triggered by things that *were* done – that is, because monitoring systems *were* introduced, there *is* still less time *being* lost, etc. The present perfect is the only appropriate tense in this case, whereas in the text on blast-furnaces the intended reference is only to the things that were done, not to any still ongoing effects they may have triggered.

Returning to the text on sheet metal, there are other slips in grammar and idiomaticity, among them the following:

ll. 6–7 'Making available samples' is at best ambiguous – does it mean 'making samples available' or 'manufacturing available samples'? The ST refers to *finding a supply* of samples; this phrase would be a suitable revision.

ll. 8–12 'A few techniques were used in order to [. . .] but they all revealed being unsuccessful' reads very oddly. It seems to be saying: 'So as to make such samples, we used a few techniques.' 'A few' is the wrong determiner – it corresponds more to 'quelques', putting the emphasis on 'techniques', whereas the ST emphasis is on the fact that they tried several. 'Used' loses the essential notion of 'tried out'. 'In order to' does not accurately render 'pouvant conduire à', which corresponds more to the preposition 'for'. 'Revealed being unsuccessful' is not even a literal translation of the ST expression. It seems to be modelled on something like 'se sont révélées infructueuses'. An acceptable revised TT would be : 'Several techniques for the artificial creation of such samples were tried {without success/but all proved unsuccessful}.'

ll. 13–14 'The USINOR Plant Chatillon at Isbergues' might be decodable for an informed reader, but it is hopelessly garbled (not to mention the missing circumflex). According to the ST, there is a company, USINOR Châtillon, which has a factory at Isbergues. The TT should be revised to: 'USINOR Châtillon's Isbergues plant'.

l. 21 '*Allowing to* calculate' is a common francophone slip in such contexts; revise to: 'permitting calculation'.

ll. 29–30 'The used ultrasonic emission' sounds like 'the second-hand ultrasonic emission'; revise to: 'the ultrasonic emission used'.

ll. 30–33 '*A same* defect/mode' is another classic French-speaker's error; revise to: 'a single defect/mode'.

ll. 32 'From a mode to another' is another faulty determiner; revise to: 'from one mode to another'.

It is not just technical TTs produced by native SL speakers that benefit from revision. Here is a literary ST with a TT produced by an English-speaker. (*Contextual information*. The text is set in rural Provence. Ugolin's new neighbour, the hunchback Jean, is explaining his plans for making money by large-scale rabbit-breeding. His wife Aimée is also there. His estimates are based on a specialist book he has read, in which it says that after three years a modern breeder should be able to get five hundred rabbits a month from a single pair. He has just been talking about the huge rabbits that have devastated large tracts of Australia. Ugolin is the first to speak.)

ST

– C'est ce genre de lapins que vous voulez amener ici ?

– Non, heureusement, non.
D'ailleurs, je pense que la force et
5 la nocivité de cette race sont dues au climat australien : ici, en deux ou trois générations, ils rede-
viendraient certainement semblables à nos lapins des
10 champs. En plus gros, évidemment.

– Heureusement ! dit Ugolin. Alors, vous comptez en faire cinq cents par mois ?

– Mais non, mais non ! dit le
15 bossu, sur le ton d'un homme qui ne croit pas aux chimères. Non. Il faut être modéré en toutes choses. De la mesure ! De la mesure ! Les chiffres que nous proposent
20 ce technicien sont sans doute exacts. Mais ce ne sont que des chiffres, et il arrive que la réalité leur donne un démenti. Cependant, vous conviendrez avec moi que si
25 je réduis ces prévisions au quart, je suis absolument sûr de mon affaire. Je compte donc obtenir 125 à 150 lapins par mois d'ici deux ans, et je limiterai mon
30 élevage à ce chiffre.

– Pourquoi ? dit plaintivement Aimée... Tu m'avais dit au moins 250 !

– Il posa tendrement sa main
5 sur l'épaule de son épouse, et dit en souriant :

« Les femmes, mon cher voisin, ont toutes les qualités, sauf le bon sens ! Ma chère amie, il faut
0 maîtriser l'enthousiasme en tenant à deux mains les rênes de la

TT

'Is that the kind of rabbit you want to bring here?'

'No, fortunately not. Besides, I think the strength and harmfulness of this race is due to the Australian climate; here, in two or three generations, they will certainly become more like our field rabbits, though noticeably bigger than them.'

'Fortunately!' said Ugolin. 'So, you plan to raise five hundred a month?'

'Oh no, no!' said the hunch-back, in the tone of one who does not daydream. 'No. One must be modern in all things. Within limits! The figures the technician suggests are no doubt exact. But they're nothing more than figures, and reality will give the lie to them. However, you will agree that if I reduce these forecasts to a quarter, I'll be quite safe. So I reckon to get a hundred and twenty-five to a hundred and fifty rabbits a month in two years and I'll keep my breed to that figure.'

'Why?' said Aimée plaintively, '. . . you told me at least two hundred and fifty!'

He put his hand tenderly on his wife's shoulder, and said, smiling:

'Women, my dear neighbor, have all the qualities except good sense! My dear friend, one must master one's enthusiasm, while holding the reins of Reason in both hands. We will keep only six males and about a hundred females, which will assure us of

Raison. Nous garderons seulement
dix mâles et une centaine de
femelles, qui nous assureront
45 1 500 naissances par an, ce qui
sera bien suffisant !
  – Pour sûr, dit Ugolin. Ça vous
donnera déjà un brave travail...
Rien que pour nettoyer les cages,
50 ça ne se fait pas tout seul ! »
        (Pagnol 1988: 137–8)

fifteen hundred births a year,
which will be quite enough!'
  'Certainly,' said Ugolin. 'Even
that will be quite a good job. . .
Even clearing the cages – that
doesn't happen by itself!'
        (Pagnol 1989: 92–3)

It is hard to know where to begin in discussing this TT. Verb tenses
are sometimes misleading. 'Will' (l. 7) is confusing, because he has just
said he is not introducing this breed of rabbit, and now he is saying they
will not grow as big in France. Similarly, in l. 21, 'will' suggests that he
is going to put the expert's figures to the test, even though he has just
said he is not.

Further confusion is caused by needless errors. It has been firmly established in the novel that Jean believes in using modern methods (see
contextual information). So why does he now *contradict* the suggestion
that he will raise five hundred rabbits a month by repeating that one must
be modern in all things? And why no 'but' before 'Within limits'? Of
course, in the ST, he does not say 'moderne', but 'modéré'. (And of course
if the TT did have 'Moderation in all things', the exclamation 'Within
limits!' would be even odder – in effect, 'moderation, but moderately'!)
Then, translating 'Ma chère amie' as 'My dear friend' ensures that the
reader will think these words are addressed to Ugolin, the 'dear neighbor'.
And the attentive reader will be mystified by the implication that six (and
not ten) males will be enough to give 1,500 births a year. Finally, the
communicative function of 'quite a good job' is absolutely unclear.

  Further errors may not be positively misleading, but they often undermine idiomaticity. A few examples:

l. 5 'Race': revise to 'breed' or 'strain'.
l. 9 'Field': revise to 'wild'.
l. 9 'Noticeably': not unidiomatic, but needs revision to 'obviously'.
l. 19 'Exact': revise to 'accurate'.
l. 20 'Nothing more than': revise to 'only'.
l. 28 'I'll keep my breed to that figure': revise to 'I'll keep it [i.e. breeding]
down to that' – avoiding the nominalization is clear and idiomatic in
context.
ll. 45–8 Revise to: 'Even then you'll have your work cut out. What about
the cages? They don't clean themselves, you know!'

  It would be useful to analyse this TT thoroughly in class. It may of
course be that the translator's strategy was not to domesticate the ST by
producing a seamlessly idiomatic English text, but to use exoticism (the

ever-present calque) to signal its French origin. But the gross errors make it hard to believe that this style was a conscious strategic choice. The whole text is like this, full of calque and downright mistakes which cannot be defended in terms of any credible strategy. Few translations are as bad as this nowadays, which makes it all the more scandalous that the publisher should have gone ahead and released such a manifest betrayal of Pagnol's work. Such an inadequate TT is really beyond revision; the only answer would be to commission a new translation.

Of course, it is one thing to criticize a translation, but another thing entirely to revise and edit it. How does one go about such a complex task? The revision and editing process comprises several activities, which broadly speaking fall into two stages. The first is checking the TT for adherence to the ST in terms of accuracy: the reviser focuses on errors, omissions, additions, names and titles, figures and tables, etc. The second stage focuses on the end-user of the TT, and attempts to achieve the 'optimum orientation of the translated text to the requirements of the target readership' (Graham 1983: 104).

At the revision or checking stage, greater emphasis is usually placed on accuracy than on style. The objectivity of the reviser should ensure that any ambiguities or unclear phrasing are dealt with before passing on to the editing stage. For editing, there are no hard and fast rules, though critical factors are certainly appearance, appeal, impact, harmony, taste, register and style. If revision is concerned with the 'bare bones' of the TT, the editing process will perform 'remedial surgery' (Graham 1983: 103), which should consist of 'upgrading the terminology, clarifying obscurities, reinforcing the impact, honing the emotive appeal to suit the target reader'. A final 'cosmetic' stage should be to ensure that the appearance and layout of the TT respect the requirements as stated by the client.

A tricky issue is style, as style and language-use obviously vary from one translator to another. In the sheet metal TT, for example, some readers will be upset by the split infinitive in lines 9–10, others will not: in technical texts, people tend not to fret about such niceties. Here is an example from another text on sheet steel which nicely illustrates the fuzzy dividing line between revision and editing:

ST	TT
Cette recherche a pour but d'étudier les propriétés d'emploi des tôles minces laminées à froid revêtues en vue de leur utilisation dans la carrosserie automobile.	The aim of this research is the study of the user properties of cold rolled coated steel sheets in view of their use in the car body.
Nos essais se sont orientés vers la caractérisation de l'aptitude au formage et au soudage, l'étude du grippage et l'influence de la déformation sur la résistance à la corrosion.	Our experiments are concerned with the characterization of *the* formability and weldability, the tendency to galling and the influence of *the* strain on *the* corrosion resistance.
(ECSC-CRM (Belgique) 1987b: 518)	(ECSC-CRM (Belgique) 1987b: 518 [our italics])

5

10

Here, the reviser will certainly want to delete the definite articles we have italicized, and possibly also in 'the car body', 'the characterization' and 'the tendency'; the last three decisions will depend on context and knowledge of the field. Ideally, the reviser will also insert a hyphen between 'cold' and 'rolled', partly to be literate but mostly to avoid ambiguity. In all honesty, though, it has to be admitted that this is another issue that tends to be ignored in technical writing; the specialist reader will know perfectly well that what is meant is cold-rolled steel, not rolled steel that is cold. Finally, again depending on the present state of research in this field, the reviser may substitute 'with a view to' for 'in view of': if these particular sorts of steel are already used in car bodies, the TT is correct as it stands; but if this is a feasibility study to see whether they *could* be used in car bodies, the revision needs to be made.

What the reviser will not be concerned with, however, is the very obtrusive alliteration, assonance and rhyme in the first sentence, and the ugly prosodic effects of the repetitions in the second. In a less technical text, an editor might very well want to tinker with such things, to make it less inelegant phonically and prosodically. But, for better or for worse, this *is* a technical text; so, as long as the message is accurate and clear, both reviser and editor will as far as possible leave the style to look after itself.

What is certainly true is that care must be taken only to change items which are in some way incorrect or unsuitable, not those which are merely phrased differently from the way the translator/reviser would phrase them. For example, there is an enormous difference in legal English between 'will' and 'shall' used in the third person, particularly in the context of contracts and agreements, but in the first person these forms are interchangeable. In a text containing direct speech, there would be little point in changing 'I shall go out later' to 'I will go out later', unless there were a particular contextual reason. However, if the TT of a contract contained the words '[The contractor] *will* complete the work by August 10th' instead of '*shall* complete', the reviser would probably have to intervene: the former TT implies that it is a foregone conclusion that the work will be completed by August 10th, whereas the latter imposes a condition that the contractor finish the work by the deadline.

Some texts are passed on to an editor before publication, and here the translator or reviser will often play no further part: in reality, it is unlikely that they will be consulted about changes to the TT. An editor may wish to prune what are considered to be irrelevancies from the TT, or to reduce the length of the text due to typographical or impagination constraints. This is a common factor in editing. Here is an example from a tourist leaflet. The TT is not altogether clear, partly because of the intrinsic quality of the translation, but partly also because of the context in which it is printed:

ST

'FRESQUES' est une promenade
dans les fresques de la
Renaissance italienne au travers
des galeries de Cathédrale
d'Images. En effet, celles-ci se
prêtent merveilleusement à la
projection à même la pierre
blanche des œuvres des plus
grands artistes de l'époque.

TT

'FRESQUES' is a stroll among
the frescoes of the Italian
Renaissance,
through the galleries
of Cathédrale d'Images.
Those lend themselves wonderfully
to projecting directly on the white
stone faces the works
of the period's greatest artists.

There are two contextual reasons why the TT is a bit obscure. First, it is the only piece of English in the entire leaflet. The French, on the other hand, is only one third of a text which explains that the Cathédrale d'Images is a huge slide show, with slides of the frescoes being projected onto vast, smooth, white limestone walls in the underground galleries of a disused quarry. The second contextual factor is impagination: there are three TTs, English, German and Italian, alternately ranged left and right. They occupy just over half a page. To keep the presentation elegant, lines 4–9 of the TT are laid out exactly as we have printed them here. But the line-breaks in the second sentence are as obstructive as badly laid-out subtitles. An editor might have made an effort either to tweak the line-breaks or, preferably, to rewrite the sentence so that it read clearly whatever the layout, e.g.

The white stone of the quarry walls
makes huge screens, onto which
the greatest works
of the period can be projected.

In effect, the editor is responsible to the translator for any changes made to the TT, whether or not the translator is consulted about them. If the TT is subsequently judged defective in some way by readers, it is the translator who will automatically be held responsible by readers or reviewers, rather than the author, the editor or the printer. It must therefore never be forgotten that revision and editing are part of the 'quality control' procedure that all translators should implement on completing their translating (or during and after translating, depending on how the translator works). Literary translators in particular are well advised to have their work checked by a friend or colleague before sending it to the publisher. This is partly because they work on their own, not in a team where there is automatic provision for revising. But mostly it is because the TT is likely only to be looked at by a copy editor; copy editors may make a few stylistic suggestions, but of course if there is nothing untoward stylistically, they will have no means of knowing whether the TT is actually inaccurate. In the Pagnol example above, it is obvious that the publisher's editors have not done their job properly. But in the following examples, the TT style offers no clue as to whether or not there is significant translation loss:

ST (i)
[Q]uelque chose de très fort me poussait à rester près de lui, à m'accrocher à lui.

    J'ai eu l'impression qu'il avait senti cet élan inexplicable vers
5 lui et que cela l'avait touché.

TT (i)
Something very strong was urging me to hang on to him.

    I sensed this inexplicable glow coming from him. Someone had moved him.

ST (ii)
J'ai senti naître la jalousie et monter le chagrin. Je crois que mes yeux qu'il regardait étaient des lacs de peine.
5   (Cardinal 1988: 261)

TT (ii)
I felt the stirring of a jealousy I had never known and showed him my grief. I felt my eyes, even as he was looking into them, becoming lakes of pain.
         (Cardinal 1984: 161–2)

    The lesson is that, whether or not the TT will be revised and edited by a third party, it is essential for translators to have their own system for careful self-assessment of the work, and that even when completing a rush job careful reading and checking is carried out to repair errors and omissions. (Excellent advice on checking can be found in Anderson and Avery 1995.)

PRACTICAL 15

15.1 Revising and editing

Assignment
- (i)   You have been asked to revise the following TT. Discuss the main types of revision challenges it poses.
- (ii) Revise the TT.
- (iii) Report on your revisions, saying what criteria you adopted for assessment of the TT, and explaining the main changes you made.
- (iv) Exchange the revised text for another student's, and edit that.
- (v) Explain your edits.

Contextual information
The texts are taken from 'La terre vue du ciel', a magazine article featuring spectacular aerial photos of various parts of the world with short accompanying commentary in French and English. This ST and TT refer to what

looks like a lacework of white channels in the desert. A particular constraint on the translator and/or editor here was the impagination. Each photo takes up about 90 per cent of the double-page spread, and the texts are printed in a single column at the extreme right. There is only space for 48 lines of text in the column. The TTs are printed directly below the STs, in a different colour, and are all, in varying degrees, shorter than the STs: the longer the ST, the shorter the TT.

ST

En se retirant, les eaux de l'oued Lemnaider, qui alimentent cette *sebkha* (lac salé temporaire) en période de pluie, ont creusé des rigoles dans le sable. Caractéristique des zones arides du Maghreb, la sebkha se trouve au cœur du Sahara occidental. Autrefois colonie espagnole, cette partie
5 de désert a été revendiquée par le Maroc en 1975. Cependant, soutenu par l'Algérie, le Front Polisario a proclamé l'indépendance de ce terri-toire et pris les armes. Une République arabe sahraouie démocratique a même été créée et admise au sein de l'Organisation de l'unité africaine. Reconnue par plus de 70 Etats, elle n'est pourtant pas considérée comme
10 administrateur officiel du territoire par les instances internationales.

(Air France 2001: 87)

TT

The waters of the Lemnaider oued, which feed this *sabkhat* (temporary salt lake) in the western Sahara, have retreated digging channels in the sand. The Polisario Front, supported by Algeria, proclaimed the indepen-dence of this part of the desert and took up arms. A democratic Sahraouie
5 Arabic republic (RASD) was created but it is still not considered the offi-cial administrator of this territory by international authorities.

(Air France 2001: 87)

15.2 Revising and editing

Assignment
  (i) You have been asked to revise the following TT. Discuss the main types of revision challenges it poses.
 (ii) Revise the TT.
(iii) Report on your revisions, saying what criteria you adopted for assess-ment of the TT, and explaining the main changes you made.
 (iv) Exchange the revised text for another student's, and edit that.
  (v) Explain your edits.

Contextual information
The text is from the management report on the 1993 financial statements of Aerospatiale. Avions, Hélicoptères, Missiles and Espace et Défense are some of the subdivisions of the company.

ST

Aerospatiale a continué à souffrir de la crise qui frappe depuis plusieurs
années le monde aéronautique et spatial.

La situation financière des compagnies aériennes reste toujours fragilisée
par une politique de dérégulation non maîtrisée et par le ralentissement
5 économique. L'année 1993 a été marquée, compte tenue des annulations
enregistrées, par des prises de commandes pratiquement nulles pour les
avions de plus de 100 places.

En outre, les pays occidentaux ont fortement réduit leurs commandes
militaires, tandis que le marché civil des hélicoptères s'est effondré.
10 Dans une conjoncture qui a été pire cette année qu'en 1992 et qui a
généré des surcapacités, la compétition s'est encore exacerbée, principalement avec l'industrie aéronautique américaine, massivement soutenue
tant sur ses marchés intérieurs que sur les marchés extérieurs, par les
pouvoirs publics.
15 Face à cet environnement, Aerospatiale a malgré tout réussi à consolider
ses parts de marché et ses alliances.

Les prises de commandes enregistrées en 1993, déduction faite des annulations, ont représenté 29 Milliards de Francs, contre 39 MdF en 1992.
Les commandes Avions sont en forte baisse. Il en est de même pour les
20 Hélicoptères, l'année 1992 ayant été il est vrai exceptionnelle, enregis-
trant les commandes du développement du NH90. Les commandes Missiles
et Espace et Défense sont en revanche en progression sensible.

Le chiffre d'affaires s'établit à 50,85 Milliards de Francs, contre 52,26
Milliards de Francs en 1992.
25 La mise en œuvre rigoureuse des actions décidées et renforcées tout au
long de l'année, afin d'adapter le potentiel de l'entreprise au contexte
économique, à savoir :

- réduction drastique des frais de fonctionnement,
- réduction des cadences et adaptation, en conséquence, du potentiel,
30 - freinage de l'investissement (1,7 MdF contre 2,8 MdF l'année précédente),
- réduction des dépenses de recherche et de développement autofinancées,
  4,3 MdF contre 5,2 MdF, tout en améliorant leur productivité et leur
  efficacité,

35 ont permis de ramener la perte d'exploitation de 1,22 MdF à 0,26 MdF
et de diminuer le besoin de fonds de roulement de 4,36 MdF.

L'endettement net a ainsi pu être réduit de 3,7 Milliards de Francs.

(Aerospatiale 1994a: 42)

TT

Aerospatiale continued to suffer from the crisis that has now reigned in the world aerospace industry for several years.

The airlines' financial position remains weakened by uncontrolled deregulation policies and the global recession. Because of the number of
5   cancellations during 1993, there were virtually no net orders booked this past year for aircraft with over 100 seats.

Furthermore, military orders from Western countries experienced a sharp drop, while the civil helicopter market collapsed.

The general economy was even worse than in 1992, generating signif-
10 icant overcapacity. This led to even fiercer competition, primarily against an American aerospace industry that enjoys massive government support on both domestic and export sales.

Despite this difficult environment, Aerospatiale nonetheless succeeded in consolidating its market shares and alliances.
15 Net orders booked in 1993 totalled 29 billion francs, compared with FF 39 billion in 1992. Orders for both aircraft and helicopters decreased sharply, although the 1992 helicopter orders integrated the major NH 90 development contract. Orders booked by the Missiles and Space & Defense divisions, on the other hand, showed a marked increase.
20 Sales for the year came to FF 50.85 billion, versus FF 52.26 billion in 1992.

The operating loss was reduced from FF 1,220 million in 1992 to FF 260 million in 1993, and working capital requirements were reduced by FF 4.36 billion, thanks to a strict year-long application of measures
25 designed to adapt the company's capacity to the economic context. These measures were as follows:

- a drastic reduction in operating costs;
- reduced production rates, and a resulting adaptation in capacity;
- a slowdown in investments (FF 1.7 billion, versus FF 2.8 billion in 1992);
30 - a decrease in company-funded R&D, from FF 5.2 billion to FF 4.3 billion, along with higher R&D productivity and cost-effectiveness.

The net debt was therefore reduced by FF 3.7 billion.

(Aerospatiale 1994b: 42)

15.3 Revising and editing

Assignment
(i)   You have been asked to revise the following TT. Discuss the main types of revision challenges it poses.
(ii)   Revise all or part of the TT (your tutor will tell you which part).
(iii) Report on your revisions, saying what criteria you adopted for assessment of the TT, and explaining the main changes you made.
(iv) Exchange the revised text for another student's, and edit that.
(v)   Explain your edits.

Contextual information

The novelist Marie Cardinal was one of France's best-known feminists. The extract is from her powerful and moving autobiographical novel, *Les Mots pour le dire*. This is the story of her gradual, determined recovery from a condition of acute anxiety, bordering on catatonia and suicide. It is dedicated to the 'docteur qui m'a aidée à naître'. The doctor who helped her put herself together was a psychoanalyst, whose consulting-room was in a cul-de-sac in Paris. The analysis, which lasted for seven years, was often stormy at first, with the patient driven to anger or sulky silence by the analyst's calm detachment. The extract comes at a point where Cardinal has finally come to terms with the strict, unloving Christian upbringing inflicted on her by her mother, and the analysis is nearing completion.

ST

La rencontre avec mes premiers vrais défauts me donnait une assurance que je n'avais jamais eue. Ils mettaient en valeur mes qualités que je découvrais aussi et qui m'intéressaient moins. Mes qualités ne me faisaient progresser que lorsque mes défauts les excitaient. Ils supprimaient le péché,
5 cette marque infamante qui désigne la méchante, la mauvaise, la damnée. Mes défauts étaient dynamiques. Je ressentais profondément qu'en les connaissant ils devenaient des outils utiles à ma construction. Il ne s'agissait plus de les repousser, ou de les supprimer, encore moins d'en avoir honte, mais de les maîtriser et de m'en servir, le cas échéant. Mes défauts
10 étaient des qualités, en quelque sorte.
     Maintenant, je venais dans l'impasse comme, jadis, j'allais à l'université : pour apprendre. Je voulais tout savoir.
     J'avais vaincu des résistances si fortes que je ne craignais plus de me trouver nez à nez avec moi-même. Les angoisses avaient totalement
15 disparu. Je pouvais (et je peux toujours) ressentir des symptômes physiques de l'angoisse (la transpiration, l'accélération du rythme cardiaque, le refroidissement des extrémités), mais la peur ne venait plus. Ces symptômes me servaient maintenant à dénicher de nouvelles clefs : mon cœur bat ! Pourquoi ? Depuis quand ? Que s'est-il passé à cet instant ? Quel
20 mot m'a frappée, quelle couleur, quelle odeur, quelle atmosphère, quelle idée, quel bruit ? Je retrouvais mon calme et j'apportais chez le docteur l'instant à analyser quand je n'étais pas capable de le faire toute seule.
     Il m'arrivait souvent de patauger, de ne pas retrouver l'origine de mon malaise, de n'être apaisée que par le fait de savoir qu'il avait une origine.
25 Sur le divan, les yeux fermés, j'essayais de démêler les fils embrouillés. Je ne m'excitais plus comme avant, je ne me laissais plus aller au mutisme ou aux injures dont je connaissais maintenant le sens et dont je savais, par conséquent, qu'ils étaient aussi éloquents que des paroles calmes mais plus fatigants.
(M. Cardinal, *Les Mots pour le dire*, © Editions Bernard Grasset, 1975: 223–4)

TT

The first encounter with my real shortcomings gave me an assurance I had never had, enhancing my virtues, which I was also discovering and which interested me less. My virtues did not allow me to progress until stimulated by my shortcomings. They took precedence over sin, that
5 infamous mark designating the wicked, the evil and the damned. My short-comings were dynamic. I felt deeply that as I learned about them they became useful tools for the construction of my life. It had ceased to be a matter of pushing them aside or passing over them in silence, still less of being ashamed of them, but rather of mastering them and in case of
10 need, making use of them. My shortcomings were in some way virtues.

Now I came to the cul-de-sac as in the past I had gone to the university to learn. I wanted to know everything.

I had conquered such resistances that I was no longer afraid to find that I was face to face with myself. The anxiety attacks had completely disap-
15 peared. I could (and I still can) feel the physical symptoms of anxiety (perspiration, accelerated heartbeat, cold extremities), but there was no longer any fear. These symptoms now served to unearth new keys: my heart is beating! Why? When did it start? What was the provocation? What word struck me, what colour, what smell, what atmosphere, what
20 idea, what noise? I would regain my composure and I would save the episode to be analysed by the doctor when I was incapable of doing it all by myself.

It often happened that I would be floundering, unable to get back to the origin of my malaise, only to find comfort in the knowledge that it
25 did have an origin. On the couch with my eyes closed, I would try to disentangle the knotted threads. I no longer got excited as I used to, I no longer sought refuge in silence or insults, whose meaning I now under-stood, and about which, consequently, I knew that they were as eloquent as calm words, though more tiring.

(Cardinal 1984: 149–50)

Contrastive topics and practicals: Introduction

The next four chapters deal with topics from the contrastive linguistics of French and English. Each chapter is self-contained, and can be used as the basis of a practical at whatever stage of the course seems most useful. There are two aims in these chapters. The first is to focus attention on some of the structural differences between French and English which most commonly offer obstacles to literal translation. The second is to increase awareness of the range of options open to translators confronted with these constructions.

There are very many such systematic discrepancies between French and English usage. We looked briefly at some in Chapter 7. Many more have been encountered in practicals, usually where grammatical transposition or compensation has been necessary. The choice of just four contrastive topics for special attention is therefore rather arbitrary. We have chosen four of the most common sources of translation difficulties, and illustrated each with a variety of exercises. It is important that these exercises be done in order, as they arise, and not out of sequence with the explanatory material they relate to.

The contrastive exercises differ in two ways from the other practicals. First, students will often be translating individual sentences taken out of context. This is so that attention can be focused on the contrastive problems themselves – problems which, when taken in context, can be masked or blurred by considerations of style or genre. Obviously, we are not suggesting that context is not important. On the contrary, where context and register are significant factors, attention is drawn to this fact. However, the aim in these chapters is to help the student develop a comprehensive awareness of available options in translation. The availability of potential options can only be properly assessed by taking sentences out of context.

Second, in the contrastive chapters the direction of translation is sometimes reversed, to translating from English into French. This is in order to bring out certain possibilities in *English* which it is easy to overlook when translating from *French*. The reason they are easy to overlook is that, with some French sentences, it is possible to translate into English without significant grammatical transposition, but at the cost of significant translation loss in terms of idiomaticity or register. Many of the English STs in the contrastive chapters contain constructions which cannot pass into French without grammatical transposition. These are instances of precisely those idiomatic English constructions which it is easiest to overlook when translating a French ST containing constructions which can be replicated in English. Our hope is that, having stumbled over these constructions as obstacles in translation *into* French, students will remain aware of their existence as options in translating *from* French.

16

Contrastive topic and practical: Nominalization

This chapter constitutes the material for all or part of a practical. The preliminary exercise should be done, and if possible handed in, before the practical. It should in any case be completed before going on to the rest of the chapter.

PRELIMINARY EXERCISE

Translate the following sentences into French, using only a monolingual French dictionary.

1 Army life seemed appallingly insipid to me.
2 These analogies recur too insistently and coherently.
3 Scandalously, they refused us any help.

4 It was a hopeless undertaking.
5 This attempted insurrection failed.
6 But Father, I was expecting you to be more understanding.

7 [*In a DIY manual*] Anyone can replace a broken window.
8 When I was in London I went round all the museums.
9 [*Imploringly*] You might stop parroting Baudelaire.

10 [*On a label on a coffee jar, announcing a competition*] Soak off and see back.
11 She motioned him in.
12 Sometimes I think back to when we met.

The preliminary exercise focuses on translation issues raised by nominal expressions. A **nominal expression** either consists of a noun or has a noun as its nucleus. Here are some examples, each with an alternative avoiding use of a noun:

With incredible speed.	Incredibly quickly.
A coat of green.	A green coat.
Implement an investigation.	Investigate.
Difficult of access.	Difficult to get to.
He shed his sandals with a kick.	He kicked his sandals off.

We shall use the term 'nominalization' to denote the use of a nominal expression which, in the same language or another, could be replaced by an expression not containing a noun. French often uses nominal expressions where English would not. An English TT that matches a French ST noun for noun tends to read unidiomatically, having a perceived static and abstract quality at odds with the English-speaker's habitual way of expressing the world. Whether such exoticism is or is not desirable depends on the genre and purpose of the TT. English legal texts, for instance, are strongly marked by nominalization (as are French ones). It is an essential element in their dignity; but this kind of gravitas would be unsuitable in many other genres. Our aim here, however, is simply to show that nominalization can have implications for idiomaticity, register and genre. The discussion is in four parts, corresponding to the four parts of the preliminary exercise.

TRANSPOSITION FROM NOUN TO ADVERB

The first sentence in the preliminary exercise is almost impossible to translate literally into French. Although grammatically possible, 'La vie militaire me semblait désespéramment fade' is implausible, even grotesque. Whereas English very readily turns adjectives into adverbs by adding -*ly*, French is more reluctant to do so by adding -*ment*. A more likely translation is:

La vie militaire me semblait d'une fadeur désespérante.

Now let us treat this as an ST. It is a good example of a very common French construction, '*de*' + *indefinite article* + *noun* + *adjective*, which is usually most idiomatically rendered into English by *adverb* + *adjective*. Following the French structure is possible in English, of course:

Army life seemed to me (to be) one of appalling insipidness.

But this sounds stuffy or pompous, whereas the French does not. This question of register is important, as we shall see. Once register is taken into account, there seems little alternative to a TT along these lines:

Army life seemed appallingly insipid to me.

What is the difference between this and the French ST? The ST is certainly not formal or stuffy, but it can be said to be more *static*, in that the insipidness is (however rapidly) analytically isolated as a phenomenon, and then *described*. In this English TT, on the other hand, the insipidness *actively appals* the speaker. So in respect of register, there are fewer possibilities open to the French-speaker than to the English-speaker, who can choose between two registers; and each register entails different nuances. Examples of this structure are common in French, and translators must remember the range of possibilities at their disposal if they are to choose an appropriate register. The deciding factor in the choice is usually the context.

Another common French structure usually calling for an adverb in English is *'avec/sans' + noun*. Here is an example (it is actually the French original from which sentence 2 in the preliminary exercise was derived):

ST	TT
Ces analogies se répètent avec trop d'insistance, trop de cohérence.	These analogies recur too insistently and coherently.

'With too much insistence and coherence' would be unusually heavy – though less implausible than a monstrous 'trop insistamment, trop cohéremment'! Here too the English may be said to be more 'dynamic' and 'concrete' than the French: the adverbs induce the reader to visualize the analogies actively recurring thick and fast. The significant translation loss lies in the fact that the TT is less of a *detached perception and definition* of what is involved, and more an *account* of what is *happening*. The distinction is a relatively fine one here, and sensitivity to it will vary from person to person. Such sensitivity notwithstanding, the whole tone of a text can be affected by how the translator renders the many such expressions as:

ST	TT
avec agitation	with excitement/agitation? Excitedly/agitatedly?
avec nostalgie	with nostalgia/longing? Nostalgically/longingly?
avec complaisance	with obligingness? Obligingly?
sans complexe	without inhibition? Uninhibitedly?
sans effort	without effort? Effortlessly?

Very often, then, a French adverbial phrase containing one or more nouns is most idiomatically translated with an adverb in English. Indeed, English-speakers are so ready to use adverbs that one adverb is often qualified with another placed next to it, something which is rare in French (at least with adverbs in -*ment*). For example:

ST	TT
Elle a été élue à la quasi-unanimité.	She was elected virtually unanimously.

Now, with this example and the question of register in mind, discuss in class the possibilities for translating the following sentences:

Le travail avance avec une rapidité rassurante.

Le travail avance avec une lenteur décourageante.

In such cases, the translator may have little or no choice. But the following example is different:

ST	TT
[*In reference to a pianist*] Elle joue avec une délicatesse étonnante.	(i) She plays amazingly delicately. (ii) She plays with amazing delicacy.

Here, the two TTs are equally idiomatic and acceptable. There is a genuine choice between adverb and noun. The choice seems to depend mostly on what register is required. As far as 'stasis' and 'abstraction' are concerned, similar remarks apply to the English nominalization as to the French one. The only difference – but a significant one – is that since French-speakers do not have this choice between a nominal construction and juxtaposing two adverbs, they will not find 'avec une délicatesse étonnante' unduly marked in terms of register: only in a colloquial context would it stand out (compare e.g. 'Elle joue avec une délicatesse ! J'en reviens pas !'). In English, on the other hand, 'amazingly delicately' is more conversational than 'with amazing delicacy', which belongs more to the critics' page or the lecture platform.

An interesting conclusion emerges from the discussion so far. Changing ST *preposition + noun* into TT adverb, or vice versa, seems inevitably to involve partially overlapping translation (see p. 140). Take 'avec une délicatesse étonnante' translated into English as 'amazingly delicately'. While the core meaning is retained, the English TT adds something and loses something. It adds something in that it makes two things more *explicit* than the ST does: the pianist actively amazing the listener, and her delicate finger-movements, which the adverb 'delicately' encourages the reader to visualize.

But it also loses something, in that it makes *implicit* the concept of delicacy, which is an abstract quality or category implied in the pianist's
playing. In the French, two things have been inferred from the experience
of listening to the playing. From the pianist's finger-movements, the quality
of delicacy has been inferred; and from people's reactions when listening
to her, the fact that her delicacy is amazing has been inferred. This is
doubtless why this nominalization often sounds academic or even pedantic
to Anglophones – it is as if French-speakers stand back from their reactions, analyse them and assess them as belonging in a particular category.
This may well not be how it happens in practice, of course, but the impression left on English-speakers unfamiliar with French is a real one.

Partial overlap is also clearly seen in another typical construction (see
sentence 3 in the exercise):

ST	*TT*
Chose monstrueuse, ils nous ont refusé tout soutien.	Scandalously, they refused us any help.

Using an adverb in this position is possible in French, but much rarer than
in English. It would in any case shift the meaning. 'Monstrueusement'
would describe the manner in which the refusing was actually done. It
would thus also convey a stronger impression than 'chose monstrueuse'
of the speaker's *first reaction* on hearing that help had been refused.
'Chose monstrueuse' is more a mature assessment than a first reaction.
'Scandalously' has a similar effect to 'monstrueusement', and is therefore
a partially overlapping translation: while retaining the core element of
scandalousness, it adds the implication of initial emotional reaction and
loses the implication of later balanced judgement. As ever, this translation loss has to be balanced against different ones incurred by different
alternative TTs, as in: 'It is/was {a scandalous thing/a scandal}, they
refused us any help.'

A symptom of French predilection for the noun is seen in the compar-
ative readiness with which it turns adverbial phrases into nouns, as in
'l'au-delà'. Here are two examples for discussion:

L'au-jour-le-jour de l'existence.
Mourir par absence et par à-peu-près.

TRANSPOSITION FROM *PREPOSITION + NOUN* TO ADJECTIVE

Translators very often find themselves needing to render French *preposition
+ noun* with an English adjective. Almost any page of French chosen at random will throw up examples. Here are a few, for discussion and translation:

C'était une entreprise sans espoir (see sentence 4).
Elle est dans l'incertitude quant à l'avenir.
J'ai l'air d'avoir de l'ordre, mais c'est une illusion.
Planté, roulé dans la prédominance de la fange (see p. 93).
C'est avec plaisir que nous accueillerons pour ses séances de dialyse votre patiente Madame Smith.

As with adverbs, the tendency to nominalization in French is such that adjectives are readily used as nouns, as in the following examples:

Ses pittoresques frappaient (see p. 93).
Il reste dans le vague.
Le tragique de l'histoire, c'est qu'elle a perdu son bébé.
Dans la mesure du possible.
Je suis sensible à l'absurde de cette hypothèse.

A symptom of this contrast between the two languages is found in such fossilized everyday expressions as 'J'ai {faim/froid/de la chance}', where there is little choice but to translate with an adjective. Fixed expressions like these may be closer to true synonymy than in the case of transposition from noun to adverb, but there is often a more obvious element of analysis and categorization in the use of a noun as opposed to an adjective. This is especially clear where there is a choice between the two, as in 'she wore a coat of green' vs 'she wore a green coat'. In translating from French into English, there is often no choice; but when there is one, it will be determined largely by what register is required, just as with the choice between adverb and *preposition + noun*. This is illustrated in sentence 5 of the exercise, which is in fact translated from a French ST, 'Cette tentative d'insurrection a échoué'. 'This attempt at insurrection' is wordy, and also carries an implication that the French does not – that a rather pathetic attempt to mount an insurrection was made, but no insurrection worthy of the name actually materialized. 'Insurrection attempt' is grammatically possible (and a common structure in English), but it is an unlikely collocation. If there is a choice in translating this French sentence, it must surely, as so often with this type of construction, be in favour of an adjective: 'This attempted insurrection failed.'

Sentence 6 is also a translation from French. In principle, there are a number of possibilities for translating this into English, among them:

ST	*TT*
Mais mon père, je m'attendais à plus de compréhension de votre part.	(i) But Father, I was expecting more understanding on your part.
	(ii) But Father, I was expecting more understanding from you.
	(iii) But Father, I thought you would be more understanding.

The choice between these versions depends on the context, and on the son's use of 'votre' rather than 'ta'. This last factor probably rules out the first two versions, because neither has the register of a junior speaking to a senior.

Our next example, from a text on replacing window panes, contains an adjectival construction that is common in French, *'de' + noun*:

> Même si le mastic est de première fraîcheur, pétrissez-le jusqu'à le rendre très malléable.

Perhaps 'de première fraîcheur' is preferred to 'très frais' because the adjective might suggest 'cold' (although 'tout frais' would have got round this). At all events, 'brand new' or 'fresh' is virtually the only possible translation of the ST expression. Here are some more examples of the same construction, for discussion and translation in class:

> Ne pas oublier les précautions d'usage.
> C'est un cas d'espèce.
> Le détail est d'importance.

The *preposition + noun* structure often translates most idiomatically into English with a noun used attributively (i.e. as an adjective), without analytic prepositions such as 'of', 'for' or 'on', as in these examples:

> mesures de sécurité; feux de circulation; équivalent de dose (cf. p. 177); locomotive à vapeur; gravure sur bois; essai de direction; vérification de pneus.

Here are two final examples for discussion and translation in class. The first is from a book on the medieval writer Chrétien de Troyes and his fore-runners. The second is from an account of the defeat of France in 1940.

> Je crois pouvoir conclure sans témérité qu'avant Chrétien la Sainte Lance n'était pas une lance qui saigne.

> L'évidence de l'effondrement s'imposait à tous les esprits.

TRANSPOSITION FROM NOUN TO VERB

Here the likely difference between 'static' noun and 'dynamic' verb is obvious. Once again, French may seem to an English-speaker to be dealing in abstract categories. There is a generic flavour about the noun, as seen for example in the French original from which sentence 7 in the prelim-inary exercise was derived:

Le remplacement d'un carreau cassé est à la portée de n'importe qui.

The French *definite article + noun* is a generic concept, 'the {replacement/replacing} of'. The natural English expression is different: 'replacing a broken window'. Here, the gerund is strongly verbal, focusing on the action, rather than the concept, of replacing a window. Keeping the ST structure in English is possible, but it elevates the register, perhaps inappropriately. Here are four alternative translations for discussion:

(i)   The replacement of a broken window is within anyone's capability.
(ii) Replacing a broken window is within anyone's capability.
(iii) Replacing a broken window isn't too difficult for anybody.
(iv) Anyone can replace a broken window.

Translating either way, rendering a noun with a finite verb inevitably gives a particularizing translation, as for instance in:

ST	TT
Quelques rides à la surface marquèrent sa disparition.	(i) A few ripples showed where she had gone down.
	(ii) A few ripples showed that she had gone down.

Only the context will make it possible to decide between (i) and (ii). It would be possible, but rather donnish, to avoid this particularization by using a noun: 'showed/marked her disappearance/descent'. The same is true of this example:

Ils poussaient d'étranges cris, comme à l'apparition d'un fantôme.

'As at the {appearance/apparition} of a ghost' is pompous; 'as if they had seen a ghost' or 'as if a ghost had appeared' is particularizing. In fact, particularization is inevitable in these movements from generic concept to specific event. This translation loss has to be weighed against that caused by using an inappropriate register.

Using a noun instead of a subordinate clause is a common way of avoiding the subjunctive constructions necessitated by such conjunctions as 'avant que' and 'bien que':

Six mois avant ma naissance.	Six months before I was born.
Malgré mon absence de Paris.	Although I'm away from Paris.

Yet again, in examples like these, keeping the French structure usually gives a more elevated register, while using a finite verb is particularizing. In translating 'malgré mon absence de Paris' with a verb, for instance, the translator is forced to select a particular tense, aspect or mood: 'although I {am/was/will be/would be}', etc.; which is chosen will depend on the context.

The following sentence shows clearly the static and generic nature of a noun as compared with a verb:

ST	TT
Dès son entrée en fonctions, en 1969, elle avait déclaré devant la Knesset qu'Israël n'en démordrait pas.	{On taking/{when/as soon as} she took} office in 1969, she told the Knesset that Israel would not back down.

The context will show which of these options is best. As this example suggests, phrases like *'lors de'* + *noun* or *'dès'* + *noun* resemble *'avant'* + *noun* or *'malgré'* + *noun* in that they are virtually always rendered in English with a particularizing translation. Take 'lors de'. This can be followed by the whole gamut of indicatives and conditionals, as with 'Lors de mon passage à Londres' (cf. sentence 8):

If I {had been/were} in London . . .
{When/while/whenever} I {am/was} in London . . .

Only the context (usually the tense of the main verb) will show which particularization is the right one. And only the most pompous of contextual registers would prompt a TT with a nominal construction, e.g. 'On (the occasion of) my passing through London'.

The relative predilection for the noun in French is neatly illustrated by two opposite tendencies in English and French. Where English can, and does, easily use nouns as verbs, French usually cannot, as in sentence 9 (originally a French ST) and similar examples:

ST	TT
Tu pourrais cesser de sortir du Baudelaire comme un perroquet.	You might stop parroting Baudelaire.
Jeter un pont sur une rivière.	To bridge a river.
Atteindre son niveau plancher.	To bottom out.
Mettre en bouteille(s).	To bottle.

Conversely, French typically uses verbs either in the infinitive, *as* nouns, or in the third person singular present indicative, *in* nouns. Some examples:

le laisser-aller; le savoir-vivre, l'être et le paraître; le parler populaire; le boire et le manger; le porte-bagages; le passe-partout; le tire-bouchon, etc.

English does sometimes use infinitives as nouns, as in 'the hijack'. But the English verbal noun is usually a gerund ('replacing', 'belonging', etc.), which has a stronger verbal force than the corresponding French noun. This is doubtless because English does not need the definite article in such cases: contrast '*le* remplacement *d'*un carreau' with 'replacing a window'.

To finish consideration of the noun–verb contrast, here are two final examples for discussion and translation in class. The first contains other modes of nominalization as well:

> J'avais plus que jamais conscience de son appartenance à la religion musulmane.

The second is a sentence from Cardinal de Retz (1613–79), with an intralingual translation into modern French (Godin 1964: 127). Among other things, it is revealing to compare the two in terms of particularization and generalization:

ST	TT
La Reine avait, plus que personne que j'aie jamais vu, de cette sorte d'esprit qui lui était nécessaire pour ne pas paraître sotte à ceux qui ne la connaissaient pas.	La Reine possédait plus qu'aucune autre personne de ma connaissance, cette sorte d'esprit nécessaire pour ne pas paraître sotte en présence d'étrangers.

TRANSPOSITION FROM PREPOSITION REINFORCED BY A NOUN PHRASE TO A PREPOSITION, PHRASAL VERB OR PREPOSITIONAL VERB

We look at two problems in this section. The first is that French prepositions cannot generally bear as much weight as English ones – think of the many possible meanings of 'à' and 'de'. This is why they are often reinforced with a noun, which does not as a rule need translating into English; for example:

ST	TT
Dans un délai de trois semaines.	In three weeks.
C'est de la part de qui ?	Who's it from/Who's calling?
Je ne suis pas spécialiste en matière de sculpture.	I'm not an expert on sculpture.

The second, and bigger, problem is that of prepositional and phrasal verbs. A prepositional verb is one that forms a combination with a preposition, as in:

refer to; apply for; live off; call on; hint at, etc.

Note that the preposition in such verbs is normally unstressed, and (except in passive constructions) must come before the prepositional object (e.g. 'I've applied for a job', and not *'I've applied a job for'). A phrasal verb forms a combination with an adverbial particle, as in:

turn down; call up; dust off; catch on, etc.

Note that the adverb in phrasal verbs is normally stressed, and can be placed after the object of the verb (e.g. 'I'll just {turn down the hem/turn the hem down}'). These adverbial particles are generally identical in form to prepositions, which is why we are considering prepositional and phrasal verbs together. But in general, it is the phrasal verbs that cause the biggest headaches. Most of the following sentences bring out clearly constructions which are common in English but do not exist in French, and which translators *from* French can therefore easily overlook. Of course, it is often possible to keep the French structure and use a noun in English, but it is very often more idiomatic to substitute a phrasal verb for the noun. The first three examples are the French originals for sentences 10–12 in the preliminary exercise:

ST	*TT*
Décoller à l'eau et voir au dos.	(i) Unstick with/in water and see back.
	(ii) Soak off and see back.
Elle le fit entrer d'un geste.	(i) With a gesture, she made/had him come in.
	(ii) She motioned him in.
Parfois je reviens en pensée au moment où nous nous sommes connus.	(i) Sometimes I return in my thoughts to when we met.
	(ii) Sometimes I think back to when we met.

In each of these cases, TT (ii) could only be put into French with the help of a noun.

   To get an idea of the great challenges these (and other) sorts of construction throw down to French translators, we can take almost any passage at random from an action-packed English narrative and see what noun-based grammatical transpositions are forced on the translator. Here is an example from a Harry Potter adventure, for discussion in class:

ST

'RUN!' Harry yelled and the four
of them sprinted down the gallery,
not looking back to see whether
Filch was following – they swung
around the doorpost and galloped
down one corridor and then
another, Harry in the lead without
any idea where they were or
where they were going. They
ripped through a tapestry and
found themselves in a hidden
passageway, hurtled along it and
came out near their Charms
classroom, which they knew was
miles from the trophy room.
(Rowling 1997: 117–18)

TT

– ON FILE ! cria Harry et ils se
mirent à courir sans se donner le
temps de se retourner.
Parvenus à l'extrémité de la
galerie aux armures, ils prirent un
virage serré et foncèrent à toutes
jambes à travers un dédale de
couloirs. Harry avait pris la tête
du groupe sans avoir la moindre
idée de l'endroit où ils se trou-
vaient, ni de la direction qu'ils
suivaient. Ils passèrent derrière
une tapisserie et s'engouffrèrent
dans un passage secret qu'ils
parcoururent sans ralentir l'allure.
Ils se retrouvèrent alors près de la
salle où avait lieu les cours
d'enchantements et qui était située
à des kilomètres de la salle des
trophées.
(Rowling 1998: 159–60)

A back-translation of the TT would most likely give a much stodgier
narrative than Rowling's original.

Proper attention to prepositions and phrasal and prepositional verbs is
one of the surest ways of avoiding both stodginess and unwanted exoticism. It will be useful to conclude with discussion and translation of some
further examples, which also bring in other categories of nominalization:

Il marchait à longues foulées, remontant l'avenue Montaigne, et Tony
devait trotter pour se maintenir à son niveau.

[*Of a swimmer underwater*] D'un coup de jarret il revint à la surface.

[On retrouve la] même philosophie en matière de rémunérations : là
encore, il s'agit de donner la priorité aux moins favorisés, tout en évitant
les rigidités.

[*Tokor is taking his guest for a drive through the city*] On dévala en
trombe une rue large où Tokor klaxonnait comme un fou, se frayant de
la force du poignet un fulgurant passage dans les attroupements de la
cohue bariolée, braillarde du matin.

A FINAL WORD OF COMMON SENSE

We have been talking in this chapter about a notable contrast between French and English. But this does not mean that the translator has mechanically to strip an English text of nouns, or pack a French one with nominalization! The sensible starting-point is always to try rendering noun with noun, adverb with adverb, and so on. It is just that, in the many cases where nominalization does after all turn out to require grammatical transposition, the translator is statistically more likely to transpose *from* a noun when translating into English, and *to* a noun when translating into French.

There are of course plenty of exceptions to the statistical norm. To conclude this warning word of common sense, here are some examples for discussion:

Un logiciel permettant de calculer les diagrammes de vitesse de phases.	Software permitting/for calculation of phase velocity diagrams.
Je gémis de douleur et tordis brutalement le levier.	I yelped in pain and gave the lever a savage twist.
Elle aime bien rire.	She likes a good laugh.
Mieux vaut prévenir que guérir.	Prevention is better than cure.
C'est pas dramatique.	It's not {a tragedy/the end of the world}.
Il risquait de se faire arrêter.	He was in danger of arrest.
[*On the phone*] Ça ne répond pas.	(There's) no reply.
Il écoutait, stupéfait.	He was listening in amazement.
Ça ne presse pas.	(There's) no rush/hurry.
[*In a contract*] Tout versement effectué par l'acquéreur lui sera immédiatement et intégralement restitué.	Any payment made by the buyer shall immediately be returned to him and full restitution effected.
[*From an EU Act*] Les représentants votent individuellement et personnellement.	Representatives shall vote on an individual and personal basis.

17

Contrastive topic and practical: Adverbials

This chapter constitutes the material for all or part of a practical. The preliminary exercise should be done, and if possible handed in, before the practical. It should in any case be completed before going on to the rest of the chapter.

PRELIMINARY EXERCISE

Translate the following sentences, using only a monolingual French dictionary.

1   – Rentrer en France ? dit Jeanne, pensive.
2   'Someone should tell him about the pill,' said another youth raising his head somnolently.
3   – Ça c'est une bonne idée, s'exclama Léa joyeuse.

4   Pour lui aussi, la durée s'écoule à un rythme implacablement ralenti.
5   'I've given up trying with Patrick,' said Mavis Mottram studying Eva's vase critically.
6   Ils accomplissaient leur besogne sans hâte, méthodiquement.

7   L'autre reluquait les garçons sans se gêner.
8   'Two bananas?' yelped Sherwood uncomprehendingly.
9   Tous étaient prêts à mourir, sans poser de questions, pour le IIIᵉ Reich.

10 Elle gagne difficilement sa vie.
11 You didn't laugh at Stalin and get away with it.
12 Les jeunes gens s'éloignèrent sous l'œil faussement désespéré de Raoul.

The preliminary exercise was designed to draw attention to problems arising from differences between French and English in respect of adverbials. 'Adverbials' is a cover-term for any expression having adverbial function. We shall talk simply either of 'adverbs' (e.g. 'well', 'recently') or of 'adverbial phrases' (e.g. 'in fine fashion', 'a few days ago', 'once you're there'). The English sentence in each section of the exercise contained the section's 'hidden agenda' – that is, it is a clue to an option in English which is not available in French, but which is often hidden from the translator by the fact that the grammatical structure of a given ST expression can be replicated in the TL. To adapt an example from Vinay and Darbelnet (1958: 127), the following sentence can be translated literally:

ST	*TT*
Il fait constamment allusion à ses propres sources, dont l'anonymat est compréhensible mais tout de même agaçant.	He constantly refers to his own sources, the anonymity of which is understandable but nonetheless annoying.

Because the ST grammar does have a structural counterpart in the TL, the translator's initial reaction will most likely be to reproduce the French structure, as here. The tonal register of the TT is formal, and the social register that of an old-fashioned academic. But since the ST is clearly taken from an academic work, the translator might decide that the element of stuffiness is not inappropriate. Those are two good reasons why the following English structure might not occur to the translator:

He constantly refers to his own sources, which are understandably, but nonetheless annoyingly, anonymous.

This is more idiomatic and just as appropriate. Using two adverbs to qualify the adjective is on the translator's 'hidden agenda' precisely because it is a pattern that is acceptable in English but unlikely ever to appear in a French ST: 'compréhensiblement mais tout de même agaçamment anonymes' could only be found in a comic text. Phonically and prosodically, this TT could be improved further by omitting 'nonetheless' – 'understandably, but nonetheless annoyingly, anonymous' is a terrible mouthful, and threatens to reintroduce the plummy pomposity which the adverbs were meant to get rid of. Interestingly, omitting 'nonetheless' is not as great a semantic loss as it would be in the first TT: the adverbial element in 'annoyingly anonymous' is more forceful than the less dynamic 'annoying anonymity'. Even so, and even with the comma, the juxtaposition of 'annoyingly' and 'anonymous' may still sound comic or off-putting, whereas the ST does not. If so, it would be easy to reverse the order of the adverbs: '. . . which are annoyingly, if understandably, anonymous'. This version actually incurs less semantic loss, because 'if' has a similar contrastive function to 'tout de même' and 'nonetheless'.

As this example suggests, there are two main reasons why adverbs can pose translation problems. First, English *forms* adverbs, by adding *-ly* to an adjective or participle, much more readily than French does by adding *-ment*. Second, English *uses* adverbs much more frequently than French, even to the extent of sometimes qualifying one adverb in *-ly* with another – as in 'Diana's legacy is to have repositioned the royals firmly, if hilariously uncomfortably, at the heart of public culture'. There is also a third reason: despite the more frequent use of adverbs in English, French sometimes uses adverbs in a way that would be unidiomatic or ungrammatical in English.

The four sections of this chapter reflect the four parts of the preliminary exercise. Each section is devoted to a major contrastive category. In each, comments on the sentences used in the exercise are accompanied by further examples for discussion and translation in class.

TRANSPOSITION FROM FRENCH ADJECTIVE TO ENGLISH ADVERB

Sentence 1 in the preliminary exercise is an example of a common structure in French, an adjective used in apposition to the subject. In English, the most plausible way of translating such adjectives is generally to use an adverb:

ST	TT
– Rentrer en France ? dit Jeanne, pensive.	'Go back to France?' said Jeanne thoughtfully.

Another possibility is 'said the thoughtful Jeanne'. Like the ST, this refers more to Jeanne's state of mind than to the way she says the words. However, this is a less favoured construction in English than the adverbial one, perhaps because – to take this example – the definite article implies either that Jeanne is thoughtful by nature, or simply that she was already thoughtful before going back to France was suggested. In any case, this type of construction is more common with an adjectival past participle, as in 'said the excited Jeanne'. Yet another possibility is 'said a thoughtful Jeanne'; but this construction, too, tends to occur more with an adjectival past participle; in any case, it is more likely in journalism, as in '"I knew it would work out this way", said an {elated/emotional/ clearly dejected} Bloggs'. The most unlikely solution of all, however, is to copy the ST structure: 'said Jeanne, thoughtful'.

Sentence 3 in the exercise is a variant on the construction in the Jeanne example:

ST   *TT*
– Ça c'est une bonne idée,   'That's a great idea,' cried Léa
s'exclama Léa joyeuse.   joyfully.

Here, as is commonly the case, there is no comma after 'Léa'. This often conveys a nuance of suddenness: the structure is an elliptical form of 's'exclama Léa devenue tout à coup joyeuse'. In cases like this, the impact of the adjective is often slightly closer to that of the English adverb. This is because the absence of a comma suggests a sudden change in state of mind: the reader is thus invited to picture a change taking place in the person's behaviour, especially facial expression and tone of voice. Facial expression and tone of voice are part of the way in which something is said, so the absence of a comma gives the adjective something of the function of an adverbial complement of manner.

In constructions like these, then, French has a choice that English lacks, because English is forced to use an adverb. Apart from the question of the comma, this example raises similar issues to the Jeanne ST: compare 'cried Léa joyfully', 'cried the joyful Léa', 'cried a joyful Léa' and 'cried Léa (,) joyful'.

As we have seen, French both uses and forms adverbs more sparingly than English. But of course the option of using an adverb does exist in many cases, as in:

ST   *TT*
Le chien aboya joyeusement.   The dog barked joyfully.

Comparing this with 's'exclama Léa joyeuse' brings out very clearly the difference between adverb and adjective. 'Joyeusement' directly qualifies the barking, not the dog. The reader is invited to imagine the manner of barking and, implicitly, to visualize the dog wagging its tail and jumping about. 'Joyeuse' qualifies Léa's state of mind, not the way she speaks (although the lack of a comma does give the adjective some degree of adverbial force, as we saw).

Where there is a choice in French between adjective and adverb, there is thus a further possible nuance. Here are five variants on the Léa example:

(i)   – Ça c'est une bonne idée, s'exclama Léa, joyeuse.
(ii)   – Ça c'est une bonne idée, s'exclama la jeune fille, joyeuse.
(iii) – Ça c'est une bonne idée, s'exclama Léa joyeuse.
(iv)   – Ça c'est une bonne idée, s'exclama joyeusement Léa.
(v)   – Ça c'est une bonne idée, s'exclama la jeune fille joyeuse.

In (i) and (ii), rendering 'joyeuse' by 'joyfully' gives a partially overlapping translation, losing explicit reference to her state of mind and adding explicit reference to the way she speaks.

In (iii), using 'joyfully' to render 'joyeuse' also gives a partial overlap, for the same reason; but there is less translation loss in respect of literal meaning, because the lack of a comma gives 'joyeuse' a touch of adverbial status.

In (iv), where adverb is rendered with adverb, there is even less translation loss; but the impact of 'joyfully' will necessarily be less nuanced than that of 'joyeusement', because the adverb is the only option available in English, whereas 'joyeusement' is one of three different possibilities in French.

As for (v), the choice between 'joyful' and 'joyfully' must depend on the context. If the context shows that the girl is joyful by nature, 'joyful' is an accurate choice and incurs minimal translation loss. But if she is simply exclaiming joyfully, then the English adverb, as a partial overlap, incurs a similar loss to that involved in the translation of (iii).

Sometimes, though, English does allow a closer counterpart to a French adjective used in the ways we have been examining. We can show this from the Léa sentence. To return first to (i) and (iii). Suppose the context suggested that 'gleeful' would be a more accurate rendering of 'joyeuse': then 's'exclama Léa (,) joyeuse' could be translated as 'Léa exclaimed in glee'. This, too, is a partial overlap (although less so in the case of (iii)): it *defines Léa's state of mind* as 'glee' rather than *describing Léa* as 'gleeful'. All the same, it does preserve the ST's prime focus on how she feels, instead of switching focus to how she speaks. Indeed, English *preposition + noun* is so attractive in this kind of case that, if 'joyful' were after all more accurate in context, the translator would want to consider using 'in joy'.

So it is worth bearing in mind the possibility of using *preposition + noun* ('in glee/disbelief', etc.) to translate the type of expression examined here. However, it remains true that the most usual successful solution is to choose an adverb, the translation loss in terms of literal meaning being less serious than that caused by not meeting the demands of idiomaticity and register.

A further point to be borne in mind is that the adverb is sometimes the only option in French, because the adjective would be odd for semantic reasons. In cases like this, the question of nuance between French adverb and adjective does not arise. Compare the following pairs of sentences:

(i)	*(ii)*
– Je vois, dit le colonel encore plus sèchement.	? – Je vois, dit le colonel (,) encore plus sec.
Elle aimait à le piquer, et il répliquait vertement.	? Elle aimait à le piquer, et il répliquait (,) vert.

Finally, it does sometimes happen that an English adjective (or adjectival past participle) is a serious translation option, as in this example:

ST	*TT*
– Alors vous n'avez rien compris à mes explications ? observai-je un peu vexé.	(i) 'Haven't you understood *any*thing I've been saying?' I said, feeling rather upset.
	(ii) Rather upset at this, I said reproachfully: 'Haven't you understood *any*thing I've been saying?'
	(iii) That upset me a bit, and, reproachfully, I said: 'Haven't you understood *any*thing I've been saying?'

Note that in TTs (ii) and (iii), 'reproachfully' is an example of compensation. In the ST, the verb 'observai-je' has the reflected meaning of 'observation' (in the sense of 'reproche' or 'critique'); 'reproachfully' conveys this connotation by compensation.

Here, for class discussion and translation, are some more examples which invite comparison of adjective and adverb both intralingually and interlingually:

(i)
– Combien d'hommes au travail, ce matin ? demanda le colonel (,) impérieux.

[*See sentence 2*] – Faudrait lui parler de la pilule, dit un autre jeune homme en relevant sa tête endormie.

– Vous avez du feu ? me demanda-t-il brusquement.

(ii)
– Combien d'hommes au travail, ce matin ? demanda impérieusement le colonel.

– Faudrait lui parler de la pilule, dit un autre jeune homme en relevant la tête d'un air endormi/somnolent.

– Vous avez du feu ? me demanda-t-il, brusque.

TRANSPOSITION FROM FRENCH *PREPOSITION* + *NOUN* TO ENGLISH ADVERB

Sentence 4 in the preliminary exercise is notable for two things. The first will strike any French reader immediately – the weighty adverb 'implacablement', which by its very length gives a 'relentless' emphasis to the sentence. The second will go unnoticed by most French readers – the prepositional phrase 'à un rythme ralenti' functioning as an adverbial. Here is the sentence, with two translations:

ST	TT
Pour lui aussi, la durée s'écoule à un rythme implacablement ralenti.	(i) For him, too, time was passing at a relentlessly slow pace. (ii) For him, too, time was passing relentlessly slowly.

TT (ii) is more idiomatic than TT (i). English readily uses one adverb as the direct modifier of another, but 'implacablement lentement' would be virtually unthinkable in French. The phrase 'à un rythme ralenti' is in fact a good example of a common structure in French, *preposition + noun* in the role of adverbial complement. We looked at some examples of this structure on pp. 223–6. As with those examples, rendering *preposition + noun* with an adverb results in greater dynamism in the TT. The significant translation loss lies in the fact that the TT is less of an analytic definition of the situation, and more of a description of the manner in which events unfold.

In sentence 6, there are again two adverbial complements, and again, the natural solution in English is to use two adverbs:

ST	TT
Ils accomplissaient leur besogne sans hâte, méthodiquement.	They were carrying out their task unhurriedly, methodically.

This time, one adverb does not qualify the other, but both directly qualify the verb. It would have been possible to say 'ils accomplissaient leur tâche lentement, méthodiquement', but this is unlikely, for two reasons. First, juxtaposing two adverbs in *-ment* is relatively unusual, and would therefore be rather ponderously emphatic. Second, there is a difference between 'lentement' and 'sans hâte', much as there is between 'slowly' and 'unhurriedly'. The difference is presumably important to the writer, who is describing unmolested dive-bombers in 1940. His problem is that there is no adverb in French that conveys the precise notion of unhurriedness (as applicable to aircraft at any rate), so that he is obliged to use the common *'sans' + noun* construction. 'Without (any) hurry' is possible in English, of course, and would entail less translation loss in respect of literal meaning; the translator's choice will depend on contextual factors, notably register.

Sentence 5 is another reminder of the homology of French noun-based adverbial phrases and English adverbs:

ST	TT
'I've given up trying with Patrick,' said Mavis Mottram studying Eva's vase critically.	– Avec Patrick, moi, je n'essaie même plus, dit Mavis Mottram tout en considérant d'un œil critique le bouquet d'Eva.

There is little alternative to 'd'un œil critique'. This is a partially overlapping translation, keeping the notion of critical observation, but adding
explicit reference to the look in Mavis Mottram's eye and losing explicit
reference to her general disapproving demeanour as she looks at the
flowers. In English, of course, there is a choice between 'critically' and
'with a critical eye'. That is, in this case, there are nuances available in
English which are denied the French speaker. Coping with the translation
loss caused by these sorts of restriction is the stuff of everyday life for
translators. If they judge the loss unacceptable, the only answer is to use
some form of compensation.

For further discussion of transposition from *preposition* + *noun* to adverb,
see pp. 223–6. Here are some final examples for class discussion and translation:

Il avait parlé bas, presque d'un ton d'excuse.
– Je ne sais pas nager, dit Atkins d'une voix obstinée.
– Je ne sais pas nager, dit Atkins (,) obstiné.
– Je vois, dit le colonel sur un ton glacial.
– Je vois, dit le colonel (,) glacial.
Elle les dévisageait avec une insolence incroyable.
Elle jeta un coup d'œil anxieux autour d'elle, puis, d'un pas mal assuré,
se mit à traverser la cour.

TRANSPOSITION FROM FRENCH *PREPOSITION* + *VERB* OR RELATIVE CLAUSE TO ENGLISH ADVERB

In sentence 7 of the preliminary exercise, an adverb seems the most
idiomatic way of rendering 'sans se gêner':

ST	TT
L'autre reluquait les garçons sans se gêner.	The other guy was unashamedly ogling the boys.

A *preposition* + *noun* construction is perhaps conceivable here – e.g.
'{without/with no} shame/embarrassment'. What is most unlikely in translating this sentence is a construction modelled on the ST, e.g. 'without
{being/becoming} {ashamed/embarrassed}'.

'Unashamedly', 'unembarrassedly', 'uninhibitedly', etc. are as typically
English adverbs as 'unhurriedly'. It is easy to form such compounds in
English. French, on the other hand, rarely adds the suffix *-ment* to an
adjectival past participle, and perhaps just as rarely the prefix *in-*. Instead,
as we have seen, it commonly uses *preposition* + *noun* or *preposition* +
verb. This example is thus a useful reminder that translators into English
have a stock of potential affixes which it is easy to overlook when reading
French texts that are devoid of such structures. More often than not, an

adverbial constructed with *preposition + verb* in a French ST can in fact be rendered with the same structure in English. There will often be slight translation loss in respect of idiomaticity or register, but the occasional case will probably not be unacceptable. However, as with a consistent absence of prepositional and phrasal verbs (see pp. 232–3) or unreinforced prepositions (see p. 256), a consistent lack of compound adverbs like 'unashamedly' will insidiously create a vaguely exotic impression.

Sentence 9 in the exercise contains a typical French adverbial which can be copied in English, but which can also be rendered with a single adverb:

ST	TT
Tous étaient prêts à mourir, sans poser de questions, pour le IIIᵉ Reich.	(i) All were ready to die, without asking (any) questions, for the Third Reich.
	(ii) All were ready to die unquestioningly for the Third Reich.

Because (i) is a possibility in English, the option with 'unquestioningly' (a structural impossibility in French) may not even occur to the translator. 'Unquestioningly' entails translation loss in respect of literal meaning. It is a partial overlap that loses the element of static analysis and definition of the people's behaviour, and adds an element of dynamic description (the eager manner in which they court death). The question – once again – is whether literal meaning should have higher priority than idiomaticity, register, etc.; and the answer – once again – can only be given terms of the context.

The impossibility of finding an adverb to translate 'uncomprehendingly' in sentence 8 is a reminder of a further alternative using a verb: an English adverb often corresponds to a French relative clause:

ST	TT
'Two bananas?' yelped Sherwood uncomprehendingly.	– Deux bananes ? glapit Sherwood qui n'y comprenait rien.

Here, for class discussion and translation, are some further cases illustrating the possibilities discussed in this section:

On est en droit de présumer qu'il sait ce qu'il fait.

Mais, sans qu'on ait pu se l'expliquer, il n'était pas au rendez-vous.

– Je viens de me rappeler que je voulais te demander quelque chose, dit-elle. Que veut dire « diversification transsexuelle ? » – Cela veut dire poésie pour invertis, se hâta de répondre Wilt.

La providence s'acharnait à la poursuivre.

Ce noble but, elle le poursuivait depuis onze ans, sans compter, sans s'en laisser détourner.

TRANSPOSITION FROM FRENCH ADVERB

We have looked at three common categories of grammatical transposition from French adverbial phrases to English adverbs. But just because adverbs are formed and used more often in English does not mean that transposition is all one-way traffic. The final category we examine gathers together exceptions to the statistical norm, i.e. cases where a French adverb is best transposed into a different structure in English.

Sentence 10 in the preliminary exercise is an example:

ST	TT
Elle gagne difficilement sa vie.	She finds it hard to make a living.

'Difficilement' is regularly used in this way, and usually needs to be translated with a phrase built round an adjective. Compare the similar use of 'mal', as in:

ST	TT
Je vois mal en quoi consisterait cette prétendue supériorité du rugby anglais.	I {fail/find it hard} to see just where English rugby is supposed to be so superior.

In the following example, 'mal fait' could be translated as 'badly done', but an adjective is more idiomatic:

ST	TT
– C'est du travail mal fait, dit-il d'un ton faussement indifférent.	'It's shoddy {work/workmanship},' he said in (tones of) feigned indifference.

This example also contains an instance of another regular problem case, the adverb 'faussement'. The solution adopted here, transposition from French *adverb + adjective* to English *preposition + adjective + noun*, is a classic one. Sentence 12 is another example:

ST	TT
Les jeunes gens s'éloignèrent sous l'œil faussement désespéré de Raoul.	Raoul watched in feigned/mock despair as the youngsters walked off.

In sentence 11, the two verbs can be translated with two verbs in French. However, French has an adverb which has no structural equivalent in English:

ST	*TT*
You didn't laugh at Stalin and get away with it.	(i) Qui se moquait de Staline n'en sortait pas indemne. (ii) On ne se moquait pas impunément de Staline.

Depending on the required register, 'impunément' will usually be translated as 'with impunity', or 'and get away with it', or 'without suffering the consequences'.

As at the end of Chapter 16, the conclusion to be drawn from these examples is a simple caveat. The alert translator does not seek as a matter of course to maximize the number of adverbs in an English TT. There are often cases where the more common procedure is reversed, and a French adverb needs to be transposed to a different structure in English. Here are some final examples for class discussion and translation:

Il l'avait regardée longuement.

Vous devez obligatoirement composter votre billet avant de monter dans le train.

La démarche a été diversement interprétée par les observateurs.

L'abbé ramena frileusement sur ses genoux la couverture.

Elle ouvrit brutalement la fenêtre.

Déconnecter impérativement (moteur arrêté) les deux câbles reliés aux bornes de la batterie.

18

Contrastive topic and practical: 'Absolute' constructions

This chapter constitutes the material for all or part of a practical. The preliminary exercise should be done, and if possible handed in, before the practical. It should in any case be completed before going on to the rest of the chapter.

PRELIMINARY EXERCISE

Translate the following sentences into French.

1   [*On the economic situation*] The figures are depressing.
2   Bad luck is very enriching.

3   While you're a student, you'll be travelling abroad.
4   If you'd been a student, you'd have travelled abroad.

5   When she had finished her lunch, she went out.
6   When my brother had left and Mother was at prayer, Lucile would shut herself away.

7   Emma fainted and they carried her over to the window.
8   William and Tokor had stopped the car and were sitting gazing at the city.

The preliminary exercise points the way to four types of structure that often cause translation problems. Each of these types will be dealt with in a separate section. What they have in common is that each can be interpreted as involving some form of ellipsis, and each can be conveniently described as an 'absolute' construction. As with nominalization, English does have structural counterparts to French absolute constructions, but uses them less often. Consequently, when translating a French absolute construction, the translator generally needs to use grammatical transposition if the TT is to be idiomatic. As with nominalization, the contrast between French absolute constructions and their English counterparts usually reveals a preference in English for the particular or concrete, as opposed to a preference in French for the generic or abstract.

TRANSITIVE VERB WITH NO OBJECT

In most cases of this type, it is the absence of a *direct* object that is at issue. French allows, and frequently prefers, the use of a transitive verb without a direct object, as in:

ST	TT
Ce n'est pas que les éditeurs ne publient plus.	It is not that publishers have stopped publishing.

As this example shows, the structure is also possible in English (compare 'Thou shalt not kill', 'United flatter to deceive', 'Enjoy!', etc.). However, it is much more common in French, and reproducing it every time would make for exoticism in an English TT. The following typical example does pose such a problem:

ST	TT
Au risque de scandaliser, j'avoue même qu'une femme en pantalon ne me choque pas.	(i) It may shock/scandalize you, but . . . (ii) It may {sound shocking/be scandalous}, but . . .

In most contexts, 'At risk of scandalizing/shocking, I admit . . .' will be unidiomatic. TTs (i) and (ii) are more likely. The choice between them will depend on such things as genre and register, but each option entails translation loss in respect of literal meaning. TT (i) is a particularization, because it specifies 'you' (as distinct from 'them', 'people', etc.). TT (ii) is a partial overlap: as adjectives, 'shocking' and 'scandalous' lose explicit reference to the act of shocking/scandalizing somebody, and add explicit reference to the permanent, inherent quality of shockingness/scandalousness in not being offended by a woman wearing trousers.

Similar points can be made about the next two examples, from which the first two sentences in the exercise were derived:

ST	TT
Les chiffres rendent morose.	The figures are depressing.
Ça enrichit, les coups durs.	(i) Bad luck is very enriching.
	(ii) It's enriching, (is) bad luck.

In the second example, the ST sequential focus puts strong emphasis on 'enrichit' – compare the feebler 'les coups durs enrichissent'. The obvious TL structure, *subject* + *verb* + *complement*, loses this emphasis; hence the compensatory addition of 'very' in (i). It is possible to copy the ST sequential focus in English, as in (ii), but this will be too informal for some contexts. In both alternatives, though, the transposition from verb to adjective is pretty well unavoidable. In the following case, there is a choice between a number of constructions; we list three, for discussion in class:

ST	TT
Sa nomination au poste de premier ministre surprit et rassura.	(i) His appointment as Prime Minister was (both) surprising and reassuring.
	(ii) His appointment as Prime Minister {was/came as} a reassuring surprise.
	(iii) When he was appointed Prime Minister, it {was/came as} a reassuring surprise.

Using a transitive verb without a direct object is just as common in more colloquial French, as in:

ST	TT
Fais voir, donne ! Mais dis donc, comment tu fais ?	Let's have a look, give it us! Hey, how do you do it?

Note that 'donne' here, and perhaps also 'fais', is an example of ellipsis of an *indirect* object, which is also common in French.

In translating expressions like these, there is usually translation loss in respect of literal meaning. If transposition is to an adjective, or to *verb* + *noun* (e.g. 'was a surprise'), the result is partial overlap; if an object is supplied, there is inevitable particularization. The latter case also brings out clearly a typical difference between English and French, which we have already noted in Chapters 16 and 17: English often tends to concretize and specify individual details in situations where French prefers less concrete and less specific reference to details.

TRANSPOSITION FROM A NOUN, ADJECTIVE OR VERBLESS PHRASE TO A CLAUSE

Very commonly, a French sentence will contain a noun, an adjective or a verbless phrase which needs to be rendered with a clause containing a verb in English. Here is a French ST, from which sentences 3 and 4 in the exercise were derived:

ST	*TT*
Etudiant, vous voyagerez à l'étranger.	While you're a student, you'll be travelling abroad.

Similar remarks apply to this kind of expression as to those in the previous section. Depending on context, the item 'Etudiant' may be rendered not only as 'While/when you're student', but also as 'Since/as you're a student'. Transposition into a clause containing a verb inevitably entails particularization. In our TT, the general, timeless concept of 'being a student' is particularized by reference to a specific time at which a specific individual is a student. In some contexts, the timelessness can be preserved, e.g. in 'As a student'; but of course this is still a particularization, and it may also have a causal implication that the ST does not necessarily have.

A further indication of the generic quality of a verbless construction is the fact that it can be followed by a number of different verb forms, e.g.

Etudiant, vous {voyagez/voyagiez/voyagerez/voyageriez}/{avez/aviez/aurez/auriez voyagé} à l'étranger.

Like 'lors de mon passage' (see p. 230), 'Etudiant' contains no temporal or modal indication; depending on context, it will therefore be rendered by one of the following particularizations:

{When/while/whenever/if} you {are/were/have been/had been} a student . . .

And of course 'Etudiant' could just as easily be followed by 'je' or 'il', which would require one from a whole further range of particularizations.

Similar remarks apply to the following example, adapted from Astington (1983: 52), which will repay discussion in class:

Lui président, les prélèvements obligatoires {passeront/passeraient} de 42% à 40% du produit intérieur brut.

Lui président, les prélèvements obligatoires {sont/étaient/seraient/seront} passés . . .

Any translation of 'Lui président' using a clause with a verb is an example of transposition from an absolute construction to a relatively specific, particularizing one. In this instance, however, a 'timeless' phrase is just as possible in English:

> With him as President, compulsory contributions {will go/would go/ went/have gone/had gone/would have gone/will have gone} down . . .

This solution, using 'with', is sometimes a handy one. But it still entails a degree of particularization: 'with' seems to establish an explicit *causal* relation between his being President and the reduction in contributions (cf. 'with all this snow, there are bound to be accidents'). The French 'Lui président' leaves the causal relation inexplicit, as one of several possible interpretations. A similar point could be made about two other optional English renderings: 'Under/during his presidency'.

This type of construction is common in all genres. Sometimes, the decision as to what kind of particularization to allow in the TT depends on stylistic factors, sometimes on more practical ones. Here is an example from a car handbook. It completes the instructions for changing a wheel:

ST	TT
• serrez les écrous et descendez le cric ;	• tighten the nuts and lower the car to the ground;
• roues au sol, serrez les écrous à fond.	• remove the jack and tighten the nuts right up.

'Roues au sol' can easily be translated as 'with the wheels on the ground'. But if you have never changed a wheel before, you need as much explicit information as possible, and it may be safer to particularize further, as in our TT.

A type of construction that closely approximates the French one does exist in English, as in 'He a judge, it is surprising to find such a blunder'. This example is old-fashioned and stuffy, but it does have colloquial counterparts, as in: 'And him a judge, too!' In most TTs, though, this kind of structure is either unidiomatic or in the wrong register.

The next three examples contain a construction which is related to the others in this section; they should be discussed and translated in class:

> [*In a magazine on kitchens and bathrooms*] Le désir de pouvoir conserver une bonne partie de l'électroménager existant (parce que pratiquement neuf) dans une cuisine qui est à refaire, oblige à prévoir des éléments de dimensions standardisées.
> [*On a Prog Rock band*] Leur musique est mûre, parfaite, géniale réellement, car inspirée à la moindre seconde.

[*On someone who made a documentary on the Resistance*] Harris, lui, eut son père fusillé par les Allemands, car travaillant pour l'Intelligence service.

In the first of these examples, a verb needs to be supplied in the TT, so that 'practically new' does not look as if it qualifies the owner of the kitchen. An unlikely reading, no doubt, but it is easy to let such ambiguities creep into the TT. Take this example:

Reposée – donc jolie, disaient les magazines – Lucien pourrait encore la désirer.

We note in passing that here again, 'reposée' could just as well have been followed by a future, present or past, depending on the context. The main point, though, is that a literal translation of this sentence would result in a misattributed participle, e.g.: 'Rested – and therefore pretty, said the magazines – Lucien might find her desirable again'. Misattributed participles are a common danger in translating this kind of construction. The problem does not arise for the French reader, because the feminine ending on 'reposée' prevents any ambiguity. Even so, the structure is sometimes criticized in French, because in *spoken* French feminine and plural endings often cannot be heard, so that there sometimes is a risk of ambiguity.

In translating these sorts of absolute construction, then, the first challenge is to have the confidence to use a structure that does not imitate that of the ST; and the second is to make sure that the inevitable TT particularization is consistent with the context (e.g. to make the right choice between 'as/since/when/while/although' etc.).

'ABLATIVE ABSOLUTE'

The type of construction in this section can be thought of as a survival – or an imitation – of the Latin ablative absolute, which takes the form of *noun + participle* in the ablative case, as in '(with) the sun rising, darkness flees', or '(with) the bridge (having been) built, crossing the river was easy'. The 'ablative absolute' construction in French can almost always be interpreted as implying ellipsis of 'étant' or 'ayant été', as in this example (a soldier recalls relieving a section of Catalans garrisoning the frontier town of Kirschweiler):

Les Catalans relevés, je défends Kirschweiler.

'Les Catalans relevés' is an elliptical form of 'les Catalans {étant/ayant été} relevés'. The corresponding English forms are '(with) the Catalans ({being/having been}) relieved'. These are not idiomatic in this case, but such forms are perfectly possible, as in 'arms folded, she listened intently'. Consequently, the following example presents no translation difficulty (see sentence 5 in the exercise):

ST	TT
Son déjeuner terminé, elle sortit.	Her lunch finished, she went out.

However, as with the other types of absolute construction, idiomaticity and register do often require a particularizing or partially overlapping translation. Here are some examples for discussion and translation:

> Réflexion faite, le coup de tête de Botard ne m'étonne pas (see p. 156).
> [*On how to use a food processor*] Il sera beaucoup plus facile de les hacher, le bol bien rempli.
> Déconnecter impérativement (moteur arrêté) les deux câbles reliés aux bornes de la batterie.
> [*On the retail book trade*] Les petits libraires disparus, la librairie ne sera plus qu'un circuit de dépôts à court terme.
> [*On a tennis match*] Montée au filet, elle s'est fait lober.

As with 'lors de mon passage' and 'Etudiant, vous . . .', rendering French 'ablative absolutes' with a finite verb inevitably produces particularization, or sometimes partial overlap. Henri Godin (1964) sees this type of construction as typical of a 'streamlining' tendency in modern French, and cites an early example from Chateaubriand (see sentence 6), who first wrote:

> Lorsque mon frère était parti et que ma mère était en prières, Lucile s'enfermait.

and then changed his text to:

> Mon frère parti et ma mère en prières, Lucile s'enfermait.

TRANSPOSITION FROM PAST PARTICIPLE OR ADJECTIVE TO NOUN PHRASE OR RELATIVE CLAUSE

This is another category that is very common in French, but much rarer in English. Here are two examples:

ST	TT
Ils éditeront à des tirages aussi bas que possible pour réduire le risque encouru.	They will publish with the smallest print runs possible, so as to reduce the risk incurred.
On célébra Rocroi délivré.	We celebrated the relief of Rocroi.

The structure is easily replicated in the first example. But in the second, a literal translation – 'We celebrated Rocroi (having-been-)relieved' – is out of the question. The idiomatic 'the relief of' is a virtually obligatory partial overlap.

Considerable structural recasting is often necessary with this kind of construction. Here is a straightforward French sentence with some alternative TTs for discussion:

ST	TT
[*On a bus*] Il se jeta sur une place devenue libre.	(i) Then there was a free seat and he grabbed it.
	(ii) Then he saw a free seat and grabbed it.
	(iii) He grabbed a seat someone had just vacated.
	(iv) Then someone got out and he grabbed the seat.

The French structure can be seen as a contracted relative clause, with 'être' being omitted – 'Rocroi (qui avait été) délivré', 'une place (qui était) devenue libre', etc. This kind of ellipsis is often not idiomatically possible in English, so that the translator has to look for structural alterations. The following examples will probably need significant restructuring in translation:

[*See sentence 7*] On porta Emma évanouie devant la fenêtre.
[*See sentence 8*] William et Tokor arrêtés dans leur voiture contemplaient la ville.
Michel ahuri se tut.

Another common structure has an adjective, not a past participle, as the qualifier. This amounts to omission of the verb 'devenir', as in the following:

[*In bomb-shattered Nuremberg, 1945*] Seule dans la pierraille de Nuremberg déserte, une cycliste souriante.
En tout cas, dis-je furieux, tu pourrais cesser de sortir du Baudelaire comme un perroquet.
Oh, un système ordinaire, dis-je, un peu triste.

In the last two examples, the adjectives are probably best rendered by adverbs in English, as we saw in Chapter 17.

19

Contrastive topic and practical: Prepositions

This chapter constitutes the material for all or part of a practical. The preliminary exercise should be done, and if possible handed in, before the practical. It should in any case be completed before going on to the rest of the chapter.

PRELIMINARY EXERCISE

Translate the following passage into English.

Chaque fois qu'Henri promenait son chien [. . .], il suivait invariable-ment le même chemin. Le chien le prenait docilement, et Henri suivait le chien. Ils descendaient la rue, tournaient devant le bureau de poste, traversaient le terrain de jeu et passaient sous la ligne de chemin de fer pour arriver au sentier qui longeait la rivière. Un kilomètre au bord de l'eau, puis retour au bercail. Ils repassaient le viaduc puis pénétraient dans ces rues où les maisons étaient bien plus grandes que celle d'Henri et il y avait des arbres et des jardins et les voitures étaient toutes des Volvo ou des Mercedes.

The passage in the preliminary exercise is actually taken from the published TT of an English ST (Sharpe 1988: 7). We adapted the TT slightly so as not to give away its English origins, which might have prejudiced translation choices. Here is the original English text:

> Whenever Henry Wilt took the dog for a walk [. . .], he always took the same route. In fact the dog followed the route and Wilt followed the dog. They went down past the Post Office, across the playground, under the railway bridge and out on to the footpath by the river. A mile
> 5   along the river and then under the railway line again and back through streets where the houses were bigger than Wilt's semi and where there were large trees and gardens and the cars were all Rovers and Mercedes.
>
> (Sharpe 1978: 7)

The French TT could be discussed in a number of respects, but we shall concentrate on the specific points that relate to the topics of this chapter – the relative weakness of French prepositions in comparison with their English counterparts.

In the English text, the verb 'went' is qualified by a series of eight adverbial complements, each with a preposition as its nucleus. In none of these cases has the translator been able to use a simple French preposition on its own to render the English one. In four instances, the TT has prepositions reinforced with a verb:

ST	*TT*
past the Post Office	*tournaient devant* le bureau de poste
under the railway bridge	*passaient sous* la ligne de chemin de fer
to the footpath	*pour arriver au* sentier
through the streets	*pénétraient dans* ces rues

In three other cases, the French contains no preposition, the English one having simply been replaced with a verb of motion:

ST	*TT*
across the playground	*traversaient* le terrain de jeu
by the river	*qui longeait* la rivière
under the railway line again	*repassaient* le viaduc

In the remaining case, a compound French preposition containing a noun is substituted for a simple English preposition:

ST	TT
along the river	*au bord de* l'eau

These eight grammatical transpositions are typical of a technique which French translators often have to use when confronted with English prepositions. Their job is made more difficult by another typical English device: the use of one preposition as an adverbial modifier of another. The English text has two examples of this, 'down past' and 'on to'. To these we can add further complications: the possibility of modifying a preposition with an adverb, as in 'back through'; or of using an adverb to modify an expression consisting of a preposition modified by another preposition, as in 'out on to'. In each of these cases the result is in effect a compound preposition; a symptom of this is the absence of a comma after 'down', 'out', 'on' and 'back'. Compound prepositions like these cannot usually be formed for French TTs, as is seen here:

ST	TT
They went *down past* the Post Office	Ils *descendaient la rue, tournaient devant* le bureau de poste
out on to the footpath	*pour arriver au* sentier
then under the railway line again and *back through* streets	puis *retour au bercail*. Ils repassaient le viaduc puis *pénétraient dans* ces rues

These comparisons show that an ordinary English text is liable to contain prepositional structures that have no structural counterparts in French. Now imagine an English text that had no instances of these very common and compact structures: it would be subtly, but distinctly, odd. There is a real danger of this oddness affecting a TT translated from French, because it is actually possible for the most part to replicate the kinds of structure that are used in French. Thus a typical translation of the text in the preliminary exercise might look something like this:

Every time Henri walked his dog [. . .], he invariably took the same route. The dog would set quietly off, and Henri would follow the dog. They *went down the street, turned off by* the Post Office, *crossed* the playground and *went under* the railway line, *coming at last to* the path *that ran alongside* the river. A kilometre by the water *before returning to the fold*. They *went back under* the viaduct, and *then set off through* streets where the houses were much bigger than Henri's and there were trees and gardens and the cars were all Volvos and Mercedes.

It is highly unlikely that a back-translation from the French would hit on the original preposition-based expressions that correspond to the italicized phrases – the translator would be reluctant to lose the explicit variety and deliberateness embodied in the accumulation of verbs of motion in the French text. This would be a major translation loss. (Conversely, the French text itself has suffered considerable translation loss: compared with the economical and dynamic power of the English prepositions, the succession of verbs seems very plodding.) The translator's choices must, as ever, be weighed in terms of context, idiomaticity, and stylistic considerations such as that of a racy, down-to-earth narrative. But it is hard to see how, without major compensation, a French TT could avoid losing many of these qualities of Sharpe's original.

In the text we have been looking at, the French counterparts to English prepositions are mostly verb-based phrases. This is a common correspondence between the two languages, but it is not the only one. Just as often, an English preposition corresponds to a compound French preposition containing a noun:

ST	TT
L'éditeur ne peut le vendre que *par l'entremise d'*un libraire.	The publisher can only sell it *through* a bookseller.
C'est *de la part de* qui ?	Who's it *from*?

or to a French relative clause or present participle:

ST	TT
J'avais contemplé avec nostalgie le chromo *qui représentait* sa chambre.	I had gazed longingly at the coloured picture *of* her room.
Jean-Rostand, un gros établissement *accueillant* plus de 2 300 élèves.	Jean-Rostand, a big school *with* over 2,300 students.

or to a French preposition reinforced by an adjective or past participle:

ST	TT
L'après-midi du vendredi est *consacré à* votre éducation.	Friday afternoons are *for* your education.
C'est les hurlements *venus de* la cuisine qui l'ont réveillée.	It was the screaming *from* the kitchen that woke her.

The practical work that follows is divided into four sections, corresponding to the four categories of French–English correspondence illustrated above. Each section has two stages. In stage A the task is to translate

English sentences containing prepositions that cannot be rendered into French without grammatical transposition. The point of this is to raise awareness of the relative weakness of prepositions in French. In stage B, the task is to give alternative translations of each of a set of French sentences, including a translation that renders the italicized material with a single English preposition. Stage B should be done *without a dictionary* throughout.

ENGLISH PREPOSITION CORRESPONDS TO FRENCH VERB OR PREPOSITION REINFORCED BY A VERB

A 1 What's the quickest way to the University, please?
  2 I'll come for you about seven.
  3 I managed to crawl away from the flames.

B 1 Il faudrait téléphoner *pour appeler* un médecin.
  2 On n'atteint le bureau qu'*en traversant* la chambre.
  3 La machine heurta le bureau et *il glissa* jusqu'au mur *qu'il rencontra* d'une force irrésistible.

ENGLISH PREPOSITION CORRESPONDS TO FRENCH PREPOSITION REINFORCED WITH A NOUN, OR NOMINALIZED FRENCH COMPOUND PREPOSITION

A 1 She's on the executive committee.
  2 There's only one night crossing from Ostend.
  3 She was calling him from across the street.

B 1 Un maçon laissa tomber une brique *du haut d'*une échelle.
  2 Le résultat de cette politique sera la disparition, *en l'espace de* cinq ans, de la plupart des libraires français.
  3 Une main-d'œuvre bon marché *en provenance des* territoires occupés.

ENGLISH PREPOSITION CORRESPONDS TO FRENCH RELATIVE CLAUSE OR PRESENT PARTICIPLE

A 1 I'm very touched by your concern for me.
  2 The headmaster was a batty old man with a literally moth-eaten gown.
  3 The houses over the road are much bigger than ours.

B 1 On n'est pas près d'oublier le match *qui a opposé* Agen et Béziers, l'an dernier.

2 Le taxi démarra lentement. C'était une vieille Renault *dont* le chauffeur *était* à moitié sourd.

3 [*Instruction for a food processor*] Il est recommandé d'employer cette vitesse pour les produits *contenant* beaucoup d'eau.

ENGLISH PREPOSITION CORRESPONDS TO FRENCH PREPOSITION REINFORCED BY AN ADJECTIVE OR PAST PARTICIPLE

A 1 A young man with AIDS tells us his tragic story.

2 He illustrated his argument with quotations from Shakespeare.

3 In France, passengers with tickets have to date-stamp them before boarding the train.

B 1 Le pasteur, *vêtu de* son habit noir, nous terrifiait.

2 Il ne semblait pas savoir de quel défi, et *lancé par* qui, il s'agissait.

3 Mille rumeurs vagues *relatives aux* trésors enfouis par Kidd et ses associés.

20

Summary and conclusion

The only conclusion necessary to *Thinking French Translation* is a summing up of what it is the translator is supposed to be thinking *about*. The first thing to remember is that, whatever revision or editing the TT has undergone, it is the translator who is ultimately responsible for it. 'Thinking' translation implies a clear-sighted acceptance of this responsibility, but it also implies reducing the element of chance in how the TT will be received. If responsibility entails making decisions, taking the approach presented in this book will enable the translator to make them intelligently enough and imaginatively enough to be confident of what the overall impact of the TT will be. This is why we have stressed throughout the course the need for a clearly formulated initial strategy, and for clearly formulated decisions of detail rationally linked to the strategy.

One thing we hope to have shown is that no strategy can be assumed *a priori*. Formulating an appropriate strategy means assessing the salient features of a particular ST and relating them to the purpose of the TT. A crucial question then is: 'How do I decide which features are salient?' What we have tried to do is equip the student translator with a way of answering this question, whatever the nature of the ST. For our purposes, the salient features of a text can be said to be its most *relevant* ones, those that have significant expressive function. Devising a strategy means prioritizing the cultural, generic, formal, semantic and stylistic properties of the ST according to two things: their relative textual relevance, and the amount of attention they should receive in translation. The aim is to deal with translation loss in as rational and systematic way as possible. This implies being prepared, *if necessary*, to lose features that have relatively little textual relevance in a given ST (e.g. alliteration in a technical text on mining), sacrificing less relevant textual details to more relevant ones. And, of course, it implies using compensation to restore features of high textual relevance that cannot be more directly rendered (e.g. a significant play on words in a publicity text).

'Textual relevance' is thus a qualitative measure of how far particular properties of a text are responsible for its overall impact. Textually relevant features are those that stand out as making the text what it is. Since it is the translator who decides what is textually relevant, the decision is inescapably subjective. But not necessarily damagingly so. A relatively objective test of textual relevance is to imagine that a particular textual property is omitted from the text and to assess what difference this would make to the overall impact of the text. If the answer is 'little or none', the property in question has little textual relevance. But if omitting it would imply a loss in either the genre-representative or the individual character of the text, then it has high textual relevance. So, for example, phonic features are irrelevant in 'l'endettement net' in a financial statement, but relevant in 'ces serpents qui sifflent sur vos têtes' in a poetic tragedy.

Developing a translation strategy by assessing textual relevance in an ST entails scanning the text for every *kind* of feature that might be relevant to producing a TT fit for its purpose. For this scanning to be effective, it is vital to have in mind a systematic set of questions to ask of the ST. These questions correspond to the checklist of kinds of textual feature introduced in the schema of textual matrices on p. 5. The successive chapters of *Thinking French Translation* tackle the sorts of translation issue lying behind the questions that need to be asked of texts. The idea is that the translator learns to ask the questions systematically, one after the other. As students working through the book will have found, it only takes a bit a practice to be able to do this quickly and efficiently.

Some comments are called for on aspects of the relation between the schema of textual matrices and the book you have read. First, the 'cultural' matrix is different in focus from the others. Unlike the others, it does not list types of feature that may *in themselves* be salient in the ST before the translator starts forming a strategy. Corresponding to Chapter 3, it lists types of feature whose relevance can only be decided when the translator starts to form a strategy. That is, it draws attention to features that force the translator to choose between source-culture bias and target-culture bias. As such, it does invite the translator to assess how far the culture-specificity of ST features is textually relevant – this is why we have included it in the schema of textual matrices.

The other matrices are more straightforward reminders of what sorts of thing to look for when asking what the relevant features of a text are. Chapter 5, corresponding to the 'genre' matrix, gives a set of parameters to apply in identifying textual genre preparatory to translation. Chapters 6–8 correspond to the 'formal' matrix, introducing translation issues raised by the formal properties of texts. Chapters 9 and 10 correspond to the 'semantic' matrix; the translation issues addressed here are the ones most typically raised by literal and connotative meaning. Chapter 11 corresponds to the 'varietal' matrix; the questions to ask here concern language variety and its translation implications. Chapters 12–14 then give a brief sample of the many sub-genres from which professional translators will normally choose their speciality.

Some vital topics in the book do not figure as such in the schema of matrices. This is because they either apply universally from top to bottom of the schema, or concern a translation operation, not a textual feature. Grammatical transposition, for example, is introduced in Chapter 2 but is of central relevance in every chapter and every practical. There is a case to be made for including it in the cultural matrix, but it is so all-pervasive that it is not useful to identify it as a discrete element in the matrix. It is in fact so important that Chapters 16–19 are given entirely to it – and there could have been many more than these four. The topic of grammatical transposition would have been altogether too big for Chapter 3.

Another crucial topic, introduced as such in Chapter 4 but everywhere relevant, is compensation. More than anything else, successful compensation exemplifies the combination of imagination and rigour that is the mark of a good translator. However, even though compensation very often involves cultural and/or grammatical transposition, it is a translation operation, not a textual feature. So too are revising and editing, which are introduced as such in Chapter 15, but are an integral part of the translation process and figure in many of the chapters and practicals.

One pre-eminent translation issue is neither a textual feature nor a translation operation. This is the translation brief – why the text is being translated, on whose behalf, and for what audience. As we suggest in Chapter 5, it is useful, for practical translation needs, to see the purpose of a text as very closely linked with its genre. Genre, of course, *is* a textual feature, and as such figures at the head of the schema on p. 5. The reason why it is placed at the top is precisely that it shares a prime importance with purpose: the translation *process* will result in a translation *product*, a text having specific features, and produced in order to meet a communicative demand. This demand, formulated by the work-provider, is the translation brief. As the brief is neither a process nor a textual feature, it does not have a chapter to itself. But it has decisive importance, and that is why we have everywhere stressed its role as a parameter in assessing the relevance of ST and TT textual features, and why, in practicals, you have been asked to produce your TTs as if in response to a specific commission.

It should be remembered that the schema of matrices can be used to analyse any text, not just an ST. It can be applied to draft TTs, their features being systematically compared with those of the ST so as to see which details will be acceptable in the final version. Published TTs can also be evaluated in the same way. But whatever the text that is analysed by this method, never forget that the watchword is . . . *thinking* translation. This course encourages a methodical approach based on reasoned analysis of textual features and the translation problems they pose. But 'methodical' is not synonymous with 'mechanical' or 'automatic'. As we said in the Introduction, good translators know what they are doing: for thinking translation, there has to be a thinker, an individual person using flair and rigour to take creative, responsible decisions.

To sum up, then, we have tried to do two things in this course. Our first aim has been to help you ask and answer the strategic questions we listed on p. 6: 'What is the purpose and intended audience of my translation? What is the purpose of this ST? What genre does it belong to, and what audience is it aimed at? What is its message content? What are its salient linguistic features? What are its principal effects? What are the implications of all these factors? If a choice has to be made among them, which ones should be given priority in ensuring that the TT is fit for its purpose?' And our second aim has been to help you use intelligent, creative techniques for the translation operation, the battle with the problems of syntax, lexis etc. that has to be fought in translating particular expressions in their particular context.

May the loss be with you.

Postscript: A career in translation?

Having completed the course, you may feel you wish to know more about becoming a translator. This concluding section aims to provide some preliminary information and advice for aspiring entrants to the profession. It is necessarily British-oriented, but a contact address for the United States is given. An organization that can give help anywhere in the world is FIT, the Fédération Internationale des Traducteurs (http://www.fit-ift.org).

Translators are usually either 'in-house' or 'freelance'. The in-house translator is employed by a business, or a translation company or agency, to provide translations in the workplace, on either a permanent or a fixed-term basis. The advantage of being in-house for a newcomer to the profession is the opportunity to gain experience quickly, in an environment where mentoring and feedback are usually supplied. Though it may take time to find a placement or post, this kind of experience is extremely valuable. A good place to find companies who offer placements or posts in-house is the Institute of Translation and Interpreting (ITI) Bulletin. Newspapers, such as *The Guardian* on Mondays in the Media supplement, publish job vacancies, and your local 'Yellow Pages' directory will provide you with a list of translation companies or agencies operating in your area.

Setting up as a freelance is a more complex issue. Generally speaking, offers of work are only made to translators with a 'track record' and a specific qualification in translation, such as the Diploma in Translation of the Institute of Linguists (IoL), which can be considered the first step on the professional ladder, or membership of the ITI, which is gained by examination and experience. The IoL Diploma in Translation exam is held every January, and a number of institutions offer courses, whether on site or by distance learning. For details of these exams, do not write to us or to Routledge: contact the IoL and the ITI at the addresses given below.

The optimal freelance translator will need to be able to offer two or possibly more foreign languages at a very high level of competence.

Moreover, experience and knowledge of a number of subject specialities are required; most translators concentrate on either technical translation (e.g. IT, engineering, construction) or what is called 'general translation' and usually includes legal, financial and business texts. Few translators cover a very wide range of subjects. In addition to such skills, the translator must possess suitable equipment, comprising a computer equipped with modem and e-mail (virtually all translation is sent back to the work-provider by e-mail these days), a printer (preferably laser), a scanner and a fax machine. Two phone lines are useful, so that one can communicate with work-providers while using e-mail or the Internet.

Working as a freelance means being self-employed, and it is important to find out before taking this step what self-employment entails. All translators have to grapple with taxation, pensions contributions, accounts, grants and subsidies, training, marketing and legal issues at some point. Help is at hand though, from bodies like Business Link, which exist throughout the United Kingdom and can provide information and advice (usually free of charge) about these matters. The Inland Revenue has offices in all towns and cities, as does the DSS. Your local Chamber of Commerce may also be able to provide you with useful information, and sometimes they have their own lists of translators available for work, which you may be able to join.

One disadvantage of working from home is isolation. A body like the ITI offers a valuable lifeline to affiliates and members by providing a range of services. These include: links with the world of employment (e.g. DTI and other important bodies), guidance for new entrants to the profession (e.g. a forum for new translators at the annual conference), training and professional development (also in conjunction with universities and professional institutions), information on IT and reference materials, and the promotion of professional standards of competence through the Codes of Conduct and Terms of Business. Students on an approved course of study can become Student Members on payment of a small annual sum, and those who are not students but interested in the profession may become Subscribers. Membership is gained by assessment and examination only. All categories of affiliation may attend ITI events, and Students benefit from very advantageous rates for courses and the annual conference.

The Bulletin published by ITI every two months contains useful articles and tips, job offers and a calendar of events. This is a good way of keeping abreast of developments in the field of translation. Networking is also important, and ITI has a number of networks for subjects, languages and regions, which enable translators to share their experiences, meet and pass on work. Some new entrants, in fact, are offered their first job through networking.

An excellent book giving detailed advice for aspiring and practising translators is Samuelsson-Brown (1993).

Useful contacts:

The Institute of Translation and Interpreting
Fortuna House
South Fifth Street
Milton Keynes
Bucks
MK9 2EU

Tel: 01908 325250

Web site: http://www.ITI.org.uk

The Institute of Linguists
Diploma in Translation Department
48 Southwark Street
London
SE1 1UN

Tel: 020 7940 3100

E-mail: info@iol.org.uk

Web site: http://www.iol.org.uk

In the United States, every American state has its own translators/interpreters association, affiliated to the American Translators Association (ATA):

American Translators Association
225 Reinekers Lane, Suite 590
Alexandria, VA 22314
USA

Tel: (703) 683-6100

E-mail: ata@atanet.org

Web site: http://www.atanet.org

If you do decide that you want to make a career in translation, bear in mind that you need to be enthusiastic, motivated and determined. Freelancing, in particular, is not for the faint-hearted! Work flows are usually erratic, at least until you become established and have several work-providers. Therefore, if you are considering changing jobs and abandoning the nine-to-five office job for translation, make sure you have enough funds to see you through at least the first two years, where cash-flow and income will be irregular. However, once you have become successfully established, you will be unlikely to want to return to a routine job, as the independence of freelancing makes for an interesting and stimulating occupation.

Glossary of terms used

affective meaning a type of **connotative meaning**, affective meaning is the emotive effect worked on the addressee by using one particular **linguistic expression** rather than others that might have been used to express the same literal message.

alliteration the recurrence of the same sound or sound-cluster at the beginning of two or more words occurring near or next to one another; not to be confused with **onomatopoeia**.

allusive meaning a type of **connotative meaning**; in a given **linguistic expression**, allusive meaning consists in evoking the meaning of an entire saying or quotation in which that expression figures. NB If a saying or quotation appears in full, that is a case of *citation*: e.g. 'The darling buds of May are just beautiful this year'; *allusion* occurs where only part of the saying or quotation is used, but that part evokes the meaning of the entire saying or quotation: e.g. 'Brrr . . . No darling buds yet awhile, I'm afraid'.

anaphora see **grammatical anaphora** and **rhetorical anaphora**.

associative meaning the **connotative meaning** of a **linguistic expression** which takes the form of attributing to the referent certain stereotypically expected properties culturally associated with that referent.

assonance the recurrence of a sound or sound-cluster within words occurring near or next to one another; not to be confused with **onomatopoeia**.

attitudinal meaning the **connotative meaning** of a **linguistic expression** which takes the form of implicitly conveying a commonly held attitude or value judgement in respect of the referent of the expression.

back-translation   translation of a **TT** back into the **SL**; the resulting text will almost certainly not be identical to the original **ST**.

calque   a form of **cultural transposition** whereby a **TT** expression is closely modelled on the grammatical structure of the corresponding **ST** expression; a calque is like a moment of **exoticism**, although exoticism proper is a feature of whole texts or sections of texts. NB Calque is different from **cultural borrowing**, which imports the ST expression verbatim into the TT.

code-switching   the alternating use of two or more recognizably different language varieties (of the same language or of different languages) within the same **text**.

coherence (adj. **coherent**)   the tacit, yet intellectually discernible, thematic or affective development that characterizes a **text**, as distinct from a random sequence of unrelated **sentences**.

cohesion (adj. **cohesive**)   the explicit and transparent linking of **sentences** and larger sections of **text** by the use of overt linguistic devices, such as conjunctions or **grammatical anaphora**, that act as 'signposts' for the **coherence** of the text.

collocative meaning   the **connotative meaning** lent to a **linguistic expression** by the meaning of some other expression with which it frequently collocates; e.g. 'social *intercourse*' almost inevitably acquires an association of 'sex' from the common collocation 'sexual intercourse'. Collocative meaning is thus the 'echo' of expressions that partner a given expression in commonly used phrases.

communicative translation   a mode of **free translation** whereby ST expressions are replaced with their **contextually**/situationally appropriate cultural equivalents in the **TL**; i.e. the **TT** uses situationally apt target-culture equivalents in preference to **literal translation**.

compensation   a technique of mitigating **translation loss**: where any conventional translation (however **literal** or **free**) would entail an unacceptable translation loss, this loss is mitigated by deliberately introducing a less unacceptable one, important **ST** features being approximated in the TT through means other than those used in the ST. NB Unlike e.g. an unavoidable, conventional **grammatical transposition** or **communicative translation**, compensation is not forced on the translator by the constraints of **TL** structures – it is a conscious, careful, free, one-off choice.

connotation   see **connotative meaning**.

connotative meaning (or **connotation**)   the implicit overtones that a **linguistic expression** carries over and above its **literal meaning**. NB The *overall* meaning of an expression is compounded of its literal meaning plus these overtones and its **contextual** nuances.

context (adj. **contextual**)   the rest of the **text** in which a given **linguistic expression** or stretch of text (e.g. lines, paragraph, chapter, etc.) occurs; the immediate context is a crucial consideration in making any **decision of detail**.

cultural borrowing   taking over an **SL** expression verbatim from the **ST** into the **TT**; the borrowed term may remain unaltered in form, or it may undergo some degree of **transliteration**. NB Cultural borrowing differs from **calque** and **exoticism**, which do not use the ST expression verbatim, but adapt it into the **TL**, however minimally.

cultural transplantation   the highest degree of **cultural transposition**, involving the wholesale deletion of source-culture details mentioned in the **ST** and their replacement with target-culture details in the **TT**.

cultural transposition   any departure from **literal translation** that involves replacing **SL**-specific features with **TL**-specific features, thereby to some extent reducing the foreignness of the **TT**.

decisions of detail   translation decisions taken in respect of specific problems of **lexis**, **syntax**, etc.; decisions of detail are taken in the light of previously taken **strategic decisions**, although they may well in their turn lead the translator to refine the original **strategy**.

dialect   a language variety with non-standard features of accent, vocabulary, **syntax** and **sentence**-formation characteristic of the regional provenance of its users.

discourse level   the level of **textual variables** on which whole **texts** or sections of texts are considered as **coherent** or **cohesive** entities.

editing   the final 'polishing' of a **TT**, following **revision**, and focusing on matching TT style and presentation to the expectations of the target readership.

exegetic translation   a style of translation in which the **TT** expresses and comments on details that are not explicitly conveyed in the **ST**; i.e. the TT is an explication, and usually an expansion, of the contents of the ST.

exoticism the lowest degree of **cultural transposition**, importing linguistic and cultural features wholesale from the **ST** into the **TT** with minimal adaptation; exoticism generally involves multiple **calques**. NB Exoticism is different from **cultural borrowing**, which does not *adapt* ST material into the **TL**, but quotes it verbatim.

free translation a style of translation in which there is only an overall correspondence between units of the **ST** and units of the **TT**, e.g. a rough **sentence**-to-sentence correspondence, or an even looser correspondence in terms of even larger sections of text.

generalization see **generalizing translation**.

generalizing translation (or **generalization**) rendering an **ST** expression by a **TL hyperonym**, e.g. translating 'clochette' as 'bell'. The **literal meaning** of the **TT** expression is wider and less specific than that of the corresponding ST expression; i.e. a generalizing translation omits detail that is explicitly present in the literal meaning of the ST expression.

genre (or **text-type**) a category to which, in a given culture, a given **text** is seen to belong and within which it is seen to share a type of communicative purpose with other texts; that is, the text is seen to be more or less typical of the genre.

gist translation a style of translation in which the **TT** expresses only the gist of the **ST**; it is usually shorter than a faithful translation would be.

grammatical anaphora the replacement of previously used **linguistic expressions** by simpler and less specific expressions (such as pronouns) having the same **contextual** referent; e.g. 'I dropped the bottle and *it* broke'.

grammatical level the level of **textual variables** on which are considered words, the decomposition of inflected, derived and compound words into their meaningful constituent parts, and the **syntactic** arrangement of words into phrases and **sentences**.

grammatical transposition translating an **ST** expression having a given grammatical structure by a **TT** expression having a different grammatical structure containing different parts of speech in a different arrangement.

hyperonym a **linguistic expression** whose **literal meaning** includes, but is wider and more general than, the range of literal meaning of another expression; e.g. 'vehicle' is a hyperonym of 'car'.

hyperonymy–hyponymy   the semantic relationship between a **hyper-onym** and a **hyponym**; a lesser degree of semantic equivalence than synonymy.

hyponym   a **linguistic expression** whose **literal meaning** is included in, but is narrower and less general than, the range of literal meaning of another expression; e.g. 'car' is a hyponym of 'vehicle'.

idiom   a fixed figurative expression whose meaning cannot be deduced from the **literal meanings** of the words that constitute it, e.g. 'football's a *different kettle of fish*', 'she's so *stuck up*'.

idiomatic   an idiomatic expression is one that, in its **context**, is unremarkable, 'natural', 'normal', completely acceptable. NB 'Idiomatic' is not synonymous with '**idiomizing**'.

idiomizing translation   a relatively **free translation** which respects the overall **ST** message content, but typically uses **TL idioms** or phonic or rhythmic patterns to give an easy read, even if this means sacrificing some semantic details or nuances of **register**. NB 'Idiomizing' is not synonymous with '**idiomatic**'.

illocutionary particle   a discrete element which, when added to the **syntactic** material of an utterance, tells the listener/reader what affective force the utterance is intended to have; e.g. 'dammit!', 'hélas', or 'tout de même' in 'Je ne vais tout de même pas serrer la main à un terroriste'.

interlinear translation   a style of translation in which the **TT** provides a literal rendering for each successive meaningful unit of the **ST** (including affixes) and arranges these units in the order of their occurrence in the ST, regardless of the conventional grammatical order of units in the **TL**.

intertextual level   the level of textual variables on which **texts** are considered as bearing significant external relationships to other texts, e.g. by allusion or imitation, or by virtue of **genre** membership.

lexis (adj. **lexical**)   the totality of the words in a given language.

linguistic expression   a self-contained and meaningful item in a given language, such as a word, a phrase, a **sentence**.

literal meaning   the conventional range of referential meaning attributed to a **linguistic expression**. NB The *overall meaning* of an expression in context is compounded of this literal meaning plus any **connotative meanings** and **contextual** nuances that the expression has.

literal translation   an **SL**-oriented, word-for-word, style of translation in which the **literal meaning** of all the words in the **ST** is taken as if straight from the dictionary, but the conventions of **TL** grammar are respected.

nominal expression   a **linguistic expression** which either consists of a noun or has a noun as its nucleus.

nominalization   the use of a **nominal expression** which could be replaced by a **linguistic expression** not containing a noun.

onomatopoeia   a word whose phonic form imitates a sound; not to be confused with **alliteration** or **assonance**.

partial overlap   see **partially overlapping translation**.

partially overlapping translation (or **partial overlap**)   rendering an **ST** expression by a **TL** expression whose range of **literal meaning** overlaps only partially with that of the ST expression; e.g. translating '*agents hydratants*' as 'moisturizing *ingredients*' in a text on toiletries: the literal meaning of the **TT** expression retains something of the ST literal meaning ('part of the toiletry'), but also *adds* some detail *not* explicit in the literal meaning of the ST expression ('element included in a recipe or formula') and *omits* some other detail that *is* explicit in it ('active element'); partially overlapping translation thus simultaneously combines elements of **generalizing** and **particularizing translation**. NB In this example, the overall message is preserved despite the needless partial overlap, because 'moisturi*zing*' implies agency.

particularization   see **particularizing translation**.

particularizing translation (or **particularization**)   rendering an **ST** expression by a **TL hyponym**, e.g. translating 'bell' as 'sonnette'. The **literal meaning** of the **TT** expression is narrower and less general than that of the corresponding ST expression; i.e. a particularizing translation adds detail to the TT that is not explicitly expressed in the ST.

phonic/graphic level   the level of **textual variables** on which is considered the patterned organization of sound-segments in speech, or of letters and layout in writing.

prosodic level   the level of **textual variables** on which are considered 'metrically' patterned stretches of speech within which syllables have varying degrees of *prominence* (e.g. through stress and vowel-differentiation), varying degrees of *pace* (e.g. through length and tempo) and varying qualities of *pitch*.

reflected meaning the **connotative meaning** given to a **linguistic expression** by the fact that its form (phonic, graphic or both) is reminiscent of a homonymic or near-homonymic expression with a different **literal meaning**; e.g. 'I can see you're naval' could have a reflected meaning of 'bare midriff' in certain **contexts**. Reflected meaning is thus the 'echo' of the literal meaning of some other expression that sounds, or is spelled, the same, or nearly the same, as a given expression.

register see **social register** and **tonal register**.

revision checking a **TT** against the **ST** to eliminate errors and inconsistencies; compare **editing**.

rhetorical anaphora the repetition of a word or words at the beginning of successive or closely associated clauses or phrases.

rhyme rhyme occurs when, in two or more words, the last stressed vowel and all the sounds that follow it are identical and in the same order.

sentence a complete, self-contained linguistic unit capable of acting as a vehicle for communication; over and above the basic grammatical units that it contains, a sentence must have sense-conferring properties of intonation or punctuation, and may in addition contain features of word order, and/or **illocutionary particles**, which contribute to the overall meaning, or 'force', of the sentence. NB In this definition, a sentence does not necessarily contain a verb.

sentential level the level of **textual variables** on which **sentences** are considered.

SL see **source language**.

social register a style of speaking/writing from which relatively detailed stereotypical information about the social identity of the speaker/writer can be inferred.

sociolect a language variety with features of accent, vocabulary, **syntax** and **sentence**-formation characteristic of the class affiliations of its users.

source language (or **SL**) the language in which the **ST** is expressed.

source text (or **ST**) the **text** requiring translation.

ST see **source text**.

strategic decisions   the initial decisions that constitute the translator's **strategy**; strategic decisions are taken, in the light of the requirements of the **TT** and the nature of the **ST**, as to which ST properties should have priority in translation; **decisions of detail** are taken in the light of these strategic decisions.

strategy   the translator's overall 'game-plan', consisting of decisions taken after an initial read-through of all or part of the ST before starting to translate in detail, e.g. whether and when to give **literal meaning** a higher priority than style, to address a lay readership or a specialist one, to maximize or minimize foreignness in the **TT**, to use formal language or slang, prose or verse, etc.

synonym (adj. **synonymous**)   a **linguistic expression** that has exactly the same range of **literal meaning** as one or more others. NB Synonymous expressions usually differ in **connotative meaning**, and are therefore unlikely to have identical impact in **context**.

synonymy   the semantic relationship between **synonyms**; synonymy is the highest degree of semantic equivalence.

syntax (adj. **syntactic**)   the branch of grammar that concerns the arrangement of words into phrases and **sentences**.

target language (or **TL**)   the language into which the **ST** is to be translated.

target text (or **TT**)   the **text** which is a translation of the **ST**.

text   any stretch of speech or writing produced in a given language (or mixture of languages – cf. **code-switching**) and assumed to make a **coherent** whole on the **discourse level**.

text-type   see **genre**.

textual variables   all the demonstrable features contained in a **text**, and which could (in another text) have been different; i.e. each textual variable constitutes a genuine *option* in the text.

TL   see **target language**.

tonal register   a style of speaking/writing adopted as a means of conveying an affective attitude of the speaker/writer to the addressee. The **connotative meaning** of a feature of tonal register is an **affective meaning**, conveyed by the choice of one out of a range of expressions capable of conveying a particular message content; e.g. 'Excuse me, please' vs 'Shift your butt'.

translation loss   any feature of incomplete replication of the **ST** in the **TT**; translation loss is therefore not limited to the omission of ST features in the TT: where the TT has features not present in the ST, the addition of these also counts as translation loss. In any given TT, translation loss is inevitable on most levels of **textual variables**, and likely on all. NB The translation losses only matter in so far as they prevent the successful implementation of the translator's **strategy** for the TT.

transliteration   the use of **TL** spelling conventions for the written representation of **SL** expressions.

TT   see **target text**.

References

Aerospatiale 1994a. *Rapport annuel 1993*. Paris: Aerospatiale.

Aerospatiale 1994b. *Annual Report 1993*. Paris: Aerospatiale.

Air France 2001. *Air France magazine*, April. Roissy: Air France.

Air France/Fréquence Plus 2001. 'Fréquence plus' [pull-out leaflet], *Air France magazine*, April.

Albert, J.C. 1987. 'Détection par ultrasons des amas inclusionnaires dans les tôles minces', in *Euroabstracts Section II*, Vol. XIII, No. 8, Luxembourg: Commission of the European Communities.

Anderson, A. and Avery, C. 1995. 'Checking comes in from the cold', *ITI Bulletin*, February.

Angevin, A. 2000. Unpublished report on a *table ronde* at La jeunesse d'Europe danse en Avignon.

Astington, E. 1983. *Equivalences: Translation Difficulties and Devices, French–English, English–French*. Cambridge: Cambridge University Press.

Audisio, G. (ed.) 1945. *Les Ecrivains en prison*. Paris: Seghers.

Ayres-Bennett, W. and Carruthers, J. 2001. *Problems and Perspectives: Studies in the Modern French Language*. Harlow: Longman.

Baker, M. 1992. *In Other Words*. London: Routledge.

Barham, D.K. and Cutts, A. 1987. 'Monitoring and automation for the coalface', in *Euroabstracts Section II*, Vol. XIII, No. 8, Luxembourg: Commission of the European Communities.

Beauvoir S. de 1960. *La Force de l'âge*. Paris: Gallimard.

Beauvoir, S. de 1965. *The Prime of Life*, Green, P. (trans.). Harmondsworth: Penguin.

Braun 1981. *The Cookbook for the Braun Multipractic Plus and the Multipractic Plus Electronic; Cuisiner avec Multipractic Plus et Multipractic Plus Electronic de Braun*. Kronberg: Braun GmbH.

Cabon, A. 1999. Two texts in *Tables et saveurs de Bretagne 1999*. Rennes: Association Tables et Saveurs de Bretagne.

Cadou, R.-G. 1972. *Pleine poitrine et quelques poèmes*. Périgueux: Fanlac.

Camus, A. 1946. *The Outsider*, Gilbert, S. (trans.). London: Hamish Hamilton.

Camus, A. 1947. *L'Etranger*, (2nd edn). Paris: Gallimard.

Camus, A. 1983. *The Outsider*, Laredo, J. (trans.). Harmondsworth: Penguin.

Cardinal, M. 1975. *Les Mots pour le dire*. Paris: Bernard Grasset.

Cardinal, M. 1984. *The Words to Say It*, Goodheart, P. (trans.). London: Pan Books.

Cardinal, M. 1988. *Les Mots pour le dire*. Paris: Le Livre de Poche.

Carton, F. et al. 1983. *Les Accents des Français*. Paris: Hachette.

Caste, M. 1980. 'Ma Mie', in *Le Monde*, 24 December.

Coertens, J. 2001. 'La Petite Provence du Paradou'. Le Paradou: La Petite Provence.

Cross, T. (ed.) 1988. *The Lost Voices of World War I*. London: Bloomsbury.

Dassault 1987a. *Electronique Serge Dassault. Avril 1987*. Saint-Cloud: ESD.

Dassault 1987b. *Electronique Serge Dassault. April 1987*. Saint-Cloud: ESD.

de Gaulle, C. 1956. *Mémoires de Guerre : l'Unité*. Paris: Plon.

de Gaulle, C. 1959. *War Memoirs. Unity: 1942–4. Documents*, Erskine, H. and Murchie, J. (eds and trans.). London: Weidenfeld and Nicholson.

Dutourd, J. 1972. *Au Bon Beurre*. Paris: Gallimard, Coll. Folio.

ECSC-CERCHAR 1987. 'Amélioration des moyens de fermeture des enceintes à confiner en cas de feux ou d'incendies'; 'Improvements in stopping-off methods used in the event of fire', in *Euroabstracts Section II*, Vol. XII, No. 1, Luxembourg: Commission of the European Communities.

ECSC-CRM (Belgique) 1987a. 'Influence of the form and position of the softening and meltdown zone on the blast furnace performance', in *Euroabstracts Section II*, Vol. XIII, No. 8, Luxembourg: Commission of the European Communities.

ECSC-CRM (Belgique) 1987b. 'Formabilité et soudabilité des tôles minces avec revêtement métallique'; 'Formability and weldability of thin metallic coated steel sheets', in *Euroabstracts Section II*, Vol. XIII, No. 8, Luxembourg: Commission of the European Communities.

Emmanuel, P. 1982. *L'Arbre et le vent*. Paris: Editions du Seuil.

George, K. 1993. 'Alternative French', in C. Sanders (ed.) *French Today*. Cambridge: Cambridge University Press.

Gide, A. 1958. *Romans*. Paris: Gallimard, Coll. Pléiade.

Gide, A. 1966. *The Immoralist*, Bussy, D. (trans.). London: Cassell.

Godin, H. 1964. *Les Ressources stylistiques du français contemporain*. Oxford: Blackwell.

Goscinny, R. and Sempé, J.-J. 1960. *Le petit Nicolas*. Paris: Denoël.

Goscinny, R. and Sempé, J.-J. 1976. *The Adventures of Nicholas and the Gang*, Bell, A. (trans). London: Beaver.

Goscinny, R. and Uderzo, A. 1961. *Astérix le Gaulois*. Neuilly-sur-Seine: Dargaud.

Goscinny, R. and Uderzo, A. 1969. *Asterix the Gaul*, Bell, A. and Hockridge, D. (trans.). Leicester: Brockhampton Press.

Goscinny, R. and Uderzo, A. 1973. *Astérix en Corse*. Neuilly-sur-Seine: Dargaud.

Goscinny, R. and Uderzo, A. 1980. *Asterix in Corsica*, Bell, A. and Hockridge, D. (trans.). London: Hodder Dargaud.

Graham, J.D. 1983. 'Checking, Revision and Editing', in C. Picken (ed.) *The Translator's Handbook*. London: Aslib.

Grainville, P. 1976. *Les Flamboyants*. Paris: Editions du Seuil.

Guidère, M. 2000. *Publicité et traduction*. Paris: L'Harmattan.

Halliday, M.A.K. and Hasan, R. 1976. *Cohesion in English*. London: Longman.

Hatim, B. and Mason, I. 1990. *Discourse and the Translator*. London: Longman.

Hermans, T. 1999. *Translation in Systems. Descriptive and Systemic Approaches Explained*. Manchester: St Jerome Publishing.

Hervey, S. 1992. 'Registering Registers', *Lingua*, 86.

Hickey, L. 1998. 'Perlocutionary Equivalence: Marking, Exegesis and Recontextualization', in L. Hickey (ed.) *The Pragmatics of Translation*. Clevedon: Multilingual Matters Ltd.

Hollander, J. 1981. *Rhyme's Reason: A Guide to English Verse*. New Haven and London: Yale University Press.

Holmes, J.S. 1988. *Translated!* Amsterdam: Rodopi.

Ionesco, E. 1962. *Rhinoceros*, Prouse, D. (trans.). Harmondsworth: Penguin.
Ionesco, E. 1988. *Rhinocéros*. Paris: Gallimard, Coll. Folio.
Irwin, M. 1996. 'Translating Opera', in J. Taylor *et al.* (eds) *Translation Here and There, Now and Then*. Exeter: Elm Bank Publications.
Jakobson, R. 1971. *Selected Writings*, Vol. II. The Hague: Mouton.
Katan, D. 1999. *Translating Cultures: An Introduction for Translators, Interpreters and Mediators*. Manchester: St Jerome Publishing.
Keats, J. 1958. *The Poetical Works of John Keats*, Garrod, H.W. (ed.). 2nd edn. Oxford: Clarendon Press.
Koller, W. 1995. 'The Concept of Equivalence and the Object of Translation Studies'. *Target*, 7.
Lanoux, A. 1978. *Le Commandant Watrin*. Paris: Le Livre de Poche.
Larreguy de Civrieux, M. de 1926. *La Muse de Sang*. Paris: Librairie du Travail.
Leech, G. 1974. *Semantics*. Harmondsworth: Pelican Books.
Le Figaro 1990. 'Brève histoire des compagnons de déroute', 27 September.
Léon, J.-A. 1989. *Poèmes d'un amour inutile*. Paris: Le Méridien.
Le Taillanter, R. 1990. 'Roger Le Taillanter raconte', *L'Express*, 10 August.
Lewis, R. 1982. *On Reading French Verse*. Oxford: Clarendon Press.
Michel, G. 1968. *L'Agression*. Paris: Gallimard.
Molière. 1967. *Tartuffe and Other Plays*, Frame, D.M. (trans.). Signet Classics. New York and London: New American Library.
Molière. 1990. *Le Tartuffe ou l'imposteur*, Ferreyrolles, G. (ed.). Classiques Larousse. Paris: Librairie Larousse.
Molière. 2000. *The Misanthrope and Other Plays*, Wood, J. and Coward, D. (trans.). Penguin Classics. Harmondsworth: Penguin.
Montesquieu, C. de S. 1960. *Lettres persanes*, Vernière, P. (ed.). Paris: Garnier.
Neubert, A. and Shreve, G.M. 1992. *Translation as Text*. Kent, OH: The Kent State University Press.
Newmark, P. 1981. *Approaches to Translation*. Oxford: Pergamon.
Nicholson, R.A. 1987. *Translations of Eastern Poetry and Prose*. London: Curzon Press, NJ: Humanities Press.
Nida, E. 1964. *Toward a Science of Translating*. Leiden: Brill.
Pagnol, M. 1988. *Jean de Florette*. Paris: Editions de Fallois.
Pagnol, M. 1989. *Jean de Florette and Manon of the Springs*, van Heyningen, W.E. (trans.). London: Picador.
Pinchuk, I. 1977. *Scientific and Technical Translation*. London: Andre Deutsch.
Ponge, F. 1965. *Tome premier*. Paris: Gallimard.
Reiss, K. 1989. 'Text-types, Translation Types and Translation Assessment', in A. Chesterman (ed.) *Readings in Translation Theory*. Helsinki: Finn Lectura.
Robbe-Grillet, A. 1963. *Pour un nouveau roman*. Paris: Editions de Minuit.
Rochefort, C. 1988. *La Porte du fond*. Paris: Grasset et Fasquelle.
Rowling, J.K. 1997. *Harry Potter and the Philosopher's Stone*. London: Bloomsbury.
Rowling, J.K. 1998. *Harry Potter à l'école des sorciers,* Ménard, J.-Fr. (trans.). Paris: Gallimard Jeunesse.
Salines de Guérande 1997. *Fleur de Sel le Guérandais, récolte 1997*. Guérande: Les Salines de Guérande SA.
Samuelsson-Brown, G. 1993. *A Practical Guide for Translators*. Clevedon: Multilingual Matters.
Schifres, A. 2000. 'Dix poids, dix mesures', *L'Express*, 3 August.
Schneider 1996a. *Rapport annuel 1995*. Paris: Schneider SA.
Schneider 1996b. *Annual Report 1995*. Paris: Schneider SA.
Schneider 1997a. *Rapport annuel 1996*. Paris: Schneider SA.
Schneider 1997b. *Annual Report 1996*. Paris: Schneider SA.

Serge, V. 1967. *Les Révolutionnaires*. Paris: Editions du Seuil.

Serge, V. 1968. *The Case of Comrade Tulayev*, Trask, W.R. (trans.). Harmondsworth: Penguin.

Shakespeare, W. 1967. *Macbeth*, Hunter, G.K. (ed.). The New Penguin Shakespeare. Harmondsworth: Penguin.

Sharpe, T. 1978. *Wilt*. London: Pan.

Sharpe, T. 1988. *Wilt 1*, Dupuigrenet-Desroussilles (trans.). Paris: U.G.D., Coll. 10/18.

Snell-Hornby, M. 1988. *Translation Studies: An Integrated Approach*. Amsterdam: John Benjamins.

Tardieu, J. 1990. *La Comédie de la comédie*. Paris: Gallimard.

Toury, G. 1980. *In Search of a Theory of Translation*. Tel Aviv: The Porter Institute for Poetics and Semiotics.

Toury, G. 1995. *Descriptive Translation Studies and Beyond*. Amsterdam and Philadelphia: John Benjamins.

Viguie, J.C. 1983. 'Construction et caractérisation d'un électrolyseur pour la réduction électrochimique de la vapeur d'eau à 850°C. Rapport final'; 'Fabrication and characterization of a set of electrolytic cells for the electrochemical reduction of water vapour at 850°C. Final report', in *Euroabstracts Section I*, Vol. XXI, No. 12, Part 2, Luxembourg: Commission of the European Communities.

Vinay, J.-P. and Darbelnet, J. 1958. *Stylistique comparée du français et de l'anglais*. Paris: Didier.

Voltaire 1960. *Romans et contes*, Bénac, H. (ed.). Paris: Garnier.

Voltaire 1964. *Zadig/L'Ingénu*, Butt, J. (trans). Harmondsworth: Penguin.

Index

Bold type denotes a term that figures in the glossary, and the page where it is first defined.